BRAVE

BRAVE: STORY OF A TRANS WOMAN

K.K.

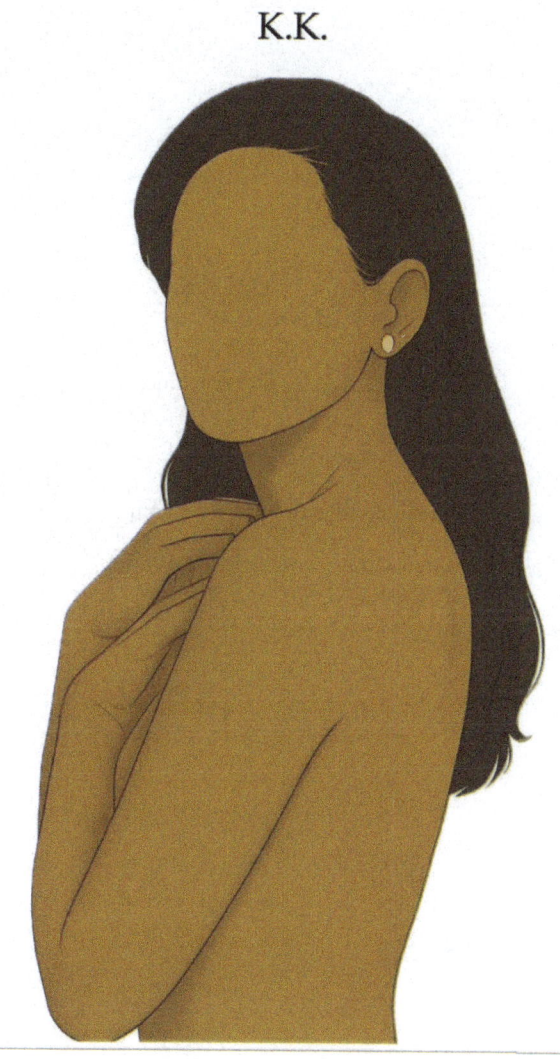

Cover Design by Ebook Launch

Contact information:

Email: kkthewriter1@gmail.com

Twitter/X username: @kkthewriter

This book is dedicated to every queer person in the world.
Your story is mine, and my story is yours.
We are not broken; we are whole, and we are one.

CONTENTS

PREFACE

What does it mean to be brave? Bravery has been defined as the ability to show courage and to face and endure danger or pain. For most of my existence, I often wondered if I possessed the capability to be brave, as I often found myself being the opposite. I lived in fear for most of my life. Fear of being myself, fear of being judged, and fear of being unwanted. I think the most fearful moment of my life was when I discovered that I was queer.

Realizing that I did not fall into the norms of society was a harrowing experience. My response was to suppress and conceal the different parts of myself. I lived in the shadows for most of my life and tried my best to go unseen. I thought it was better to be hidden than to be my authentic, queer self. However, I eventually realized that if I were ever going to find happiness and peace, I would have to practice the bravest act of all, self-acceptance. Learning to accept and love yourself as a queer person is uniquely challenging, but it can be done, and I am living proof of this and the tenacity of the queer spirit.

My name is K., and I am, among many things, a queer transgender woman. I have transitioned from a man into a woman for over ten years when writing this book. Being trans comes with its fair share of pain. Living as a trans woman means living in a state of perpetual dysphoria. Dysphoria is a constant battle between the body and the mind. Trans women often feel betrayed by their bodies. We feel like women internally, but our external appearance displays masculine traits. Living with a disconnect between your mind and body is absolute torment. Most escape this nightmare by filling their bodies with synthetic

1

hormones or enduring painful surgeries. Sadly, some escape the constant hell of dysphoria by taking their own lives.

Deciding to transition requires a level of bravery and fearlessness like no other. In my opinion, trans women are the most oppressed people in our nation, as society actively denies trans women fundamental humanity and dignity. Trans women must endure bullying, rejection, abandonment, and violence for most of their lives and are either ostracized by society or encouraged to practice self-exile.

Trans women must fight for fundamental human rights, including playing sports or using the restroom. We are often forced into survival sex work due to employment discrimination. We are also often betrayed even by our own members of the LGBTQIA+ "community."

Trans women must deal with not only our own shame, but we must also deal with the shame and secrecy of the men who date us. Trans women are murdered the most by the men who claim to love them, which is one of the main reasons for the average lifespan of a trans woman being thirty-five.

Harmful and ignorant legislation such as the gay or trans "panic defense" is also used to validate the murders of trans women by their lovers and protect the murderer instead of the victim. When we are murdered, we are victim-shamed and accused of "tricking" men who were fully aware of the sex and gender of the trans woman they slept with but who lie out of fear of being labeled gay. For these men, being labeled gay is somehow worse than murdering a fellow human being.

Trans women are vulnerable in life but also in death. We are often disrespected through dead naming and misgendering in both life and death. Our deceased bodies frequently go unidentified and misidentified. We are also often denied dignity and dressed as men by embarrassed family members at our funerals. Finally, we are told that we will be punished in the afterlife, refusing us peace even in death.

Still, while the life of a trans woman may be undoubtedly bleak at times, there is magic to being trans. Being trans can be wonderful; in many ways, being trans is a blessing. There are many things in life I regret, but transitioning is not one of them. Being transgender and deciding to transition require a level of bravery like no other. Living in your truth takes true nerve. Despite all the odds, there is a light at the end of the tunnel and a rainbow at the end of the storm.

Transitioning is a beautiful physical, mental, and spiritual metamorphosis. Trans individuals grow in a way and experience life in a manner that cisgender people will never know. We must look inside ourselves, discover who we are, and fight to become that person, which is amazing. Through this book, I detail this incredible process and journey of my queerhood, gender transition, and entire life.

In this memoir, I depict all aspects of my life, sparing none of the details. I discuss complex topics, from child molestation, domestic violence, child abuse, prostitution, and suicide, to name a few.

I also decided to pepper in some of my poetry. And I have included images of myself and my loved ones that I converted into digital art. The images created are all faceless for anonymity.

I strove to be educational and factual in my writing and use non-stigmatizing language. Still, there will likely be moments when I inadvertently use offensive language. If there are moments in which I offend, I hope the reader realizes this was in ignorance and not maliciousness.

I desire more than anything that this book helps others stand in their truth and show their sparkling true selves. This book is intended to uplift and inspire others to persevere through adversity. My memoir is meant to touch the lives of all people but, more importantly, the lives of my fellow transgender brothers and sisters and nonbinary siblings.

While there are similarities between the lives of queer and transgender individuals, each story is unique; queer and transgender people are not a monolith but a beautiful and broad spectrum of color and life experiences. I used the opportunity to write this book so that my voice could be heard and to contribute to the literature on transgender individuals. I wanted to give a glimpse into the life of a transgender woman from childhood to adulthood.

For so long, trans stories have been told by non-trans people. Transgender individuals are often not trusted to tell our own narratives and our truths. We are usually seen as mentally unstable and psychiatrically deranged due to our struggles with gender dysphoria and identity. With this book, I am reclaiming the power taken away from so many transgender individuals by telling my story from a first-person perspective.

In short, this book is an opportunity to get a glimpse into the radically candid tale of a trans woman. I narrate my sorrows, joys, failures, and accomplishments through this testimony. I felt I needed to keep my writing as blunt and honest as possible to portray the struggles of a trans woman accurately. Most importantly, I wanted to highlight the human experience that is often neglected when discussing the life of transgender people; that is, transgender people are much more than just our gender transition.

Writing this memoir was no easy feat, as it required me to dig deep into myself and face all of me: the good, the bad, and the ugly. At many points, I contemplated whether I should even publish my memoir. However, I realized I did not want my voice to go unheard or my story untold. One of my idols and favorite musicians, Dr. Nina Simone, says freedom is having "no fear." With this memoir, I am liberating myself from the shackles of fear. I am unveiling myself for the world to see. I am standing up and saying look at me; look at the amazing person I am; look at what I have overcome. With this book, I am being what I always knew I could be: brave.

THE QUEENS DICTIONARY

➤ Ballroom: Noun. Queer subculture event in which people compete (or "walk") for trophies, prizes, and peer recognition. ("I compete in ballroom and walk realness.")

➤ Beard: Noun. Someone who, knowingly or unknowingly, dates someone else romantically to conceal that person's sexual orientation. Beards can be male or female, but typically, beards are women who serve as a social cover for a closeted gay man. Just as a beard of hair covers and conceals a face, a human beard conceals a closeted queer person's sexual identity. ("John is really gay, but he is dating Janet; Janet is John's beard.")

➤ Beat: Adjective. Synonym for beautiful ("She's beat"). As a verb, it's used to describe the tapping or beating motion when applying makeup. ("I'm going to go beat my face.")

➤ Bottom: Noun. Person who enjoys receiving anal penetration or who is the receiver in a sexual encounter. ("I'm a proud bottom.")

➤ Boy pockets: Noun. A term used to describe the common anatomical indentations on the sides of the male buttocks. ("Those are some deep boy pockets.")

➤ Cis-het: Abbreviation for the phrase cisgender-heterosexual. The opposite of queer. ("She's not gay or trans; she's cis-het.")

➤ Clocked: Verb. Calling out someone's flaws. ("I clocked her crooked teeth.") Revealing or realizing the gender of someone who identifies as trans. ("I got clocked; he knew I was trans.")

➢ Closet: Noun. A metaphor for queer individuals who have decided not to disclose their sexual orientation or gender identity to others. ("Nobody knows he's gay. He's in the closet.")

➢ Dip: Verb. One of the five recognized elements of vogue, especially in Femme Vogue. A floor-level vogue move that is usually paired with spinning or spiraling down, tucking one leg, and extending the other to create the illusion of touching the ground. Sometimes referred to as a "death drop." ("Bitch, that dip was ovah!")

➢ Down-low: Adjective. Term used to describe a man who is secretive or discreet about his sexual preferences. ("He's on the down-low about liking trans women.")

➢ Face: Ballroom category in which contestants compete against each other to determine who has the most aesthetically pleasing facial features. ("I walk face.")

➢ Faggotry: Noun. Used for activities unique and secluded to the queer community. ("Let's go out and get into some faggotry.") Can be considered derogatory if used by someone who is not a member of the queer community.

➢ Gaff panty: Noun. Undergarment often used by trans women and drag queens that compresses and flattens male genitals to give the illusion of female genitals. ("I'm tucked and wearing a gaff panty.")

➢ Gag: Noun. A shocking or disturbing event. ("That movie was a gag.") As a verb, it means to be shocked or speechless. ("I was gagged when I found out she went back to being a man.")

➢ Gay mother: Noun. The maternal figure of a ballroom or queer house. ("Alyssa is the gay mother of the House of Gucci.")

➢ Getting my life: Phrase used to describe having a good time. ("I am getting my life at this ball.")

➤ House: Noun. Ballroom concept used to describe a queer chosen family. ("The House of St. Clair.")

➤ Kiki: (pronounced key-key) Noun. A party or social gathering. A fun time amongst friends. ("Let's have a kiki.")

➤ Labels: Noun. Ballroom category in which contestants compete to see who is wearing the most name-brand garments. ("I'm wearing Chanel, Louis Vuitton, and Prada tonight because I'm walking labels.")

➤ Ms. Thing: Noun. Used to describe someone deemed sassy, mouthy, and/or brazen. ("Calm down, Ms. Thing.") Can be used as a compliment ("Ms. Thing, you are stunning") or an insult ("Ms. Thing, you look a mess"). Also frequently used to describe a queer person when one does not know said queer person's name. ("Ms. Thing over there in the blue.")

➤ Queen: Noun. Used to describe a member of the queer community. ("That's a queen.") Also short for the term "drag queen." ("Our next queen coming to the stage is Sapphire Sparkle.")

➤ Queer: Noun. An umbrella term for individuals who identify with and belong to the LGBTQIA+ (Lesbian, Gay, Bisexual, Transgender, Queer/Questioning, Intersex, Asexual) communities. Sexual and gender minorities. ("We're here, we're queer, get used to it.") As an adjective, it's used to identify a person, place, or thing belonging to the LGBTQIA+ community. ("That's a queer bar, honey.")

➤ Read: Noun. Clever or witty insult. ("Don't make me read you.")

➤ Realness: Adjective. Used to describe likeness or similarity. ("Lady Gaga gives me Madonna realness.") As a noun, it's used as a ballroom category in which contestants give an illusion of a specific person, concept, or gender. ("The category is schoolgirl realness.")

➢ Runway: Noun. Ballroom category in which contestants imitate walking on a catwalk. ("I am a fierce runway walker.")

➢ Sat down: Phrase used in ballroom indicating that you have beat a fellow contestant. ("I sat her down in the realness category.")

➢ Sex siren: Noun. Ballroom category in which contestants compete against each other to determine who has the greater sex appeal. ("He's a sex-siren legend.")

➢ Shade: Noun. An act or behavior that is deemed rude, judgmental, or insulting. ("What you said was shade.") As an adjective or adverb, it's used to describe demeaning behavior. ("She was throwing shade; she was being shady.")

➢ Snatched: Adjective. Used to describe something or someone highly feminine. ("She looks snatched.") Also used to describe something tight and pulled back. ("My face is snatched when my hair is in a ponytail.")

➢ Stealth: Noun. The state of a transgender individual living and presenting their gender identity without disclosing their transgender status to others. ("I don't tell people I'm trans. I'm stealth.")

➢ Tea: Noun. Personal information about oneself. ("I'm trans, that's my tea.") Also: gossip, entertaining news. ("Spill the tea about his affair.") Also: truth. ("What's the real tea?")

➢ Tell: Noun. Physical trait on a trans woman that can be viewed as masculine. ("My voice is my tell.")

➢ Top: Noun. Person who generally prefers to be the more active, dominant, or controlling partner during sex. ("He's a top.")

- Versatile: Noun. Person who participates in anal sex who is both penetrated by their partner and penetrates their partner. ("I'm versatile in bed.")

- Vogue: Verb. Dance originated from ballroom culture. Consists of characteristic poses struck by a model on a catwalk. ("Let's go out and vogue tonight.")

PART I: CHILDHOOD

In Plain Sight

Wake up
I fake myself
Go out
I split myself
Come home
I touch myself
Go to bed
I hate myself
What's the point?
I kill myself
Take a pill
I numb myself
Take another pill
To feel myself
Try and try
To change myself
But if I could
I'd be myself
But I can't
I hide myself
But I can't
I hide myself

CHAPTER 1

TRUST VS MISTRUST

It has been said that the only winner in the drug war has been the drugs. America's relationship with drugs and substance use disorder has always been complicated. The criminalization of substance use disorder and controlled and dangerous substance distribution (or selling drugs) has devastated the lives of countless individuals and families, mine included. When I was less than one year old, my father was deported from America back to his home country of Guyana for selling drugs.

Our family was poor, and my father and his family had recently immigrated to America at the time. I never spoke to my father about why he sold drugs, but he had just become a father, was a poor immigrant, and likely saw selling drugs as fast and easy big money. I don't think he ever realized how selling drugs would ruin his life and the lives of his family.

One of my earliest memories involves my father's deportation. While it was traumatizing for most members of my family, it was most devastating to my grandmother. The day that my father was deported, my grandmother was crying hysterically in her bed. Numerous family members surrounded the bed and tried to comfort her, but this was in vain. She began screaming my father's name over and over again. I was named after my father, so some of my family members thought she was calling for me and placed me in bed with her, but she continued to wail for my father. I hugged her but quickly realized that it wasn't me she wanted to hold.

Before my father was deported, he, my mother, my brother (his then-stepson), and I lived together in a rented home. But after my father got deported, my mother moved in with my father's family into my grandparents' big, two-story home in Paterson, New Jersey. My father's family is huge, as my paternal grandparents had eight children. During this time, most of my father's family (well over ten people) lived in the same large house in Paterson.

My mother is biracial; her father was Black, and her mother is White. My mother was raised in foster care, as her parents abandoned her shortly after her birth due to her White maternal family's issues with their daughter being impregnated by a Black man. My brother is also mixed race; his father is a Black Jamaican man who had been incarcerated indefinitely shortly after his birth. My brother was born with a rare developmental disorder called Williams syndrome, which also mildly impacted his intellectual functioning.

My father's family was from Guyana, but our ancestors came from India. My father was the first person in the family to date and have a child with a Black person, which is often considered taboo in Indian households. Many people are unaware of the prevalence of racist views that people of Indian descent have toward Black people.

Most of my father's family despised Black people. As I mentioned, my mother and brother are both biracial, mixed with Black and White. I have heard the tales regarding the racism that my mother and brother endured from racist family members, from being called racist epithets to sustaining actual physical violence. I did not endure the same racism that my mother and brother faced from my father's family, for some reason. I guess my father's family viewed me as being more Indian than Black, so they accepted me. However, to my father's family, my mother and brother were simply "niggers."

Thankfully, not all of my family members were racist and hateful. Some of my aunts helped my mother get a job with them, working at a battery factory for a short period. My mother would leave for the factory in the morning and come home in the afternoons, and my grandmother would watch me while she worked. When recalling these times, my mother tells me that she would argue with my grandmother when she came home from work because she would find me dressed in girl's clothing.

Once, my grandmother and I were on the porch relaxing when my mother got home from work. My mother walked up the porch stairs and said, "Oh, what a cute little baby girl!" until she realized the cute little girl was me dressed up in baby drag!

I'm unsure why my grandmother kept dressing me in girl's clothing. She loved me more than life itself, so I'm sure she had no malicious intentions. Maybe she saw the girl in me before I or anyone else did, or perhaps she just wanted to utilize my female cousins' hand-me-downs; whatever the reason, my mother says she got into countless arguments with my grandmother over this.

When discussing the time she lived with my father's family, my mother also often tells me of an incident in which one of my uncles slapped my brother in the mouth and called him a "nigger." Shortly afterward, my mother decided to venture out of my father's family home and explore the state of Delaware.

My mother had heard great things about the job market, school system, low crime rates, and taxes in Delaware. She went to scope it out when I was two years old and left me behind with my father's family. Her foster mother, who also lived in New Jersey, agreed to take in my brother. My mother was raised by a Black foster family, so they understood her wanting to escape the racism from my father's family. My mother vowed to return to New Jersey quickly to collect my brother and me and take us to Delaware to be raised but soon realized that it would be hard to find employment with her limited education level. She would eventually come back to New Jersey to retrieve my brother and me about two years later when I was around the age of four.

When my mother left, I was raised, for the most part, by my grandmother and my aunt Malinie (whom I referred to lovingly as

Auntie Lini). I quickly became my grandmother's favorite grandchild, as I was the only piece of my father that she had left after he was deported. Auntie Lini took favor to me as well, as she was very close to my father too. Also, I was a pretty adorable baby.

My tight relationship with my Auntie Lini would continue for the rest of our lives, and she would go on to become an additional mother figure to me. When I think of my relationship with Auntie Lini, I am overcome by her kindness, and I will never forget all she has done for me. However, my time with my father's family was not all roses.

At an early age, I began displaying signs of gender dysphoria. Gender dysphoria is a mental health condition in which one experiences feelings of discomfort or distress due to an incongruence between one's gender identity and one's sex assigned at birth or sex-related physical characteristics. Not all people with gender dysphoria go on to become transgender, and not all transgender people have gender dysphoria. Still, most transgender individuals experience gender dysphoria at some point in their lives, if not the majority of their lives. Gender dysphoria can occur at any age, but for most individuals with the condition, gender dysphoria begins in childhood, which was the case with me.

Shortly after I started talking, I would tell my father's family that I was not a boy but a girl. I only wanted to play with my female cousins and their toys. I would also steal and wear my female cousins' clothing, as I felt more comfortable wearing girl's clothes. Some of my family members thought nothing of this and wrote it off as a phase, while others recoiled in horror and shock at seeing what they presumed to be a gay child.

There is a deep-seated history of homophobia embedded in the West Indian Caribbean culture, which I discovered at an early age. Some of my first memories involved being called homophobic slurs by some of the men in my father's family. One homophobic slur specific to the Caribbean culture that I was frequently called was "antiman," which, I guess, means the opposite (or anti) of a man (feminine). Occasionally, I would also be called a "battyboy" (pronounced bha-ti-boy).

Some of the men in my father's family thought it was their duty to toughen me up and beat the gay out of me. One of my earliest memories is of my older male cousins dragging me to the barbershop, kicking and screaming, to cut off all my beautiful, curly hair and make me look more like a boy. For the men in my father's family, it was easier to be cruel and attempt to discipline and bully the queer and femininity out of me than to practice acceptance. Having your family as your first bully is a type of trauma that no one should ever encounter.

Not all of my father's family bullied me, though; some allowed me to express my gender identity and even supported me. My aunt Maureen often tells me how she gave me a small purse I would walk around with as if it were the only Coach bag. She even showed me pictures of myself as a toddler walking around with the small purse. (These pictures have since been lost.) It seemed the men were the only ones who had issues with me expressing my chosen gender, as there are countless incidents I can remember of the women in my father's family being supportive of my gender expression.

I'm not sure why the men in my father's family were so disgusted with me. Maybe I confused them. Perhaps I forced them to question their own sexuality in a way that they could not cope with. Maybe I reminded them of the thoughts they secretly had, thoughts that only a fearless child could express.

Chapter 2

Warm and Fuzzy

There was one older cousin of mine who constantly terrorized me. He had to be in his mid- to late teens when I lived at my father's family home. He was one of the cooler older cousins who all the cousins of my generation looked up to and aspired to be like. He would often randomly beat me up, mainly punching me in my thighs, sometimes so hard my thighs would cramp. The beatings would usually come when I would act feminine or refuse to play with the boys. Sometimes, the beatings would make me cry, but I quickly learned not to cry, as this made the beatings worse and his satisfaction greater.

One evening, I was cruising through my grandparents' large house. I had to be no more than three or four years old then. I passed by my cousin's room and saw that he was in bed watching television. I wanted to watch whatever he was watching, so I entered his room and risked being exposed to his cruelty. Strangely, he allowed me to stay in his room to watch television. I closed the door behind me.

I don't remember what show was playing, but my cousin let me come into bed with him. I couldn't believe my cool older cousin, who usually was very mean to me, was letting me stay in his room, watching TV with him, and even lying in bed with him. Even though my cousin tormented me, I still looked up to him and wanted desperately to be his friend.

I remember lying down with my head by his feet, continuing to watch TV in silence, when my cousin began groping himself in front of me. I had never seen someone do that and had no concept of what sex or self-pleasure was. Still, I knew he was doing something he shouldn't be doing as I had come to understand those parts that he was fondling as "private parts," and I knew that he should not be rubbing them in front of me. So, I knew my cousin was doing something forbidden, which fascinated me. Although, what he did next intrigued me even more.

He then pulled out his penis and started masturbating. I was confused as to what he was doing and was surprised at how much bigger his penis was than mine. I must confess a lot of this memory is fuzzy, but what I remember next involved me touching his penis with my hands. He became aroused, and I also became aroused. I held his erect penis with my small hands. I did not understand what was going on. Still, I felt happy that my cousin was being so kind to me and wanted to have this secret experience with me of all people: the faggot, gay, antiman, battyboy.

I got lost in euphoria: the excitement of a sexual experience and the warm feeling of being accepted and loved. Being left by my mother, not having a father, and being bullied by the men in my father's family, it is no wonder why I was so eager for acceptance and love. Maybe my cousin knew this and took advantage of this, but then again, perhaps he was just a horny teenager. I'm not sure why he did what he did, but I do know that what he did next would change how I viewed relationships and sex for the rest of my life.

My cousin then began pushing my head toward his penis and guiding me to put his penis in my mouth. I did it, wondering if this meant we could finally be friends. He closed his eyes and pulled the covers over me so he couldn't see me. I remember enthusiastically licking and sucking his penis like a lollipop and peeking from under the covers to see him continuing to lie back with his eyes closed in silence.

I remember looking down, seeing his feet, and watching his toes curl inside his white socks. I felt proud of myself for being able to bring pleasure to my cousin. As I lay there with his penis in my mouth, I thought maybe this would finally stop the beatings; perhaps this would finally stop the name-calling.

That is all I remember. I do not remember how long it went on or if my cousin ejaculated or not; hopefully, he did not do that, at least. I do not remember if there were more incidents like that with this cousin either. What I do remember is that I was wrong. It did not stop the beatings or name-calling.

FOG

Try to remember
And if you can't
Imagine

What it felt like
For your innocence to be taken
For a part of your soul to die

Open the dark box
For it, too, is a gift

It will hurt
When the fog lifts
You will cry
You will wish you could die

But eventually, little bird
You will fly
Out of the dark
Into the sunrise

From this gloom
Like a flower
You will bloom
And fill the world
With your wonderful perfume

And remember
That you are strong
For you have persevered
My dear child
You are here

CHAPTER 3

DELAWARE BOUND

The time at my grandparents' house was ending, and no one in the house knew it. My mother had established housing and employment in Delaware a couple of years after leaving New Jersey, and she was ready to collect her children. However, she soon learned that regaining custody of her children would not be easy.

My grandmother had grown incredibly close to me and did not want to see me, the remnants of her son, taken away from her. Curiously enough, my foster grandmother also did not want to return my brother to my mother, and this fight became so ugly that my mother had to pursue legal remedies to regain custody of my brother. My mother was able to regain physical custody of me in one day, but not without a fight.

It was a warm, sunny day when my mother came to collect me from my father's family. She had shown up unannounced. I remember a commotion outside on the front porch that I could barely see through all my adult family members' legs. My mother told them she was ready to take me home to Delaware, and my father's family responded in protest. In all the commotion and emotion, my female teenage cousins managed to sneak me away from the crowd and took me upstairs to the attic.

Downstairs on the front porch, my family continued to object and argue with my mother. They told her she could not take me away from them, as I was comfortable living with them, and removing me from their home would destabilize me. The commotion was loud, and I could hear the adults arguing downstairs. My female cousins became nervous and tried to distract me by telling jokes and talking loudly among themselves to drown out the arguments outside. However, I could still hear all the adults arguing. My cousins gave me a coloring book and some crayons and continued talking loudly to try to drown out the adults downstairs.

Eventually, my cousins realized they had to explain what was happening. They told me my mom was downstairs trying to take me away from my father's family, including my grandmother and Auntie Lini. I did not know whether to be scared or excited by this news. I always wanted a mother, but this lady making all this commotion seemed scary.

The girls asked me if I wanted to continue living with them or to live with my mother. I thought about it, and because I was frightened of being with this stranger in a new and strange environment, I told them I wanted to live with them. So, they told me to color and stay quiet, and I did.

Downstairs, outside on the porch, my family and mother continued to argue. My family had quickly fabricated a story, saying I had been sent to live in Guyana with my father and was not in the house. They apologized for not telling her sooner, but they said they had not known how to break the news to her. My mother became enraged at the blatant lie. She demanded to be let into the house to look for me, and my family declined. I then remember hearing my mother yelling my name. I repeatedly listened to the woman calling me from the attic, but the voice was foreign.

I did not remember my mother at that point. I knew I had a mother because everyone has one, but I had no idea who or where mine was. I knew I had a grandmother and an Auntie Lini who looked after me, but they told me they were not my mother. The same was true with my older female cousins. I often asked them if they were my mother, and they would say no. So, I had no idea who my mother was at that point in my life. What I did know, however, was that I missed this woman incredibly, and no matter what, there was always something deep inside of me longing for my mother's love. Sometimes, I would wander my grandparents' house looking for her. Now, she was right downstairs.

I was coloring in silence when one of my aunts came upstairs, saying it was time for me to go downstairs to meet my mom. Once my mother threatened to call the police, my family agreed to surrender me. I remember my family telling me to say goodbye to my grandmother, who was lying in bed crying. At that point, my grandmother had issues walking due to severe rheumatoid arthritis. She lay there screaming my name repeatedly, almost as loud and bloodcurdling as she did when my father was deported. I climbed into the bed and cried with her, hugging her and kissing her. Then I was taken from her, crying and confused, to the front porch, where my mother was waiting for me.

The sight of my mother was strange. I had been told she was my mother, but she was still a stranger to me. But when she kneeled down and hugged me, it felt like I was finally home. She hugged me for what felt like an eternity as she cried joyfully. I did not know if I should smile or cry, so I stayed silent but hugged her back. The woman I had searched for had finally found me. She was my mommy.

She smelled lovely and was so pretty and light skinned. She stood at five-foot-five, but to a four-year-old me, she seemed like a gorgeous giant. She told me she was my mother and was there to take me away to live with her. The fear I felt earlier melted away. I knew this woman was my mother and loved me.

My father's family packed my belongings, and we said more goodbyes. Then, it came time for me to leave. Despite the joy that I felt being reunited with my mother, being separated from the family and stability I had come to know was still painful. My mother could sense this and tried to cheer me up by telling me I would live in Delaware with her and my big brother. I had no idea I had a brother! So, even though I still felt sad, I was excited to start this new life in Delaware with my mother and brother.

***

Our first home was in Dover, Delaware. My mother eventually regained custody of my brother, and we all lived together in a tiny one-bedroom apartment, which was located on the second floor of a two-family home. There was a kind, elderly Black woman who lived on the first floor who we often spent time with, watching classic black-and-white movies. I took fondly to the elderly woman, who had the same caring spirit as my paternal grandmother from New Jersey.

The pain of being separated from my paternal family became immense, and it felt foreign being in such a new and small family consisting of only my mother, brother, and myself. While I was happy to be back with my mother again, she still felt like a stranger to me, and my brother felt even more like a stranger.

I did not know much about my brother's condition, but his appearance initially frightened me. He did not look like the other children I had grown up with at my grandparents' house, as individuals with Williams syndrome develop distinct facial characteristics. Also, my brother spoke and behaved differently than the children I had grown up with. Sometimes, he would watch TV, rock back and forth, and drool, which scared me. My mother picked up on my initial fear of my brother and encouraged us to bond through playing. Eventually, I learned that my brother was harmless and fun, and I would spend all day playing with him, laughing and having a great time.

Eventually, my timidity toward my mother dwindled, and I grew to love her immensely. I don't believe I ever held resentment toward her for leaving me for those couple of years; children are very forgiving in that way. Although, she did not always return the same level of love as I did. My mother often made me feel like I was a nuisance to her. Many times, I wondered why she even gave birth to me or questioned why she took me away from my grandparents.

After moving to Delaware, I soon discovered that my mother was a strict disciplinarian. I realized it was necessary to study my mother the way a battered woman studies her abuser. Most victims of abuse learn their abuser's idiosyncrasies out of protection, as a particular facial expression, such as a furrowed brow, could result in a slap across the face. I studied her facial expressions, body movements, how she spoke, and her posture. I learned to be in tune with my mother's temperament as well, as certain moods of hers resulted in a higher risk of being disciplined.

My mother was raised in an abusive household. Her foster parents were physically and emotionally abusive to her, so my mother had no knowledge of childrearing that wasn't abusive, and she definitely had no knowledge of raising a special needs child. My brother would often act out, and she would usually discipline him by giving him spankings. I would witness the spankings and become terrified that she would beat me the way she beat him.

Although I had often been "popped" or slapped across the face, she only gave me one spanking in my whole life. My mother soon realized that physical discipline was unnecessary to parent me. She only needed to yell at me or tell me she was disappointed in me to bring me to the point of uncontrollable crying. As a sensitive child, words hurt me more than any type of physical punishment ever could.

As a child I was baffled by my mother's treatment of me and my brother, but now I realize that she was not a monster. She was a young, single mother of two boys, one of whom had special needs. She had no family, no social support, and an eighth-grade education, trying to make the best out of the situation she had been dealt. She was nowhere near a perfect mother but continued despite her shortcomings, as she had vowed not to abandon her children like her parents had.

Expressing my gender was even more complicated living with my mother. I still wanted, more than anything, to live as a girl. I had once thought I was a girl, but most of my father's family had convinced me that I wasn't and never would be. You see, I knew I was a girl; it was everyone else who did not know. However, I had come to learn that expressing myself femininely was dangerous; as with my father's family, it led to bullying, beatings, and disciplinary actions.

Therefore, I decided to try to hide the girl in me from my mother and brother as best as possible. I concluded at that young age to only express my femininity in private, behind closed doors, or when no one was around, where I was free to tie my T-shirts in a knot to expose my tummy, like Janet Jackson, or pretend to be Mary J. Blige, putting on a show. Always behind closed doors, where no one could see the girl I saw in myself.

Chapter 4

The Cycle

I was four going on five, and the time had come to enroll in preschool. My mother had taught me a great deal of reading and writing at home, so I was well prepared for scholastic success when I entered preschool. Social success was a different story. I have many memories from the daycare program, including the bright fluorescent lights, the joyous yelling of children, the horrible lunches, and the even more horrible smells. The environment overwhelmed me for the most part. In response, I shut down, choosing not to speak much or socialize with the other children.

I did not know where I fit in. I had been told repeatedly that I was a boy, but I felt more comfortable being a girl. I had come to learn through all the bullying and beatings and discipline from the men in my father's family that being a girl, or expressing myself as a girl, or playing with the girls and not the boys was wrong and in some ways dangerous, as it placed me at risk for more bullying and violence.

So, I decided at this point that I would not speak; I would not let anyone hear my soft voice and tell me I sounded like a girl. I would not move and play and have someone tell me I acted like a girl. Lastly, I would not socialize with girls as I did not want to risk having someone reprimand me and tell me I belonged with the boys.

I was avoiding many things, but at the root of it, I was avoiding pain. At such a young age, I had decided that it was best not to express anything, especially gender, so I would play by myself, do my schoolwork by myself, eat lunch by myself, and then go home. I continued this way for most of my childhood. Even though I was lonely and longed for friendship and to play like the other children, I was too scared to come out of solitude. I learned to become content in my isolation.

Although I separated myself from the other children, one older, bigger boy named Gregory had taken a liking to me and insisted on trying to interact with me. He always wanted to play with me, but I would not engage with him. Eventually, he would leave, but he would always come back. Gregory was one of the only children who showed a persistent interest in me, which annoyed me. Sometimes, Gregory would sit next to me during lunch while we ate silently. Also, occasionally, he would put his mat next to mine during naptime. There was one naptime with Gregory that I will never forget.

It was sometime in the evening. I typically stayed the whole day at the daycare from morning until the evening, as my mother would get out of work around 5 p.m. She worked as a telemarketer at the time. The room was pitch dark as it was naptime. There were other children in the room, but not many. I had fallen asleep, but Gregory apparently lay there awake. The adults had left us children alone in the room to sleep. I'm sure they thought leaving children alone to sleep at that age was safe, but they were wrong.

I awakened to Gregory on top of me, pinning me down to the mat. He was fondling me, groping my genitals through my pants with his hands. I had no idea what was occurring and was still half asleep. When I realized that Gregory was touching my private parts, I felt humiliated and powerless. I felt shame that I was not strong enough to push Gregory off me. I believe it was also shame that prevented me from screaming out for help.

Powerless and confused, I lay on the naptime mat, pinned down like an animal. "What are you doing?" I asked Gregory in a whisper, but there was no response. "Stop," I begged, struggling to move. His body was heavy, much heavier than mine, and he smelled of sugar and sweat; it was repulsive.

"No means yes, and yes means no," Gregory said with a laugh as he rubbed his privates against mine. I was bewildered. What was Gregory doing, and why was he doing it to me? Then he unbuttoned my pants and stuck his hands down them. He began rubbing my genitals. I still remember how gross his touch felt. This was much different than the experience I had with my cousin. This time, I felt dirty and afraid.

I lay there, hoping it would end, and felt shame coursing through my body. The confusion increased as I became aroused. The juxtaposition between pain and pleasure became apparent. I did not want Gregory to touch me. I did not wish to have Gregory on top of me.

Mentally, I was distressed, but physically, my body responded to what Gregory was doing to me. His touch made me feel humiliated, but at the same time, it brought me pleasure. The pleasure from being unwantedly physically stimulated only further heightened my shame and feelings of self-loathing.

I have replayed this event many times throughout my life, and through the shame and disgust, I often wonder who made Gregory a victim the way he had made me one. Gregory and I were both children, and children are typically naïve to such sexual acts or experiences. Children who molest other children are often victims of molestation and sexual abuse themselves, either from other children or adults. It has often been said that molestation creates a cycle of repetition in which one victim goes on to victimize another.

As an adult, I see that the obvious truth was that Gregory most likely had been touched the way he touched me. He, too, most likely had been told that "no means yes, and yes means no." The cycle of molestation had been continuing, and I was the next recipient. It makes me wonder, was my cousin also a victim of this cycle?

The door opened, and a dull yellow light peeked through. Gregory quickly got off me and returned to his mat. The daycare worker saw nothing. A voice called my name and said my mother was there to pick me up. I quickly buttoned my pants and ran to the door to greet her.

I wanted to tell my mom what had happened. Somehow, I knew what had happened to me was wrong, but I still questioned myself. The shame was intensified by a feeling of guilt and disgust. I had felt pleasure from what the boy had done to me. It was as if my body had betrayed me. I did not want to be touched like that, but the awful truth was I liked it.

I held my mother's hand as we walked to the car. I looked at her face. *She seems too tired to be bothered with me*, I thought. I wanted to avoid getting into trouble, but I needed her help. I needed to know that what had happened wasn't my fault. I needed to be held and told that everything was all right. I simply needed the embrace of my mother. But how was I to say to her what had happened to me? How was I to tell her that I had been touched by a boy like that? How could I tell her that he felt my private parts? Privates are just that: private. They are not to be revealed to anyone.

For some reason, I thought that what had happened was my fault. That I had caused Gregory to violate me. I believed that something I said or did made him feel that what he did was acceptable. I should have fought harder. Maybe, as I had been told so many times before by adults in my life, I wasn't tough enough and had been acting like a girl. Perhaps if I were a girl, there would have been more invested in protecting me from perverts and predators. Could this have happened because I was behaving like a girl again?

I wondered what to say to my mother as we walked to the car, but I remained confused. I needed help. So, indirectly, I admitted my guilt and sought her support. I asked her, "Mommy, did you know that no means yes, and yes means no?" I hoped she would ask me where I heard such a ridiculous thing. I would tell her what happened, and she would punish Gregory and possibly me, but instead, she just said, "Okay, Boo-Boo." I waited for her to say more. I waited, but we continued our walk to the car in silence. We got in the car and drove home. I decided I wouldn't try telling anyone what had happened between me and Gregory again.

CHAPTER 5

FIRST GRADE CROSS-DRESSER

The first grade was a standout time in my childhood, as it was one of the first times in my life that I discovered I could pass as a female. I had been mistaken for a genetic female for most of my childhood, as my androgyny was at its all-time high. Even though I had a boy haircut and wore boy clothes, people would still frequently misidentify me as a genetic girl, even in front of my mother.

My mother would get visibly frustrated with repeatedly correcting people and telling them I was a boy. Her irritation with me being gendered as a girl led me to conclude that I could not tell her how I truly felt. I knew I could not reveal the girl inside of me to her, or else it might end up like it did with my father's family. Nevertheless, whenever someone would mistake me for a girl, I experienced a sense of happiness that I seldom felt.

First grade was tough for me. My isolation had become much worse after the incident with Gregory. Even though it only happened once, it would lead me to mistrust other children and people for a long time. For most of the school day, I would lose myself in my schoolwork and excel so much that, at one point, it was suggested to my mother that I skip a grade to be more challenged. My mother decided that it would be best to not have me skip a grade, as she felt that it would cause social stress for me to be placed in a setting with older children. The teachers suspected my aloofness and distance were from boredom, which in part they may have been. However, my detachment came from being unable to be my authentic self, a girl.

More than anything, I wanted to be like the girls in my class. I admired their outfits and pretty, long hair and desperately wanted to be one of them. When I entered first grade, I had begun to accept that I couldn't live as a girl. I stopped telling people that I was a girl, and I had learned to stop expressing myself as a girl as well. So, I fell deeper into isolation and withdrew almost entirely from socializing with my peers or participating in class. The adults interpreted this as me needing to be academically challenged, but I didn't need to be challenged; I needed to be accepted.

No one knew it, but even though I was wearing boy clothes, had a haircut, and stopped behaving femininely, I was still struggling with gender dysphoria. When I look back at my childhood, I become upset at how the adults in my life did not trust me when I told them that I was a girl. Adults often underestimate the power that children have in forming their identities. Some think of a child's identity as being impressionable to external sources. Still, truthfully, identity formation is a natural internal process that begins as early as two years of age, which was evident as I started identifying as a girl and displayed clear signs of gender dysphoria at the age of three. The dysphoria did not go away because I got older or was disciplined; I simply learned to conceal it better.

In the beginning of my time in Delaware, I hid the girl in me from the world and only allowed her to come out in secret when I was alone in my room. Still, I wanted to be recognized and seen as a girl. Whenever I was mistaken as a girl by someone, it would always bring a rush of euphoria over me. This feeling of happiness led me to begin to dare to publicly express my femininity at school, behind my mother's back.

I couldn't have been more than six or seven when I began to live a double life: a boy at home and a girl in school. My mother would drop me off at school, and I would run inside and quickly feminize myself before going to the classroom.

I hid a brush in my backpack and would take it out, brush the front of my medium-length curly hair down, and fluff my curls in the back. My hairstyle must have been inspired by the short hairstyle of the '90s girl group Total. Clothing options were limited, but sometimes I would wear tank tops to school, which made me look like a tomboy. For the finishing touch, I would take out the air freshener that I had stolen from my home and spray it on my body as if it were the most expensive perfume in the world.

Even though I had entered the school year identifying as a boy, some students had already mistaken me for a genetic girl, making the social transition even smoother. I don't remember how the adults responded to this. Maybe the adults viewed me as a queer child, and they allowed me to express myself freely because it was the kind thing to do. Or maybe the adults just weren't paying attention or didn't care. Regardless, I have no memory of adults objecting to my new identity.

I had finally started to live and be recognized as the girl I always knew I was. I began isolating myself less, socializing with the other children more, and even playing amongst the girls. I started to feel like I was finally one of the girls, and I was living for it.

***

Shortly after I began expressing my gender identity at school, I started exploring romantic attraction. My first crush was a blond-haired, blue-eyed boy named Alex. I would admire him from afar, and eventually, I gained the courage to speak to him. He was soft, gentle, and kind to me, something I had not experienced before from a boy.

Shortly after I began spending time with Alex, it became official that we "like-liked" each other, and we would spend the day innocently playing and sometimes even holding hands. Once the puppy love with Alex started, I realized I would have to work even harder to commit myself to my double life. However, I could not keep up the façade that I had been a genetic girl for much longer.

There were special times for the class to use the restroom. Boys would line up in one line, and the girls would line up in the other. It was optional to line up to use the restroom, and of course, I opted out, as I did not want to have to choose between going into the boy's or girl's bathroom. So, I stood in the hallway with the other students who did not need to use the restroom. I knew that I couldn't go into the forbidden girl's room, as I had been told so many times that I was not a girl by various adults in my life at that point. However, I knew my cover would be blown if I entered the boy's room. My double life would be exposed, and I would no longer be able to express myself as a girl at school anymore.

One day, when the class lined up to use the restroom, I felt like my bladder would explode, and I had no choice but to use the restroom. I stood in the hallway in agony as my full bladder contracted. I began panicking, as I knew if I did not use a restroom—any restroom—I would undoubtedly wet myself, which would possibly be more embarrassing than outing myself as a boy.

What was I to do? I could go into the girl's room, but if my cover got blown, my mother would undoubtedly get called, and I would be punished. Therefore, I had no choice but to go into the boy's restroom. So, with my bladder on the verge of popping, I cut in front of the line and darted into the boy's room. I went to the first urinal I saw and began urinating.

As I stood at the urinal, Alex stood beside me at the next urinal with his mouth wide open. "You're a boy?" he said in shock. I had no idea what to do or say, so I continued to urinate in silence and shame. I finished, zipped up my pants, washed my hands, and walked out of the bathroom with my head down in pure embarrassment.

My cover was officially blown. Alex and eventually the entire class discovered I was not a girl but a boy. The other children began to ridicule and bully me mercilessly. So, I knew I had to put the girl in me back into hiding. I was exhausted from living the double life, but I was heartbroken to find out yet again that I could not express my gender freely or safely anywhere.

Of course, following the bathroom incident, Alex distanced himself from me, but this did not stop my feelings toward him. In fact, it made my feelings even stronger. After discovering I was a boy, his interactions with me ceased. I was also being bullied, so I'm sure he figured out it was best to avoid being around me. Nonetheless, I still admired him, but from afar, as we finished first grade and moved on to second grade.

Chapter 6

The Second Time Around

By second grade, I had entirely stopped identifying as a girl. However, I struggled to let go of one small way I could express my femininity. I no longer changed my hair but continued to gussy up myself with air freshener. My mother started to use plug-in air fresheners instead of spray air fresheners at home. However, I would continue to steal the plug-in air fresheners to use as perfume. I would break off the wick of the plug-in container and rub the air-freshener liquid on myself.

One day in particular, I was really feeling the fantasy, and I went extra heavy with the air-freshener perfume. I entered the classroom and sat in my assigned seat behind Alex. Even though we sat close to each other, Alex continued to ignore me. I sat down and took out my books, and class began. Then, out of nowhere, Alex's eyes started to water and turn red.

Alex and the other children around him brought the alarming reaction to the teacher's attention. She began to comfort him and questioned if he was allergic to anything. Alex responded that he was allergic to perfume.

I immediately felt my heart drop. The teacher began sniffing around the room and asking if anyone was wearing perfume. I sat in silence and horror, realizing the potential harm I had caused, as the teacher tried to figure out who was wearing perfume. This went on for about ten minutes, but in my seven-year-old brain, it seemed like hours.

Eventually, the teacher identified that it was me who smelled like perfume. She asked me why I was wearing so much perfume, and I told her it was air freshener. The class erupted in laughter. The teacher became frantic and sent me to the bathroom to wash the air freshener off. I was humiliated. When I returned to class, Alex was gone. I found out later that he had been sent to the school nurse, and I felt tremendous guilt for causing his allergic reaction. So, I stopped wearing the air-freshener perfume after that day.

I kept trying to interact with Alex, but he continued to ignore me. I became frustrated with this and began teasing him. Children often have difficulties expressing their feelings, and children who bully other children are usually struggling with internal issues and use bullying as a way to deflect from facing those issues. However, I did not bully Alex because of my inner struggles with gender. I had started teasing Alex because, at that point, it was the only way that he would pay attention to me. I began calling him names and playing pranks on him. There was one prank that I played that I genuinely regret.

It was a warm day, and we had just returned from recess. I had come in early and discovered a thumbtack on the floor. I immediately hatched a scheme to play the ultimate prank on Alex, which involved placing the thumbtack on his seat. I had seen this done many times in cartoons and always thought it was funny. So, I quickly put the thumbtack on his seat, rushed to my seat, sat down, and waited excitedly. I snickered softly for a minute but managed to contain my laughter as the rest of the students entered the classroom.

Alex came in, sat down in his seat, and, of course, landed on the thumbtack. He immediately jumped up and began screaming in pain. The thumbtack had stuck him as planned. I could no longer remain quiet and started laughing uncontrollably. "It's not funny!" Alex cried. Everyone else in the class began laughing as well. The teacher asked me if I had placed the thumbtack on

Alex's seat. I shook my head no. Alex then stood up, and I realized that the thumbtack had pierced his jeans and was stuck in his buttocks. Well, that never happened in the cartoons. I began feeling very bad as I didn't mean to hurt him to that extent. The teacher sent him to the nurse, and I never attempted another prank like that again.

Eventually, I stopped bullying Alex. I realized that teasing him was pointless, as he still ignored me. Frustrated with this but still wanting to express my feelings, I started writing about him in a diary that I had purchased at a book fair. I loved the show *Hey Arnold!* and fancied myself after the character Helga. I would write passages and poems about Alex in my diary and lock it. Writing about Alex was one of the highlights of my day. Still, I would reserve writing primarily during school hours out of fear of my mother discovering me writing about him at home.

One day, my teacher saw me writing in my diary instead of doing my schoolwork and took it from me. I was mortified. It was unlocked, so she would be able to read what was inside if she wanted. I became very frightened about what would happen if she read it. Would she discover my love for Alex and tell my mom that I was gay? Would I get into trouble? Would she think I was weird? My mind was racing in fear. Then, the following day, while we were doing an assignment in silence, I looked up, and the teacher was at her desk, kicked back in her chair, reading my diary. I was so terrified that I couldn't focus on the assignment and just continued to stare at her in horror.

Highly stressed about the situation, I decided to tell my mother. When my mom picked me up from school that day, I told her I had a diary my teacher had taken from me, and I saw her reading it. I began crying. My mother became very upset. She told me to inform the teacher the next day that she wanted her to return the diary to me.

I did what my mother told me to do, and I got the diary back, but shortly after, I destroyed it. Looking back on this situation, I get angry at the teacher for invading my privacy. The teacher never said anything about my writing to me. However, I remember the sheer terror I felt at the idea that my teacher would discover I was gay.

I had somehow managed to discover that being gay is when one boy "like-likes" another boy. I also had been told, in so many ways, by family members, other children, and society that being gay was wrong. Having been told so many times that I was a boy and knowing that I "like-liked" other boys, I knew I was gay and must hide this information.

I only wrote about it in the diary because I believed no one would ever read it. The fact that my teacher read my diary and discovered I was gay mortified me. It's possible that she couldn't read most of what I had written, since I have always had terrible handwriting. Still, even the possibility of my teacher discovering I was gay frightened me. I feared my teacher would disclose to my mother what she had read in the diary, but luckily, she never did.

Despite knowing being gay was taboo, I could not deny how I felt toward Alex, at least not to myself. Meaning that even at that young age, I knew what my sexuality was. Sexuality is truly innate, and the reality is that children know a lot more about themselves and their romantic attraction than we give them credit for. Discussing sexuality in children, understandably, makes the majority of people uncomfortable.

Most people, excluding Freud, do not view children as sexual beings because children are not sexual beings. However, children understand the concept of attraction and know who they are attracted to. A gay child should never be told that it is wrong to be attracted to the same sex or gender, just as a child who is not gay should never be told it's wrong to be attracted to the opposite sex or gender. The parents and adult figures in the child's life must help them navigate these feelings and attractions and assure them that nothing is wrong with them.

K.K.

Knowing that I was this thing that everyone said I shouldn't be drove me further into secrecy and isolation. I had learned to keep my attraction to boys to myself, just as I had learned to keep my desire to live as a girl to myself. I had been pushed into the closet and lived there for the remainder of my childhood.

CHAPTER 7

PASSIVE

In third grade, the other children continued to bully me mercilessly, and I continued to be socially reserved and avoid interaction with other children after I realized I could not present as a girl. Most of the children from my first and second grade classes followed me into third grade. They had witnessed my failed attempts at feminizing myself and socially transitioning. My attempt at social transitioning provided plenty of fodder for childhood bullying, and I was labeled as gay. Shortly after I entered the third grade, the other children in my class began teasing me unrelentingly and calling me homophobic slurs. I was called "faggot" more times than I can remember by the other children.

Even though I had stopped attempting to present as a girl, concealing my femininity was still challenging. The other children regularly told me I acted and talked like a girl. I did not respond to the bullying and tried to ignore it. I did not tell any adults about the bullying either, although I'm sure the bullying was witnessed but ignored. Back in those days, the perspective on bullying was that it was a social norm and a part of childhood growing pains. If you did report bullying, you were sternly told by adults not to be a "tattletale." So, I kept the bullying to myself and did not seek help.

Eventually, the children who bullied me became frustrated with my lack of response to their verbal teasing and began physically harming me. One day, our school had a fire drill, and the procedure was to exit the building and line up on the playground. As we stood in line, the children in my class began calling me homophobic slurs. I ignored them as usual. Then, a boy came up to me and started shoving me. I did not know how to respond, as I did not know how to fight, so I began laughing and smiling so as not to seem distressed.

My laughter was also meant to not alarm any teachers outside with us on the playground. I did not want the teachers to know that I was being bullied and report it to my mother. I did not want my mother to discover that I was being called homophobic slurs and refused to defend myself. I did not want it to be known that I was weak and helpless.

I smiled and laughed as the boy shoved and antagonized me. Eventually, he pushed me to the ground. As I lay on the ground, I felt my eyes beginning to tear up, which made me laugh harder in an attempt to conceal my crying. Then, the boy started dragging me by the coat that I was wearing, and I went limp. Eventually, he dropped me and walked away. No one intervened to get the boy off me. I lay in the dirt and grass, still laughing and crying.

Being bullied remained a regular occurrence throughout the rest of my childhood. I never responded to the bullying and went deeper and deeper into isolation. I did not know how to reach out for help, and it did not seem that anyone was interested in helping me.

I had no friends, which made me dread lunchtime and recess, as I would eat alone and had no one to play with on the playground. I was truly alone, and loneliness is inhuman. To the adults, I was seen as being shy, but the reality was I was not shy; I was a queer child who had been ostracized. I feared interacting with my peers because I knew that they would pick on me, tell me I was acting like a girl, call me gay, and bully me. So, I stayed on the outskirts, always watching and wishing I could be normal and happy like the other children.

***

When I was in third grade, my mother began dating a man named Kelly, and he moved into our home shortly after they started dating. While my mother was strict, my brother and I soon discovered Kelly was an even stricter disciplinarian. Kelly did not use physical punishment; instead, he would punish us by grounding us and taking away our privileges. Kelly also gave us a slew of chores to do. Kelly took it upon himself to act like a father figure to my brother and myself. I'm sure he picked up on my queerness because of my effeminate nature, and he encouraged my mother to enroll me in sports activities to toughen me up.

Kelly had first suggested that my mother enroll me in karate classes. When we entered the building to sign up, I saw all the children and adults doing karate and became terrified. I had no idea what was going on, and it felt disturbingly familiar. I saw people being hit and flung to the ground. I did not understand why my mother and Kelly wanted me to be in this building with people fighting.

I began having flashbacks of all the physical and verbal bullying I endured at school. I knew that if I was placed into karate classes, I would not only be bullied but others would be encouraged to hit me. I began to weep uncontrollably, and had a panic attack, and begged my mother to take me home. She did not understand why I panicked, but she agreed to take me home immediately. In the car, my mother tried to ask me what made me cry, but I did not know how to explain my feelings.

My reaction at the karate studio did not dissuade my mother and Kelly from enrolling me in sports to toughen me up. The next attempt was soccer. Kelly bought me a soccer ball and tried to get me to play soccer with him, but I disliked it and made my displeasure obvious. I also protested the idea of being enrolled in sports in school. Eventually, my mother and Kelly gave up on trying to get me to play sports.

It wasn't just the fear of more bullying that made me protest sports so much. Even though I was living as a boy, I still felt like a girl deep down. It seemed strange to be around boys and try to act tough, so I objected to every attempt that Kelly and my mother made to get me to play sports.

Being bullied as a child would impact me for the rest of my life. To this day, I still fear social interaction. I fear allowing strangers to get close to me because I do not want to be hurt if they objectify my queerness. I still remain passive in most areas of my life as well, and I still struggle with avoidant behavior. Since childhood, I have learned that to entirely prevent myself from bullying, discrimination, and physical harm, it is best to avoid people altogether. Still, there is always something deep inside of me that longs for human connection. I have felt this longing since childhood. Of course, I did not want to be alone. Of course, I wanted to have friends, play sports, and be normal like all the other children, but socializing meant risking being bullied. Instead, I determined it was best to remain alone.

Chapter 8

Oh Deer!

One night when I was about nine and my brother was about eleven, we were driving through pitch dark to my mother's friend's house. Those Delaware back roads never had any streetlights. Driving through back roads in Delaware requires the constant use of high beams.

My brother and I sat in the back seat, calm and quiet. We had to be patient because car rides in Delaware could take up to an hour, as everything is so spread out. We would spend the long car rides mostly in silence, except for my mother occasionally singing along to the radio. My mother had an eclectic love of music that spanned multiple genres, but she would mostly listen to smooth jazz back in those days.

Suddenly a loud thud hit the top of the car, and an animal smashed against the windshield. We all screamed in horror as a dead deer slid from the windshield to the hood of the vehicle. My brother and I thought we had hit the deer head-on and killed it, but my mother explained the deer was already dead when it hit the top of the car. My mother figured out that a pickup truck that had passed her must have been hauling the dead deer, and it somehow managed to fly off the truck and onto our car.

My mother pulled over and calmed us down. Everyone was alright, but the windshield had a crack in it. The pickup truck driver never pulled over. I don't think the other driver even realized what happened. After we had all composed ourselves, we laughed about the ridiculous incident and continued our drive to my mother's friend's house.

When we arrived, there was some type of party going on. We came in and said hello to everyone. Then, my brother and I went to play with the other kids while the adults went to do whatever it was that adults did back then.

Later in the evening, my mother pulled my brother and me to the side to meet a new friend she had met. He instructed us to call him "Mr. W," which sounded like a cool nickname to us. He seemed very friendly, and my mom told us he would be coming home with us later. My brother and I were excited to have company, and Mr. W seemed fun and funny.

My mother had always been unlucky in love. Shortly after Kelly moved in, he moved out. My mother was single again, raising two boys on her own, although my mother's bad luck with men started way before Kelly entered the picture. As someone who had dealt with loneliness extensively at that point, I recognized that my mom was lonely, and I knew just how much sadness and pain this brought her. So, seeing my mother interacting joyously with Mr. W made me happy.

After that night, my mother and Mr. W began dating. My mother was a stunning beauty, and she was even more beautiful when she was in love. That's what this was…apparently. My brother and I began regularly seeing Mr. W at our house, and he would often stay overnight. He had been staying with us for a few days when my mom started debating whether he should move in, and she even consulted my brother and me before making a final decision.

One day, she sat my brother and me down in the living room and asked if we wanted Mr. W to live with us. She explained that they were in a relationship and that they wanted to live together. My mother said we could say no; if we did, Mr. W would not live with us, and she wouldn't be mad or sad about it. While I believed my mother wouldn't get angry, I knew she would be sad if I said no to Mr. W living with us.

While the main reason for my mother wanting Mr. W to move in was love, I'm sure she thought it would be beneficial to have a male figure around to help raise her two boys. The idea of having Mr. W as a stepdad was exciting, as all the time we had spent with him up to that point was pretty enjoyable. He seemed like a kind and caring man, and he even began calling me by my nickname, "Boo-Boo," just like my mom did, which somehow made me trust him more.

However, at age nine, I barely knew my elbow from my ear. Still, I knew that my mother was happy, and I loved her, so I said yes. Of course, my brother said yes too, and shortly after, Mr. W moved in with us. I had no idea what power was given to me that day, and I had no idea how I would regret my decision for the rest of my life.

***

Shortly after our family meeting, Mr. W moved in with us. We had long moved out from the small apartment and now were living in a spacious and quiet three-bedroom house. In the beginning, life with Mr. W was amazing. My brother began calling him "Dad," but I continued calling him Mr. W. It felt odd to call someone I hadn't known that long my dad. Luckily, he didn't push me on it. Ultimately, Mr. W began acting like a father figure to my brother but continued to treat me as a friend. He showed my mother love and affection; seeing her in a relationship was nice.

However, Mr. W could not keep up his façade of being a loving stepfather and boyfriend for long. Within a month, his true character began to show. Mr. W would become a demon, terrorizing my mother, my brother, and myself. Our lives became a tumultuous hell full of violence, abuse, and disharmony. Mr. W started to reveal his true self through verbal aggression toward my brother.

Mr. W began taking his role as my brother's father figure seriously and became a strict disciplinarian. He would verbally abuse my brother regularly by putting him down and calling him names in an attempt to discipline him. Eventually, his discipline tactics progressed beyond verbal abuse to physical abuse. Mr. W began beating and torturing my brother for his behavioral issues in school. Sometimes, Mr. W would beat him for other things, like bedwetting or if he caught him fibbing. I was in a constant state of anxiety and fear living with Mr. W, waiting for him to hurt me like he did my brother.

Mr. W would sometimes beat my brother privately in his room. However, I could clearly still hear my brother from behind the closed door, screaming and crying with each echo of the slaps and hits he received. Eventually, the beatings became public, and Mr. W would beat my brother in front of me, and then in front of my mother as well, who would usually say nothing out of fear.

One winter night when it was snowing outside, Mr. W had beaten my brother mercilessly in the living room, and after the beating, he stripped him naked, threw him outside into the cold, and told him to find a new home. Shocked by this scene, I immediately began cleaning my room and doing my homework. Mr. W saw my reaction and thought it was hilarious, laughing at my response. "I guess you don't want to be thrown outside, too, huh?" Mr. W laughed. Fearfully, I smiled and laughed back as I continued to clean my room with my head down. Eventually, he let my brother back inside, shivering uncontrollably from the cold.

Clearly, Mr. W beat my brother in front of me to display his power and as a warning. These psychological tactics worked because I decided that night that I would become the golden child. I would be nothing like my brother and excel at school and home, and Mr. W would never have an excuse to treat me the way he treated my brother. My plan worked, and I was never beaten or abused by Mr. W as he did my brother.

What always puzzled me as a child was why my mother did not step in to stop Mr. W when he beat my brother. As an adult, I realize she was most likely terrified of being harmed in the crossfire of intervening to stop Mr. W from beating my brother. Just like my mother, Mr. W was also raised in an abusive household, and I'm sure he believed the abuse, which went beyond discipline, was needed to address my brother's behavioral issues. For Mr. W, beating a child was the only way to discipline.

Also, Mr. W was raised by parents who not only abused him but also abused each other. Eventually, the cycle of abuse continued, and Mr. W became verbally abusive toward my mother, calling her obscene and explicit names during their arguments and putting her down. Despite all this, my mother continued her relationship with Mr. W and soon became pregnant with my sister. One would think the pregnancy would cause some peace, but it did not. In fact, it was shortly after my mother became pregnant that Mr. W began to physically abuse her as well.

The first time I can remember witnessing Mr. W hitting my mother came at night. I was fast asleep in my bed when suddenly I was awakened by bloodcurdling screams of a woman coming from the living room. I quickly realized the woman was my mother, and I was stricken with terror as I realized that she was in danger. Then, a second voice came. It was Mr. W: "Shut up, bitch!" I began to panic, wondering what was going on. My mother's screams were piercing. She sounded like she was being murdered.

Filled with bravery and terror unbeknownst to my then-nine-year-old self, I jumped out of bed and ran into the living room. What I witnessed has haunted me to this very day. My mother was on the floor face-down, screaming and crying in pain. She kept repeating, "Get off of me, please!" Well into her second trimester, she had a visible baby bump. Mr. W was on top of her, punching her sides, including her stomach. I was shocked at the sight. The living room was painted red, which only intensified the scene. There were barely any lights on, only dull lamp lighting. Mr. W looked like a literal demon pinning down my mother.

While he beat her, he continued to scream at her and tell her to shut up. I was in the doorway, frozen in fear. Then I began crying and shouting, "Get off my mom!" I turned around and saw that my brother was standing behind me. He had been awakened by the noise as well and seemed shocked into silence.

Mr. W ignored all of my pleas to get off my mother. I knew then I would have to fight Mr. W. Still, I knew that nine-year-old me could not win a fight against a grown man with muscle alone. So, I ran to my bedroom and grabbed a computer keyboard. I ran back into the living room and began hitting Mr. W with it, begging him to get off my mom. It was like he was made of metal; it didn't even faze him. Then he got up, grabbed me, and threw me (and the keyboard) into my room and slammed the door. Terrified, I sat in my room and listened to my mother scream and beg for mercy. Then, an eerie silence fell over the house.

I sat in a corner of my room with my legs pulled to my chest. What had happened? Was my mother dead? My mind was racing, thinking of all the horrible things that Mr. W could have done to silence my mother. Then a frightening thought came to me: Did he kill her? I wondered what to do. Was I next? What would he do to my brother? Where was my brother? I did not know what to do, so I waited there for Mr. W to come and kill me. Finally, after what seemed like hours, I regained my bravery and came out of my room. I had the computer keyboard in my hand again and was ready to fight if I had to.

I discovered Mr. W, my mom, and a large, kind-faced woman talking in the living room. I wondered who this woman was and where she came from. "Come over here, baby," she said as she signaled me to sit beside her. "I'm Grammy," she told me. She explained that she was Mr. W's mom. She embraced me, and I felt a sense of calmness and security in her hug. I did not know this woman, but I felt she had a pure heart and could be trusted. They continued their conversation.

After the fight, Mr. W and my mother had called Grammy to help settle the peace and offer guidance on what to do next. Grammy began detailing how Mr. W's dad used to beat her and how incidents like these just happen sometimes. Even at a young age, I knew that Grammy had somehow normalized abuse, which was wrong.

I looked at my mother. She looked like hell. Her face was reddened from the slapping, and she had some noticeable bruising on her arms. Mr. W sat there with his arms crossed, a stern look on his face. I hated him. I wished that I never agreed to allow him to move in. I wished we had never driven to my mom's friend's house that night. I thought back to the dead deer hitting our car. Maybe it was some type of omen, some message from God telling us to go home because a demon awaited us at our destination.

Grammy continued talking and asked my mother if she still wanted to be with Mr. W. I thought for sure that she would say no, but instead, she said yes. I realized her predicament was complicated, even at my young age. She was pregnant, with two older children and no family support. She had already lost my brother's father and my father to the legal system. Mr. W was the only father figure around. What could she do? Was my unborn sister to be raised without a father? I could only imagine the thoughts that rushed through my mother's head.

I never found out what my mother and Mr. W were fighting about that night. Although, Mr. W often got upset when my mother talked to him with sass and attitude, so this probably led to the physical altercation that night. Still, this was no excuse for beating a pregnant woman.

Grammy scolded Mr. W and told him that he had to control his anger, especially considering that my mother was pregnant. For a short while, it seemed Mr. W had listened to his mother, and the violence ceased. However, this peace was brief, and the violence became even more regular and even more ugly.

CHAPTER 9

NUTS

It was another typical day. I had just arrived home from school, and my mother was in the living room watching TV. It seemed like another ordinary evening. I headed off to do my homework. Then would come dinner, then bed. My brother had come in shortly after me, and so did Mr. W. My brother and I attended different schools, so he would usually arrive later than I did. Because my brother had a learning disability, he attended special education classes. We were both entrusted to walk ourselves to and from school. Luckily, our schools were about a ten-minute walk away from our house.

Usually, my brother was pretty jovial, but today, he looked worried, as if he knew something terrible was about to happen. At school, my brother was known as a bit of a troublemaker. He had some mild behavioral issues, most likely due to his genetic condition, but was a good kid overall. He would often act out in class, and my mother frequently received phone calls from his teachers.

My brother's behavior at school was one of the main reasons for his frequent physical punishment. However, eventually, it came to be that nothing my brother did was good enough. Worse, my mother and Mr. W compared my brother's functioning and development to mine, a blatant injustice. How could you compare the functioning of someone with a developmental disability to someone neurotypical? As a result, my brother was beaten constantly, and this day was no exception.

"I got a call from your teacher today. She told me you stole a pack of peanuts off her desk. Is this true?" my mother demanded. My brother nodded in fear. My mother continued, "You know stealing is wrong?" My brother remained silent and nodded again.

Mr. W decided to chip in, "Why are you stealing shit like we don't feed you? Huh?" My brother's face was expressionless and blank. It was as if he had become used to the verbal and physical abuse at that point and was unfazed by it.

"I'm a beat your ass!" Mr. W yelled. "You know better than to be stealing!" He charged my brother, who winced and guarded his face with his arms in fear. Then, in one swift motion, Mr. W grabbed my brother and threw him against the living room wall. He began kicking him in the sides, then slapping him in the face.

My brother begged Mr. W to stop, but he continued. The slaps echoed throughout the room loudly, like a tree branch breaking. Then, the slapping stopped, but Mr. W kept yelling at my brother. "Stop crying like a bitch! Since you want to cry like you are in pain, I'm going to show you some real pain." He charged into the kitchen, leaving my brother on the floor.

I heard the kitchen sink running. Mr. W returned. "I'm going to show you some real pain, bitch!"

"Stop it!" my mother yelled from the living room couch.

"Shut the fuck up!" Mr. W yelled back. My brother was on the floor in a fetal position, sobbing. Mr. W reached down and picked my brother up by his arms and dragged him from the living room to the kitchen.

As if he knew what would happen next, my brother started screaming and begging for forgiveness. My mother and I ran behind them. The hot water from the kitchen sink was running on full blast. Steam had begun to fill the room. I wondered what Mr. W would do with this hot water. Since my brother was stealing, I thought he might put his hands into the scalding water.

But, instead, Mr. W picked my brother up off the floor, grabbing him by the head and flipping him right-side-up. Mr. W then shoved my brother's face under the scalding hot water. My brother screamed for mercy, choking, but Mr. W showed him none. My brother, who was light-skinned, began to turn bright red from the hot water. He closed his eyes and continued wailing and thrashing his body against the sink. He tried to escape, but Mr. W's grip was firm and unrelenting. "Open your eyes," Mr. W commanded.

I did not think it could get any more gruesome, but it did. Mr. W took his fingers and pried open my brother's eyes. I still remember seeing the pinks of the inside of my brother's eyelids and the whites of his bulging eyes. Mr. W then forced his eyes under the faucet, filling them with burning hot water.

My brother's thrashing increased, and he wailed, "No, Dad!" I watched the ghastly scene in horror and shock. My mother also remained silent in fear. Finally, Mr. W turned off the water and threw my brother to the floor; his face was red and swollen. I had never seen my brother's face and eyes look like that. He had saliva and water all over his clothing. "Now, steal again!" Mr. W said, and he left the kitchen.

As Mr. W exited the kitchen, my mother quietly comforted my brother, who was still on the floor, wet and weeping. I stayed in the room in silence, attempting to process what was probably the most violent incident I had ever seen. I was too shocked and afraid to move and did not know how to respond or comfort my brother. Fortunately, he didn't sustain any permanent physical injuries from the incident. However, the psychological damage that he, my mother, and I all experienced that day would never heal.

***

Mr. W's inhumane and torturous abuse toward my brother intensified, and eventually the evidence of abuse became apparent to outsiders. DYFS (Division of Youth and Family Services), now known as DCP&P (Division of Child Protection and Permanency), quickly became a consistent presence in our lives. My brother's school regularly called DYFS to report the abuse, as my brother would go to school with markings from the beatings, and when asked what happened, he would tell the truth.

After multiple visits, DYFS eventually removed my brother from our home and placed him into foster care. However, my brother would act out in the foster homes, and he would subsequently be returned to our house. Most parents would see the issue of my brother acting out in the foster homes as a cry for help. However, Mr. W saw it as an opportunity to tell my brother that nobody wanted him and that he should stop telling his teachers about the beatings because no one cared.

Despite my brother being returned to our home, DYFS's presence remained in our lives, and they required Mr. W and my mother to do counseling and family therapy, which I also had to participate in. Respite care was also offered, which allowed my brother to go away for the weekend to give Mr. W and my mother a break from caring for him. Still, ultimately, none of the interventions of DYFS made a difference, and the abuse continued.

After experiencing the foster homes asking for him to be removed and being returned to live with Mr. W and my mother time and time again, my brother eventually learned that what Mr. W told him was true: No one was going to help him, and no one cared. So, he stopped reporting the abuse to his teachers, and he became another child that DYFS failed to protect.

***

The presence of DYFS frightened me. I had been interviewed multiple times by DYFS workers to confirm my brother's reports of his abuse. However, my mother and Mr. W had told me not to say anything to them. Otherwise, I would be taken away to live in foster care. Being raised in the foster care system, my mother had survived a plethora of abuse. She told me that if I was placed into foster care, I could be exposed to abuse the way that she was. The picture of foster care that was painted by my mother somehow seemed much scarier than the toxic environment I was living in. So, I never told the DYFS workers or anyone of the abuse that was happening in my home.

My fear of Mr. W was unimaginable, and I tried my best to remain unseen and non-problematic. I stayed well-behaved and obedient out of fear of being punished like my brother had been, which seemed to work as Mr. W never abused me. In fact, he was always very kind and loving toward me. Mr. W admired how well I did in school and how quiet and well-mannered I was. However, this filled me with pity and anxiety.

I saw how Mr. W wanted to make more of his life. He had no career, worked odd jobs, and never knew any form of stability. I was always worried that his admiration would turn into envy and that he would beat me out of sheer jealousy. He had no idea that the main reason I was so well-behaved was not out of free will but out of fear.

I was the golden child and had to be constantly polished and perfect. I could not enjoy being a child because I was too busy living up to such high expectations. I lived in fear that I would end up like my brother, who was labeled a bad child. I had to remain good. Otherwise, I would have the life beaten out of me.

Mr. W admired me because he saw in me what he wanted to be: obedient and successful. He hated my brother because he saw himself in him: a troubled child. So, Mr. W dealt with my brother the way that he had been dealt with as a child, with violence. Mr. W's father was highly abusive, not only to his mother but to him and his brothers. Seeing what Mr. W did to my brother, I could only imagine the horrible things that were done to him when he was young.

I had met Mr. W's father before and was forced to call him "Pop-Pop." In his old age, Pop-Pop had become paralyzed after a stroke and could no longer walk. As messed up as it sounds, I believe wholeheartedly that the stroke and subsequent paralysis were pure karma. Karma for the violence toward his family, and karma for the endless cycles of violence that he spawned.

Despite the abuse, my brother remained perpetually cheerful and kind to Mr. W, which seemed to disturb Mr. W more than anything. No matter what, my brother always remains unwaveringly happy. Individuals with Williams syndrome are generally unshakably happy and highly social, which is why some refer to the disorder as a "friendly" condition. Even though Mr. W would beat my brother to the point of hospitalization, my brother would still want Mr. W to be his friend. The forgiving and friendly nature of Williams syndrome has caused my brother endless pain and suffering. He would frequently find himself in situations in which a cruel person would abuse him.

For example, when he was about twelve, he became "friends" with some older kids who would urinate on him, burn him with cigarettes, and even explode firecrackers in his ears. A neurotypical person would understand to avoid people like this, but someone with Williams syndrome does not. That is the danger of Williams syndrome: indiscriminate friendliness and forgiveness paired with an absence of innate caution.

We live in a cruel society in which people prey on the weak, and individuals with Williams syndrome are among our most vulnerable. Mr. W hated my brother because his joy was unbreakable. Yet, my brother would still treat Mr. W like a friend and a father despite all of his abuse. Mr. W, like most abusers, wanted the satisfaction and power that come from their victim's fear. My brother wouldn't give it to him because he simply did not know how to, which only worsened Mr. W's rage. What a miracle. What a curse.

CURSE

He is lovely
He is kind
He is perfection personified

He is strong
With gentle hands
He is everything you'd want in a man

But don't be fooled
He is ugly
He is cruel
He will use you like a tool

He is evil
He's demonic
He's a poison disguised as tonic

He will beat
He will scorn
He will kill your firstborn

What an angel
What a devil
Evil, on another level

He will love you
He will hate you
He will hold you down and rape you

BRAVE

But you didn't know
You opened the door
Now
You are his
And he is yours

What a lesson
What a blessing
What a curse

CHAPTER 10

THE CAR CHASE

When I was around ten years old, we moved out of our home due to financial difficulties. Mr. W was unemployed but continued to work odd jobs. The telemarketing company that my mother was working for had closed, and she was now unemployed as well. With only an eighth grade education, she found it difficult to find work. Previously, she had been able to lie about her education, but as technology progressed, potential employers were able to verify it and turn her away. I had always admired my mother's hustle. Despite her lack of education, she always managed to land in managerial positions. The job loss was tough on her. It was hard seeing my mother in this state: unemployed, depressed, and pregnant.

We moved in with Mr. W's mother in her tiny, comfy, two-bedroom home. Soon after, my mother gave birth to my sister. We all lived in one room: My brother and I slept on the floor, and my mother, Mr. W, and my sister slept on the bed. It was cramped, but being close to my family was nice. Being in Mr. W's mother's house seemed to have stopped the abuse and violence for some time, but this did not last. Although, this time, it seemed that my mother was not willing to tolerate Mr. W's abuse any longer.

I'm not sure what switched in my mother. Since Mr. W's abuse started, my mother was too afraid to protect my brother or herself, but something changed. Perhaps some instinct took over when she gave birth to my sister, and she had begun to be courageous. Finally realizing that Mr. W's abuse was not love, my mother started to seek ways of escaping the doomed relationship. Eventually, she gained the bravery to seek safety at a battered women's shelter. This was my first of many times staying at a battered women's shelter.

The first shelter where we stayed was an old Victorian home in the middle of nowhere. At least four other women were staying there, and they all welcomed us. It was the first time in a long time that I actually felt safe. We all stayed in one room with two beds. My mother and sister would sleep on one bed, and my brother and I took turns sleeping on the floor. We even had our own bathroom. My mom is a germaphobe and made me robustly clean the bathroom with bleach. I remember her yelling at me for not bleaching the back of the toilet. I didn't know the back of the toilet needed cleaning!

We were the only people of color staying in the shelter. All the other ladies in the shelter were White and very kind. I remember one lady having a black eye, undoubtedly from an abusive man. A sweet older lady took a liking to me, and I loved spending time with her. For some odd reason, I have always found comfort in being in the company of an elderly person. My love of older people undoubtedly came from being raised by my grandparents. My mother often said I had an old spirit. I enjoyed watching old black-and-white movies and listening to classic jazz musicians like Billie Holiday.

I loved the women's shelter and wanted to stay there forever, but my mom said we could only stay there for one month. I soon discovered this would be a rule at all the shelters where we stayed, as we ultimately navigated from one shelter to another. We would eat dinner together every night with the other women and children. It felt as if I was a part of a large family.

One morning, my mother woke up my brother and me to run downstairs. A costume jewelry company had donated a vast supply of costume jewelry to the shelter. Everyone was allowed to take whatever they wanted. It was so fun to try on the jewelry and help my mom pick out some jewelry. My brother picked out a dog tag necklace. I only had my left ear pierced then, so I got stud earrings. On the surface, the jewelry donation seems like a superficial opportunity to look flashy. However, for my family, it was so much more than that. It was an opportunity to lift our broken spirits and prove to ourselves that we were worthy of beautiful things, from jewelry to love.

We all enjoyed the shelter, and, of course, we were very happy to be protected from Mr. W. We knew what peace felt like again. We had not known that level of peace for almost two years. It almost felt too good to be true, as we knew that Mr. W could show up at any moment and resume his reign of terror over us.

Soon, my mother was contacted by Mr. W. He begged her to have us over for some sort of apology dinner at his mother's house. For some reason, my mother agreed and told us not to tell anyone at the shelter because contacting abusers was against the rules. My mother was caught in the cycle of abuse, and she dragged us right along with her.

Most of my childhood would be filled with these repetitious cycles of leaving and returning to Mr. W. My mother's excuse for returning was always about wanting a family for us. However, the reality is she wanted a family for herself. I soon began to resent my mother for keeping us in that hellish cycle of abuse. I did not understand what was so important or so special about Mr. W, nor did I understand how my mother could endure being beaten and watch her special needs son be severely abused. I think that is what upset me the most: the abuse against my brother.

My mother tolerated being abused by Mr. W, which is sick to think about, but she was an adult. My brother, on the other hand, was a child and had no option to escape Mr. W's abuse. My mother not stopping Mr. W from abusing my brother and repeatedly placing us back into a toxic environment was inexcusable. Still, I understand that many victims of domestic violence struggle to leave their abuser out of fear and sometimes, such as with my mother, out of hope that things will change for the better. However, the reality is they seldom do.

It was a Sunday when we left to meet Mr. W. Walking out of the shelter, I stared at the shelter's emergency cell phone. We were encouraged to take and use it if we thought we would be endangered. Something deep inside me told me to grab the phone and take it with us. I knew I should have taken the phone, but I didn't. We all piled into the car. My brother and I sat in the back seat, and my sister would sit in the passenger's seat with her car seat facing backward. We drove silently to Mr. W's mother's house with the windows down. It was summer and very hot.

"We're only going to have dinner, then we're leaving—no more than two hours. I promise," my mother said. We parked, rolled the windows up, and exited the car.

We were met by a smiling Mr. W. "Hey, y'all. Dinner's about to be done, come on in," he said. I despised him. I remember the day my mother asked my brother and me if he could move in. I wish I had said what I truly wanted to say. I wish I had told her no, and we could have avoided this nightmare of a life.

Grammy, Mr. W's mother, was out, so we were alone in the house. When I discovered that Grammy wasn't home, I knew something terrible was about to happen, as Grammy often served as a source of protection from Mr. W's violence. The dinner was awkward, needless to say. I could barely eat because I was terrified the entire time. Not only was the food (ham, rice, lima beans) nasty as hell , but I was sitting across from a complete psychopath.

I watched Mr. W eat his food in sheer delight. I'm sure he was happy to have his victims back. I'm sure this was a true victory for him. "So, how's the shelter," he asked us mockingly.

"Good," we all answered. Then, he began talking about how he went to church and how things would be different. He spoke as if he thought we were coming back to stay, and I started to get the feeling that we were.

My mother understood this and clarified, "You know, I just stopped by so you could see the kids." Even I knew that was a lie. Clearly, Mr. W's hold over my mother was strong and unrelenting. This was true dysfunction.

Shortly after, we finished dinner, and my mom told us to start heading to the car. She gave me the keys to start the car; this always made me feel like a grown-up. My brother and I walked to the car, and I carried my baby sister in my arms. I put her in her car seat, and she quickly fell asleep. The sun was starting to go down, but it was still hot. My mom frowned upon using the AC, so my brother and I rolled the car windows down.

We waited impatiently for my mother in the hot car. Then, she finally came outside in a rush. As she walked down the stairs to the car, we could hear her arguing with Mr. W. "You're not going to take my daughter!" Mr. W yelled.

My mom ran to the car, got in, and backed out quickly. "Roll up the windows," she instructed us. My brother and I began rolling up the car windows in pure terror. In those days, you had to manually open and close the windows. We cranked the levers for our backseat windows as quickly as we could. My mother reached over and started rolling up the passenger seat window, where my sister was, but it was difficult for her to grip the lever.

Mr. W was running toward the car at full speed. My sister's window was still half down, and Mr. W tried to force his hand into the window, but the car was moving so fast that he couldn't. Then he grabbed the passenger door handle from outside the car and tried to open it, but luckily the door was locked. My mom continued to back out of the driveway and roll the passenger window up. Finally, all the windows were rolled up. Mr. W kept running after the car and punching the passenger-side window where my sister was. Finally, my mother finished backing out of the driveway and began speeding back to the shelter.

"I'm so sorry, you guys. He's crazy!" she said, out of breath from all the excitement.

I tried to relax, but I knew the disaster was far from over. I had seen too many Lifetime movies by then. I knew Mr. W had a car and thought he might follow us to the shelter. Then, out of nowhere, we felt a car slam into our rear. It was Mr. W! He was following us at full speed.

"Pull the fuck over!" he screamed out his car window.

My mom rolled her window down some, and then she screamed back, "You're crazy!" He pulled up to the driver's side and tried to grab the door. He was leaning over in his car, reaching through his passenger window (he was very tall). My brother and I began to scream in sheer and utter horror. *This is it. This is how Mr. W is finally going to kill us*, I thought.

To make matters worse, we were on a backroad. Backroads in Delaware were typically long and deserted. Ditches are usually on each side of the road to allow rain to drain. I feared Mr. W would hit our car and force us into one of the ditches. My mother had the pedal to the metal, but we could not escape him. He went back to driving behind us. Then boom! He smashed into us again from the back.

He then returned to the left side of our car and began slamming into us from the side. We were getting dangerously close to driving into the ditch, and Mr. W knew that. My mother managed to get in front of him again. "Hold on, y'all, we're close to the main road," she told us.

Then he sped up to us again and slammed into our left side once more. "Pull over!" he yelled through his passenger window.

He kept slamming into the rear of our car until we finally made it to the main road, where there were plenty of witnesses. However, even with all the witnesses, Mr. W slammed his car again into the back of ours. Bystanders looked at the scene in shock. Finally, a Good Samaritan called the police and reported what was happening. Miraculously, we began to see the flashing of police lights, and my mom finally pulled over. Mr. W had pulled over as well.

There were two cop cars, one by my mom's car and one by Mr. W's. My mother explained everything that had happened to the police. They asked if everyone was okay, and somehow we were, despite being slammed into multiple times. The officers spoke with my brother and me, and we confirmed my mother's report. Surprisingly, my sister had stayed asleep throughout the whole nightmare. Shortly after, Mr. W was arrested.

Seeing Mr. W being handcuffed evoked a strange sense of ambivalence in me. I had a deep-seated hatred for him and did not want him to harm my family anymore, but I also didn't want to see him punished, even though I knew he deserved it. Despite everything, he was my only father figure. This must have been a similar predicament to what my mother found herself in.

So, Mr. W was taken to jail that day. I felt relieved that someone was finally protecting us from Mr. W, even though it took him almost killing the entire family. However, I knew the cycle of abuse was not over and that soon enough, he would be released and resume his reign of terror. But for now, we had some peace. Incredibly, my mother's car was still drivable, and we drove back to the shelter in silence.

PART II: ADOLESCENCE

CHAPTER 11

SUMMERS IN PATERSON

The abuse in my home continued for the remainder of my childhood. The pattern of Mr. W being incarcerated and then released for domestic violence also continued. I would get a break from the chaos over the summer break, though, when I would be sent to stay with my father's family in Paterson, New Jersey, under the supervision of my Auntie Lini. I started spending summers there when I was around age six. Going to New Jersey for the summer was always the highlight of my year.

When I was about nine or ten, my father somehow returned to the U.S. undocumented. He came back before 9/11, so airport security wasn't as strict. From what I have been told, he borrowed the passport of one of my cousins who looked similar and impersonated him at the airport. My family also told me that he was severely depressed from loneliness after being deported back to Guyana, as, at that point, the majority of his family was in America. So, he did everything and anything he could to make his way back to the U.S.

The day I met my father was virtually unremarkable. When my father first came back to the U.S., he lived in my grandparents' house but eventually moved out after finding a place of his own. So, the summer that I met my father, he had since moved out of my grandparents' house. I remember playing video games in one of my older cousins' rooms when Auntie Lini called me to come downstairs into the living room.

I came down promptly and was greeted by a slim, plain-looking, dark-skinned man. I did not know who the man was, but Auntie Lini quickly introduced him as my father. "This is your father!" Auntie Lini said with excitement. My father said hello, but I just stared at him in silence. I did not know how to respond and was in disbelief that this man was truly my father, as he looked nothing like me, and he definitely did not exude queerness in the way that I did.

My father seemed jovial and friendly, but his masculinity overpowered these personality traits and intimidated me. I stood silently until Auntie Lini nudged me toward my father to hug him, and I did. My father's embrace felt foreign to me; it was not the same reaction I had when I reunited with my mother. No, the embrace felt superficial this time, as if I was being hugged by a stranger. After the hug, I asked Auntie Lini if I could return to playing video games. Shocked, she asked me why I wasn't more excited to see my father for the first time, but I did not respond. Frustrated with my lack of enthusiasm, Auntie Lini told me I could return upstairs.

My father felt alien to me, and I believe the feeling was mutual. I was clearly a queer child, and I don't think he knew how to navigate parenting a child like me. Despite this, my father would try to interact with me and make me laugh whenever he was around me. However, I would usually remain silent and distant, as his masculinity continued to intimidate me.

With my father being so masculine, I assumed that having an effeminate and gay son would be difficult for him to accept. I had been told by virtually every man in my father's family that I was gay, which, according to them, was a bad thing to be. Reasonably enough, I assumed my masculine father would also harbor these homophobic views. So, to prevent him from rejecting or ridiculing me, I avoided him.

Despite my attempts to avoid him, my father continued to try to interact and spend time with me. Still, I would either remain silent in his presence or disengage. Eventually, he took the hint, and after much rejection, he also began avoiding me. So, I did not spend the summers in New Jersey at my father's residence. Instead, I would spend the summers living at my grandparents' house with Auntie Lini.

Auntie Lini continued to take responsibility for me and watch over me in my parents' absence. She would always drive to Delaware to bring me back to New Jersey. My relationship with Auntie Lini began during my infancy when my mother left me under her care, and her support of me continued throughout my life. Auntie Lini would spoil me all summer, buying me whatever my heart desired and taking me on fun outings with my cousins.

Summers in Paterson were filled with parties, barbecues, and family outings that filled the warm days and made the season fly by. Although, these summers were not wholly carefree. Auntie Lini was a kind and generous woman, but she was also very strict and tried to instill class and structure into me and my cousins. We would often make fun of her behind her back and mock her famous saying, which was "You guys have no 'etiquit'" (not etiquette, *eti-quit*).

Auntie Lini had no children of her own, but she quickly became my maternal figure while I stayed at the house. All of my cousins who lived in the home lived with their parents, so she did not have to watch over them the way she did me. Auntie Lini truly treated me like her child by not only spoiling me with gifts but also trying to instill values and discipline in me through her giving me various rules, chores, and homework.

Homework would be assigned in the morning before she left for work and was expected to be completed by the time she returned home in the afternoon. She would give me, and sometimes my cousins, various assignments, including looking up the definitions of words and even writing short stories. My cousins and I relished it when Auntie Lini and the rest of the adults were at work because it was an opportunity for us to run wild. We would spend most of the day carefree, getting into all kinds of mischief. Still, we knew we had better have our stuff together by the time Auntie Lini came home.

Auntie Lini was most strict when it came to bedtime. My cousins' parents did not give them a bedtime, as it was summer, but being under the care of Auntie Lini, my bedtime was around 9:00 p.m. When I was younger, I would sleep with Auntie Lini in her room with her, sharing her bed. However, when I became older, around age nine or ten, I began sleeping in my grandparents' room, which was next to Auntie Lini's room. My grandparents would sleep in their two twin beds, and I would sleep on the floor between them. My grandparents were heavy sleepers, so sneaking out of their room was easy.

While I stayed in my grandparents' room, my cousins would watch Auntie Lini's room, waiting for her to turn off the lights, which meant she was asleep. Then they would tiptoe to my grandparents' room and tell me the coast was clear, and I would quietly exit my grandparents' room. However, to my surprise, Auntie Lini would often come and get me later, scolding me for sneaking out and making me return to bed. All this sneaking out of bed and getting caught by Auntie Lini was actually pretty fun, and my cousins and I would always laugh about it the next day.

Despite Auntie Lini's strictness, she still managed to provide me with care. No one else in my life had ever given me that level of attentiveness or comfort, and to this day, no one ever has. What I was receiving from my Auntie Lini was love, true, pure love. In many ways, my relationship with my Auntie Lini made up for the deficits in care that I had experienced with my mother and father, which is nothing short of miraculous.

Auntie Lini never asked for money from my mother or father, or anything for that matter, and would take care of me all summer on her own. I never knew why she did this for me, and I suppose I never will, but I genuinely believe she did not want me to feel forgotten. Most importantly, perhaps, she wanted me to know that she saw me: a sad and lost child.

Toward the end of the summer, Auntie Lini would take me school clothes shopping, which was always somber as it meant that my time in New Jersey was ending. I never revealed to Auntie Lini, or anyone else for that matter, the toxic environment I was living in with my mother and Mr. W. My mother had told me that revealing the dysfunction in my household would be an ultimate act of betrayal, so I kept the secret to myself.

When summer ended, Auntie Lini would drive me back to Delaware in her fancy green convertible BMW with the top down, rocking her oversized, glamorous sunglasses with her hair blowing in the wind. I would sit quietly in sadness in the passenger seat throughout the ride. I think Auntie Lini was also sad during the ride back to Delaware, but she always put on a brave and happy face.

Each year, Auntie Lini would try her best to make the trip back to Delaware joyous, making jokes, laughing, and playing music. She would also make frequent stops, stretching the trip and giving us more time with each other. However, getting me to cheer up on that Delaware car ride was nearly impossible. After about an hour of driving, I would inevitably start crying. Auntie Lini would reach over and squeeze my hand and promise that she would pick me up again the following summer, which always brought me some comfort.

FRIEND

She was a star that shone in the night
I was lost and looked to her for light

She was the calm
During the storm
Kind and careworn
She was my friend

Someone who gave a damn
Somone who told me I can
Someone who believed in me
And made me believe in myself
She was my friend

She was my world
She was my girl
A sister, aunt, cousin, and mother
There will never be another

A lasting impression
The saving grace
During my darkest depression

A warm embrace
A smiling face
A place to call home
A companion when I was all alone
She was my friend

Comfort during the pain
Shelter during the rain
Love in a world full of hate
Support when I felt I might break
She was my friend

CHAPTER 12

SHEMALES IN LEATHER

When I was around eleven, my mother and Mr. W decided to move to Ohio for a fresh start. We were still living with Mr. W's mother, Grammy, but Mr. W had some friends in Ohio and thought it would be an ideal place to relocate. Mr. W and my mother took my brother and sister with them to Ohio but figured it would be best if they sent me to live with my father's family temporarily until they were stabilized. I was thrilled by the idea of living with my father's family again, as long as I did not have to live with my father.

My relationship with my father continued to be awkward. I did not feel comfortable calling him "Dad" or even referring to him as "my father" because, truthfully, he never really was a father figure up to that point. He had been absent for most of my childhood, and the bonding period had come and gone. Shortly after he returned to the U.S., he became involved with a Guyanese woman with whom he had two daughters. To me, it felt like he had moved on with his life to bigger and better things, and I was a constant reminder of his ugly past. Our mutual avoidance worsened once he established his new family. So, when it came down to deciding where I would stay, I voiced that I wanted to live at my grandparents' house with Auntie Lini.

The prospect of living in New Jersey again was exciting. Whenever Mr. W would start his reign of terror, I would always mentally escape to New Jersey and reminisce on my summers in

Paterson. New Jersey had become a psychological retreat for me, my happy place. My mother had spoken to my father and Auntie Lini before I returned to New Jersey, and they agreed that I would live with Auntie Lini. My mother gave Auntie Lini temporary guardianship over me, although this never went through the courts.

I returned to New Jersey at the end of the school year, with only one month left of fifth grade. I still remember when Auntie Lini took me to enroll in school. She took me to the school's front office.

A secretary asked Auntie Lini questions regarding where my parents were, how old I was, what grade I was in, and so on. My mother had sent me my birth certificate and Social Security card, which Auntie Lini gave to the secretary. She also gave the secretary a letter, which the woman thought was written by my mother, that stated that Auntie Lini was my legal guardian and that I would be residing with her in Paterson. What the secretary did not know was that Auntie Lini had written the letter herself and forged my mother's signature. Back in those days, it was a lot easier to get around governmental red tape. The school accepted the letter, enrolled me, and shortly after, I began class.

I went to school with my other cousins who lived in my grandparents' house. Since they were all older than I was and were enrolled in higher grades, I rarely saw them in school. Shortly after I started sixth grade, the children started bullying me. I didn't experience bullying in fifth grade because I was only with the class for about a month. However, when sixth grade began, the bullying was heightened. What I experienced in Paterson was somehow much more cruel and violent than the bullying I had received in Delaware, which frightened me into a higher level of isolation. I continued my pattern of keeping the bullying to myself and never told anyone at home about it.

Although I was bullied at school, I had a lot of fun spending time with my older cousins, especially my cousin Devin, who was about two years older than I was. Devin was my cool older cousin whom I aspired to be like. He was the complete opposite of me: cool, masculine, and able to socialize with others. He was also bright, excelling in school, and a talented artist. Devin and I would spend our days getting into all kinds of mischief, playing pranks on people. We had separate rooms but frequently stayed up all night, talking and laughing, watching television, playing video games, and discussing our future.

Devin stayed in a room with his mother and younger brother, and I shared a room on a different floor with an older male cousin. I hated having to share a room, but luckily, the older cousin was away at college and only came home during school breaks. So, for the most part, I had the room to myself. With my older cousin being away at college, Devin and I were free to look through his belongings, and we discovered his pornography collection.

Despite being molested, I was pretty ignorant to the concept of sex at that point. Devin, however, seemed knowledgeable about sex, and had even watched pornography before, and seemed enthusiastic to share this experience with me. I had never seen pornographic material up to that point but was excited to see adults "doing it."

We began watching the pornography videos in secret and soon discovered that we would become aroused when we watched the videos. We started to masturbate side by side, watching the videos in bed with the covers over our private parts so that we couldn't actually see each other masturbating. When we reached climax we were confused as to why white stuff didn't come out of our penises like it had with the men in the videos. Frustrated with this, we confessed to my older cousin who I shared my room with that we had watched his videos and explained our confusion. My older cousin, laughingly, clarified that this would happen when we got older.

Then one day, when we were watching porn and masturbating, Devin ejaculated. He pulled the cover back to expose his penis and showed me what had happened. Even though I secretly wished I was a girl, I was jealous that Devin was able to ejaculate because it meant he was closer to being an adult than I was. Still, I was happy that he was moving on to manhood.

Watching porn with my cousin was odd. I never really became aroused from watching the heterosexual sex in the videos. I had no interest in watching nude women or women having sex with men; it did nothing for me. However, I found that I could become aroused if I focused solely on the man. Then, I began envisioning myself as being the girl in the video, which would bring me to a climax. My reaction to watching straight porn with Devin only confirmed to me that I was gay, although I did not tell Devin this.

After finishing all the porn stashed in my room, Devin and I began looking for porn in other older cousins' rooms. Then we stumbled across a video called *Shemales in Leather*. We had no idea what "shemale" meant, but we figured it was a word that meant males and females having sex, so we stole the video and went back to my room to watch it.

The video began in a men's restroom. The video showed a woman in a leather bra and skirt, looking into the mirror at herself. The woman wasn't very pretty but appeared to be a woman. We were confused because the woman was standing next to a urinal, which meant she was in the men's restroom. Confused but intrigued, we continued to watch the video. Then the woman went over to the urinal, lifted her skirt, and began urinating! At this point, Devin's mouth and my mouth were wide open in shock. It became pretty clear to us what "shemale" meant!

Then, a man came to the urinal next to the trans woman's urinal, and they began to perform oral on each other. "What the fuck?" Devin said as he began to laugh. I did not know how to respond. I was intrigued to see two people with penises having sex. Still, I was more fascinated with seeing the nude trans woman. Then I began to wonder if I, too, could be a "shemale." "Yo! This shit is gay!" Devin said as he continued to laugh. I mirrored Devin and began laughing too, but all the while, I was still focused on the trans woman in the video.

I was experiencing a variety of emotions: confusion and excitement at the possibility that I could be a "shemale," shock at seeing two people with penises having sex, and embarrassment and fear at Devin's response to the video. Seeing Devin laughing and making fun of non-heterosexual sex and a trans woman only made me more fearful of revealing to him that I was struggling with being gay and wanted to be a girl. Moreover, it made me feel embarrassed that I had become aroused at something Devin found comical. I hid my feelings with laughter. We turned off the video and began questioning why my older cousin would have a video like that. After sneaking the video back into my older cousin's room, we decided we would not watch any more of his videos.

Seeing *Shemales in Leather* was a memorable moment for me for many reasons, mainly because it was the first time that I ever witnessed non-heterosexual sex. But it was not the first time that I saw a trans woman. We had a neighbor two houses up from us, a Black transgender woman named Jasmine.

Jasmine was the first transgender person I had ever seen. She was not "passable," meaning she was visibly trans. She was close friends with my older female cousins and sometimes stopped by the front porch to chat with them. However, my older male cousins would bully her and dead-name her, which quickly drove her away.

I did not know much about Jasmine, besides the fact that she was trans, but I was captivated by Jasmine and saw myself in her. My interactions with Jasmine were limited, as I was too shy to speak to her, but I would often wave at her whenever she would pass by our house. I often wondered if I could grow up to be like her, to be trans. Still, the idea of growing up to be like Jasmine terrified me because I had witnessed the harassment that she endured from my male cousins. Even so, I wondered if I could be as brave as Jasmine and live as a woman.

DID YOU SEE HER?

I saw her once or twice on the block

Rocking ripped-up jeans and a crop top

She was quite a lovely sight

Hair blonde and long

Skin smooth and dark as night

Tall and voluptuous

With curves and swerves

Her lip gloss was popping

Her doorknockers were knocking

That body was rocking

Damn

Did you see her?

She's pretty hard to miss

CHAPTER 13

PUNKED

Because I was being bullied so badly at school, my time with Devin became the best part of my time in New Jersey. Devin was not just my best friend; he was my only friend.

We would spend most of our time together getting into all types of mischief, including making prank calls. At the time, making prank calls was a trendy thing to do. We used the landline in my grandparents' room to randomly dial numbers but always used the typical New Jersey area codes like 201 or 973. We would also block our number using *67. In the beginning, the prank calls were mainly goofy and corny, with jokes like saying, "Hey, is your refrigerator running? Well, you better go catch it!" and hanging up, but soon, our prank calls turned dark.

I remember making a prank call once, but no one picked up the phone, and it went to voicemail. The answering machine message stated, "Hey, this is Ashley; leave me a message!" I decided to leave a voicemail and went into a monologue, disguising my voice by whispering and making it deeper. The prank was intended to scare the life out of whoever this Ashley was by leaving a fake, creepy stalker message.

"Ashleyyyy," I whispered in a husky voice, "I've been watching you…I watch you while you sleep….I watch you when you take a shower….I even watch you while you take a shit …Ashleyyyy I'm coming for you, bitch!" I hung up the phone, and Devin and I burst into laughter, imagining how frightened Ashley would be of the ridiculous message.

Our mischief was not limited to prank calls; we also played stupid pranks on our family members. A typical prank involved our grandfather's supply of alcohol. He had a hopeless dependence on alcohol and spent most of the day and night drinking vodka, which he sometimes would send us to the liquor store to buy. He would call the liquor store and tell the owner we were coming to buy his favorite vodka, Laird's charcoal-filtered vodka, which cost about $5. My grandfather was disabled and did not work. He also had no control over his finances. He would get his money primarily by begging family members and sometimes strangers passing by the house for change. So, it took work for him to come up with $5 for his vodka, but he always managed to do it somehow.

Well, Devin and I had no consideration for any of this. Our pranks often involved hiding or tampering with his vodka. Sometimes, we would put his vodka on the roof. Other times, we would empty out the vodka from the bottle and fill it with water. We would catch all types of hell once we got caught, but our grandfather yelling and chasing us with his cane did not deter us from our pranks.

Once, I even worked up the gumption to play a prank on Auntie Lini. I had bought a stink bomb from the bodega that my cousins and I frequented and decided that I would sneak it into Auntie Lini's room and set it off: the ultimate prank! So, one day while Auntie Lini was in the shower, I crept into her room, squeezed the metallic bag that the stink bomb was in, put it under Auntie Lini's pillow, ran for dear life out of her room, and told Devin what I did.

"Are you crazy?" he asked me with fear on his face. Devin sensed I was taking the pranks too far, as Auntie Lini was not to be messed with. About fifteen minutes later, I heard Auntie Lini cursing up a storm, bulldozing her way to Devin and me. Devin had ratted me out and told Auntie Lini it was me who did the prank. The next thing I knew, Auntie Lini was chasing me down the stairs. She managed to catch me and fiercely scolded me and took away most of my privileges for a while. After that, we took a break from the pranks.

***

School was becoming unbearable for me. I could no longer tolerate the daily bullying I was receiving from the other children, and I started to show up to school late. Thirty minutes late turned into one hour late, then two hours late, and, eventually, I stopped going to school altogether.

Auntie Lini would leave for work early in the morning and trusted me to walk to school alone. When I started skipping school, I would just hide in my room, sneaking out occasionally for food and to use the bathroom. I was never alone, as the house was filled with my other aunts, grandparents, and adult cousins, but I managed to go unseen. Skipping school was scary, but at the time, I decided I'd much rather deal with the anxiety of getting caught skipping than get bullied.

After about a week of skipping school, my older cousin Lolly figured out what I was doing. After Devin, I was perhaps closest to Lolly. Lolly seemed to accept me for who I was from a young age, never put me down for being effeminate, and would often defend me from the harassment I received from my male family members. Still, Lolly was an adult, so I did not spend much time with her the way I did with Devin.

Lolly tried to talk to me about why I was skipping class, but I denied the skipping. Then, one day, when I was hiding in my room, Lolly knocked on my door. I figured she wanted to lecture me on why I should attend school. So, I ignored the knock and stayed silent.

"Open up...I know you're in there!" Lolly continued to knock. "The police are here, and they want to speak to you."

The police? I thought. *Shit, they must be here to take me to school.* I opened the door.

Lolly was upset. "Come downstairs right now! I knew you were skipping school! The police are here!"

I went downstairs to find three police officers standing in my living room, tall and intimidating. The room was chilly, as it was winter. The officers were mostly silent, besides their radios going off occasionally. I presumed they were there to take me to class, but to my surprise, they were there for other reasons.

"You are in a lot of trouble," Lolly said as she signaled everyone to sit on the couches.

"Do you know why we're here?" one of the officers asked me.

"To take me to school," I stated plainly as I rolled my eyes.

"No, we're here because of your voicemail on my daughter Ashley's answering machine."

I was totally confused. Then it clicked. *The prank calls!* I thought. *The police are here because of the prank calls me and Devin made!* My heart was beating out of my chest, and I was shitting bricks.

"I don't know what you're talking about," I said to the officer.

"We traced the call back to this house, and your cousin Lolly here tells us that you and your other cousin like to make prank calls. Is that true?"

"Sometimes," I confessed. "But I didn't leave a voice message," I lied.

"Well, someone from this house did, so if you know who did it, you better tell us now, or else you could be in big trouble," the officer told me.

My heart felt as if it was going to explode as the blood rushed to my head and the room spun. I began envisioning myself being taken to jail. I couldn't survive in jail; I was too pretty!

I did not know what to do. I couldn't confess, even though it was me who left the voicemail, as confessing meant I would definitely go to jail. So, I did what I thought was best in my eleven-year-old brain; I lied and said Devin left the voicemail.

"Are you sure it was your cousin?" the officer asked.

"Yes," I said, "it was him."

"Alright then, we'll have to speak with him to clear this all up," the officer said. Then everyone left.

I could not believe I just sent my best friend to jail for something I did: This was the ultimate act of treachery.

***

"Why are you lying?" Devin yelled at me.

"I'm not lying. You did it!" I yelled back.

All of the adults in my family surrounded us, telling us to tell the truth. Otherwise, they said, we would be taken to jail. Devin was on one end of the living room being comforted by his mom; he was crying and screaming at me to tell the truth. I stood my ground in the other corner of the living room and continued to declare that Devin left the voicemail, not me. While I was fiery on the outside, inside, I was frightened. I had never known this level of fear before in my life. I could not go to jail, and I would do anything to prevent myself from going to jail, even if it meant letting Devin take the blame for something I did.

As we continued to protest, I could not help but feel guilty seeing Devin so emotional. I had never seen him cry up to that point, which made me feel a deep pity for him. Nevertheless, I could not confess.

How could this happen? What were the chances that we would dial some random number and leave a prank (but threatening) voicemail on the answering machine of an underage girl, who also just so happened to be the daughter of a police officer? Also, it had been weeks since we made that prank call.

Apparently, there had been a whole investigation into the voicemail. Ashley, the police officer's daughter, was terrified, and rightfully so, as she had no idea it was a prank; she just received a random voicemail with some creepy guy saying he was watching her take a shit. Despite the police officer and his family now knowing it was two stupid boys making prank calls, they still took the voicemail seriously and threatened to pursue legal action. What was going on in my life? I was skipping school, doing poorly academically, possibly going to jail, and had just lost my only friend.

Devin continued to profess his innocence, and I continued to lie and say he left the voicemail. For some strange reason, everyone in my family believed me and unjustly scolded Devin.

Eventually, Ashley's family said they would drop everything if Devin confessed and apologized. Everyone in my family pressured Devin to just abide, and he did. So, Devin ultimately apologized formally to the family, and everything was dropped. However, things did not go back to normal between Devin and me. We both knew the truth: I had let Devin take the blame.

Devin stopped talking to me. My only friend in New Jersey was now gone. I was devastated and tried my best to make up with Devin. He did not speak to me for weeks, and I understood why, so I gave him his space.

Eventually, however, Devin did what most kids do: forgive. Somehow, he forgave me for lying and potentially sending him to jail. I promised him that I would never do anything like that to betray him again, and I kept that promise.

CHAPTER 14

GYM

School continued to be difficult for me. The bullying and constant ridicule of my sexuality became too much to bear. I was previously able to skip class because I had sick days that I could use. But now I had run out of sick days, so I couldn't skip classes anymore. Otherwise, I would fail sixth grade. Still, I struggled to participate in school, especially gym class.

In gym, I had to act in a manner that I was unfamiliar with. I generally did not do well at sports. They required a certain confidence and social skills that I did not possess. Also, the other boys in my class were rough and tough, and I was anything but that. I was a meek and shy child, and being forced to play sports with the other children truly brought me out of my comfort zone.

Besides being timid, I was also still struggling with gender dysphoria, which only heightened my problems with gym class. I still wished more than anything that I could wake up one day and be a girl, but the reality was that I was a girl trapped in a boy's body.

Gym class was the time in school when I was most strongly reminded that I was not a girl. I would be forced to play with the other boys and change in the boy's locker room, which felt strange. Even though I had the body of a boy, I felt uncomfortable exposing it to the other boys in my class.

To avoid changing in front of the other boys, I would come to gym class already in my gym clothes. However, I still had to spend the first ten to fifteen minutes of gym class waiting in the locker room with the other boys. I would sit on a bench in the middle of the locker room as the other boys laughed, rough-housed, and changed. I would stare at the floor the entire time, in a state of high anxiety, which made the short time waiting seem like an eternity. Of course, I would get teased in the locker room and called homophobic slurs. I did not respond to the bullying and remained silent out of fear of being physically harmed.

While I felt comfortable around my cousin Devin, I generally felt uneasy around other boys, as I had learned that males were mostly not safe to be around. I wholeheartedly believed that most boys wanted to cause me harm, and this was not just a theory, as up to that point, the bullies in my life were predominately male. Furthermore, whenever I was exposed to violence, it was mostly from males like Mr. W. So, putting me in a class where I was forced to interact with other boys and play sports with them was terrifying to me.

For most of my life, I had avoided participating in gym class, which was never an issue because in Delaware up until that point, I was never graded for gym class. However, in sixth grade in Paterson, I was now graded on my performance and participation in gym class. Still, my fears of being harmed by the other boys outweighed my fears of failing.

While I could not get out of physically being in gym class, I would not be forced to participate. I would simply not play with the other children. Instead I would sit on the bleachers or stand and not participate. My refusal to engage frustrated my gym teacher, who interpreted this as disobedience. Although, truly, I refused to play because I feared the other children, especially the boys, in my class. I knew I was not good at sports, so I did not want to display this weakness and give the other children even more of a reason to call me gay and bully me.

After some time, my gym teacher began to accept that I would not participate in class and left me alone to sit on the bleachers in peace. I had considered this a victory until it came time for report cards. On my first report card for the school year, I got mostly As and Bs, but there was a big red F next to physical education. I could not believe it; I had never received an F on anything in my life up to that point.

Failing physical education frightened me for many reasons. I knew that failing a class could get me left back in the sixth grade. I also knew that failing a class could get me into a lot of trouble with Auntie Lini and my mother.

I did not want Auntie Lini to discover that I was failing a class. As my guardian, she was supposed to sign my report card. However, I never took my report card home for her to review. Instead, I just forged her signature and returned it to my teacher, who never questioned it.

Even though I feared failing gym class and the sixth grade, my fear of participating in gym class won out. In the second quarter of the school year, we received report cards again, and again, there was a big red F next to physical education, but I didn't care. I did well in all my other classes, so I thought everything would balance out and I would still be permitted to move on to the seventh grade.

I forged Auntie Lini's signature on the report card again and handed it back to my homeroom teacher; she accepted the signature, but this time, she decided to have a sit-down with me. She had a private meeting with me after class and clarified that if I failed gym class one more time, I would be held back and unable to go to seventh grade.

I couldn't believe it. *Held back for gym?* I thought. *Failing sixth grade for gym, of all things?* Of course, the idea of being held back scared the life out of me. I began panicking that Auntie Lini and, worse, my mother, would find out about my poor performance. They would be disappointed, and I would be disciplined. Also, possibly being held back was an embarrassment for me and brought me a great deal of shame.

How did I slip so far from being encouraged to skip a grade to being told I would be held back? I had no idea what had become of my life, but I knew I had to do something about it. I realized I could not continue to fail gym class and be held back. I could no longer allow my fears to consume me. So, I did what I had to do, put on a brave face, and finally began participating in gym class.

Surprisingly, the other children did not bully me further for my poor physical performance and encouraged me to play with them. I still sucked at sports, but I was trying, and that's what mattered. My gym teacher seemed pleased with my new attitude and encouraged me.

Then came time for the third-quarter report cards, and next to physical education, there was an A, along with all types of positive comments from my gym teacher praising me. Despite this improvement, I still forged Auntie Lini's signature, as I did not want her to see the other two red F's from the previous semesters.

I continued to excel in my classes and give my best in gym class until the school year ended. On my final report card, I passed gym class and all other subjects with flying colors. I could move on to seventh grade, although it turned out I wouldn't attend seventh grade in New Jersey. The time had come for me to go back to living with my mother. It had been nice, having a break from living in such a toxic environment, but Auntie Lini had told me my mother was ready to take me back to live with her again, and I had to go.

Shortly after my mother and Mr. W had moved to Ohio, they discovered the state wasn't for them. They were unable to secure steady employment or housing in Ohio, so they then moved to South Carolina to live with my mother's foster family. My mother's foster family had long relocated from New Jersey to South Carolina. Of course, my mother's foster mother was excited to have my brother live with her again, as she adored him. My mother's foster family also welcomed my mother, baby sister, and Mr. W into their home.

However, soon after they moved to South Carolina, my mother's foster family kicked Mr. W out of their home for being physically violent toward my mother and brother. Mr. W returned to Delaware to live with his mother, and my mother, brother, and sister remained in South Carolina for about a year. Of course, eventually, my mother got back together with Mr. W, and she and my siblings returned to Delaware to live with Mr. W at his mother's house again.

***

It was a warm summer evening when my mother and Mr. W picked me up from New Jersey to return with them to Delaware. They did not bring my brother and sister with them to allow more room in the car for my belongings. My father's family welcomed Mr. W and my mother with open arms and even had a big dinner for them and for my farewell.

While everyone was joyous, I could not feel happiness at seeing my mother because I knew she was coming to take me back to live with her and Mr. W in their own private hell. But I did what I knew best at that point: I faked it. I told my mother I had missed her and was excited to return to Delaware with her.

Truthfully, I was sad and afraid to return to Delaware, but I decided to show no fear. I packed my bags, holding back tears and smiling. I even lied and told my cousins how excited I was to return to Delaware. I sat down with the grown-ups, my mother, and Mr. W to eat one last dinner with my family before I bid them goodbye. Then, the night ended, and I said my goodbyes to everyone.

I climbed into the back seat of my mother's car, and we drove back to Delaware. I wasn't with Auntie Lini on this drive to Delaware, but the melancholy was pretty much the same. I sat in the back seat, mostly silent, allowing a few tears to escape when no one was looking.

CHAPTER 15

BILLY AND THE BEARD

Shortly after I moved back to Delaware, Mr. W was arrested for armed robbery. He and some of his friends thought it would be a great idea to rob a convenience store. Of course, they got caught and were incarcerated following. My mother was now a single mother again, except this time, she was raising three kids: myself, my brother, and my little sister. While Mr. W was incarcerated, we lived with Grammy, Mr. W's mother, in her tiny home in Felton, Delaware. My mother and sister lived together in one of the small rooms, while my brother and I were permitted to stay in the basement.

Living with Grammy in her little home was wonderful. In contrast to her son's violence, she was a gentle and loving woman who filled her small home with warmth and kindness. I experienced comfort when I was around Grammy, and I viewed her as another grandmother. Her lovely home was even more lovely in Mr. W's absence.

As you can imagine, I did not miss Mr. W while he was incarcerated. No Mr. W meant peace. I did not keep in contact with him during his incarceration, but I did write him a letter once, in which I detailed how glad I was that he was incarcerated, how much I hated him and wished he was dead. On the envelope, I even drew a knife where it was sealed, indicating that I wanted Mr. W to kill himself.

Looking back on this, I am shocked how I could wish someone death; however, at that age, it seemed the only way to completely eliminate Mr. W's threat of violence toward my mother and brother. When he got the letter, he told my mother what I wrote. My mother scolded me and ordered me to write another letter apologizing, which I told her I would, but never did. I believe deep down my mother understood my hatred toward Mr. W.

After Mr. W was incarcerated, I started seventh grade. Seventh grade in Delaware was a completely different experience compared to Paterson, New Jersey. Of course, I was still bullied by the other children, and I continued to struggle with my sexuality and gender identity, but something was changing in me. I had started to grow weary of being passive and tolerating the bullying. I began to talk back and defend myself when I was bullied by the other children.

I'm not sure what brought on this bravery. Perhaps living in rough Paterson toughened me up and prepared me to finally defend myself. Moreover, I think I was just tired of being verbally and physically abused by my peers. Also, I had had somewhat of a growth spurt and put on some weight from New Jersey, so I was no longer the lanky boy of my childhood, unable to defend himself.

Although I was finally standing up for myself, one boy continued to bully me relentlessly. He was a White boy with curly brown hair named Billy, who decided to call me all kinds of homophobic slurs. Our desks were aligned in squares, almost like a table, and he sat across from me. He would often throw things at me and even kick me under the desk, where the teacher could not see.

One day, when school was over for the day, the other students and the teacher left the classroom to go home. Billy and I were still in the classroom by ourselves, putting our coats on and packing up, when he started calling me a gay faggot and kicking me in the shins. Well, I had had enough of his nonsense and punched him in the chest and pushed him to the floor. I had snapped. After years and years of allowing myself to be verbally and physically bullied, I finally fought back, and it felt incredible.

I was proud of finally standing up for myself and fighting back. Billy stayed on the floor, lying on his back, crying.

While I felt pride at the moment, I also feared getting in trouble for beating up Billy, so I ran out of the classroom to the bus, before the teacher could come back and discover what I had done. Of course, Billy told on me, and the next day, I was punished. Still, I didn't care; I had defended myself, and that was all that mattered to me. After I fought back, Billy stopped bullying me, and once the other kids heard what I had done, they stopped bullying me as well.

***

After about one year of living with Grammy in Delaware, my mother started looking for a home. She had started working for Bank of America and could now afford to move out. She found a place in the nearby state of Maryland.

I didn't think it could get more country than Felton, Delaware, but Marydel, Maryland, took the prize. We were literally in the middle of nowhere. The area was so rural that there was a cornfield across our street and a farm in our backyard. I felt like I was in a country prison. Despite its small size, though, Marydel still had three liquor stores, all within walking distance from my house; perhaps the townsfolk figured you needed to drink to cope with the boredom of living in that tiny town. We lived in a decently sized three-bedroom house there, which we rented at first, but eventually, the owner decided to sell the house to my mother.

I went to eighth grade in a middle school in Denton. Shortly after the school year started, I got involved in a relationship with a girl named Megan, a beautiful mixed-race (Black and Latina) girl who asked me to be her boyfriend. I thought having a girlfriend would be the perfect way to avoid being bullied for being gay; how could I be gay if I had a girlfriend? Duh! She didn't know it, but Megan had become my first beard.

Even though Megan was beautiful, I had no physical attraction toward her (or any other girls). I knew I was gay but still struggled to admit to myself and others that I was gay. My relationship with Megan was highly superficial. We were in separate classes, so we did not see each other that much outside of passing in the hallway. Even though I was in a relationship with Megan, I avoided being around her as best as I could because I was worried she would expect me to kiss her or hold her hand, both of which made me feel extremely uncomfortable. I thought maybe after a while, I could learn to be attracted to Megan because she was, after all, a fairly attractive person.

I would mostly just see Megan in the hallway and sometimes stop to talk to her—and occasionally kiss her, which felt so wrong to me. Then Valentine's Day came, which was a strange experience. Now that I was in a relationship, I was expected to get Megan a Valentine's Day gift. So I got her a small basket with a teddy bear, a candle, and a small heart-shaped balloon (actually my mother bought the gift). I was excited to tell my mother that I had a girlfriend and ask her to buy the gift because I wanted to convince her that I was not gay.

However, I could not gain the courage to give Megan the gift on Valentine's Day. I kept it in my locker and avoided Megan for the entire day; then, at the end of the day, I threw the gift in the trash. I feared that if I gave her the gift, she would give me a passionate kiss or embrace, even the thought of which made me deeply uncomfortable.

After I failed to pay her any attention or give her a Valentine's Day gift, Megan had enough and broke up with me. She wrote me a breakup letter and had a friend give it to me. I welcomed the breakup with giddiness, as it meant I no longer had to live with the pressure of showing Megan fake affection. Being dumped by Megan was not a painful experience at all. Still, it did make me worry that the other kids might start calling me gay again, but surprisingly, being in a relationship with Megan brought me some level of social credit as being heterosexual.

I went on to have two more girlfriends that school year, both of whom were pretty White girls. However, the relationships did not last that long. The other two relationships were pretty much the same as the one with Megan: fake affection, avoidance, me feeling uncomfortable, and then me being dumped. After my third try at puppy love, I decided I would not make another attempt at having a girlfriend again. The discomfort and anxiety from the relationships just weren't worth it.

Nonetheless, my plan to have a girlfriend to avoid being called gay had worked, and I went through eighth grade without being bullied. I couldn't believe it: I had managed to convince everyone that I was not gay. I had learned to find comfort in the closet.

Chapter 16

The Thirteenth Summer

Starting when I was thirteen, traveling to Paterson was a different experience for me. Auntie Lini did not drive to Maryland to pick me up. Instead, I took a Greyhound bus all by myself from Dover, Delaware, to Newark, New Jersey. My mother would drive me from Marydel to Dover, and from there I would take the Greyhound. At that age, my mother trusted me to travel responsibly and make it to my destination safely. I loved taking the Greyhound from Delaware to New Jersey; it was fun and exciting and made me feel like an adult. Once I made it to Newark, Auntie Lini would pick me up and drive me to my grandparents' house in Paterson.

Returning to Paterson was always a thrill for me, as Paterson was the exact opposite of hokey-pokey little Marydel. Paterson was so big and lively. There were people everywhere, tall buildings, and lots of noise. Even the air smelled different in Paterson. There were things to do and people to see in Paterson.

In my mind, Paterson was uptown Manhattan. Of course, as an adult, I now recognize the grim reality of Paterson: the high crime rates, ghettos, poverty, homelessness, violence, and drugs. Still, to this day, there is a certain magic that I feel when in Paterson.

I stayed at my grandparents' house, under the care of my Auntie Lini as usual, but that summer, we seemed to bump heads a lot. I was now thirteen, which meant I was a teenager and, in my mind, practically an adult. I didn't want anyone to tell me what to do, including Auntie Lini. I hadn't been rebellious in Marydel, but being in Paterson, without my mother's presence, emboldened me to test boundaries and act out.

I would stay out late with my older adult cousins on the front porch, drinking their vodka and having a great time until Auntie Lini would come down and tell us to stop making so much noise and to go to bed. At the time, it seemed like Auntie Lini just wanted to spoil our good times with her discipline and prudish ways. So, I began to feel resentment toward her.

I even started to rebel against taking care of my grandparents. I had started taking care of them around the age of nine, assisting both my grandmother and grandfather, though my bedbound grandmother required the most care.

In the early 1990s, my grandmother was diagnosed with rheumatoid arthritis. From what I've been told, shortly after her diagnosis, my grandmother began seeing a doctor who performed a procedure on her in which he would stick needles into her knees and aspirate out synovial fluid. The rationale was that the fluid contributed to the rheumatoid arthritis, so the symptoms would have improved if the fluid had been removed. However, what the doctor didn't realize was that when he was aspirating fluid, he was aspirating and damaging muscle. The procedure left my grandmother with excessive muscle damage, which made it impossible for her to stand. I am not sure why, but she never got a knee replacement.

Auntie Lini provided most of the care to my grandparents. But, over the summer, I was expected to help and provide care. I would feed, bathe, and dress my grandmother every day. I would also assist her in using the restroom. Caring for my grandfather consisted mostly of preparing his meals, keeping him company, and running errands for him. It used to bring me joy to care for my grandparents, but when I turned thirteen, taking care of them became a burden. Taking care of my grandparents now meant spending less time with my adult and adolescent cousins, having fun and getting into mischief.

Also, I started to find providing care to my grandparents to be unfair because I was the only kid in the house who was expected to do it. Of course, I was consistently praised by the adults in my family for being kind and compassionate and tending to my grandparents. Nevertheless, for my thirteenth summer, I wanted to have as much fun as possible before returning to ho-hum Marydel. So, I stopped helping Auntie Lini out with my grandparents, which caused a lot of fighting between us.

One day, Auntie Lini came home from work and discovered I had not given my grandmother her lunch. I had been so caught up hanging out with my cousins that I forgot to feed her that afternoon. When Auntie Lini realized this, she started to scold me. I argued back at her, telling her how unfair it was that I was the only kid in the house expected to care for my grandparents. She was shocked at my rebellion. Up until that point, I would mostly stay quiet when she yelled at me. Auntie Lini was clearly upset by my behavior and told me to stop "acting like a nigger."

As I mentioned earlier, my father's family had a history of racism toward Black people, and during this time in the early 2000s, racism was still high amongst my father's family. Thankfully, my father's family's racism has since dissipated, but this did not happen easily. Despite my father's family's deep-seated racist views against Black people, the younger generations of my father's family would go on to establish numerous interracial relationships. The initial response of the older generation was to protest and demand that the younger generation avoid romantic relationships with Black people, but the younger generation rebelled. Eventually, the various interracial relationships established by the younger generation and the mixed children they conceived sort of forced the older generation into acceptance and, thankfully, rid them of their racist views and ways.

At the time, I was aware of the racism in my father's family as I had been called a "nigger" by other family members, but hearing it from Auntie Lini was genuinely shocking. I had no idea that Auntie Lini also harbored racist views, as she had always adored me, and I was part Black. Regardless of her reasoning, Auntie Lini calling me a nigger hurt me. It felt like she had stabbed me in the heart. I don't know if she realized the weight of the word or the impact that it would have on me, but I truly felt betrayed by Auntie Lini at that moment.

I had always viewed Auntie Lini as a loving figure in my life, and for her to hurt me in that way was something I struggled to respond to. My initial response to being called such an ugly name was shock and silence; then I became enraged. I had decided that if Auntie Lini was going to hurt me, then I was going to hurt her right back, so I told her to go to hell. We argued back and forth, and I continued to curse at her. Then, fed up with my behavior, she kicked me out of my grandparents' house that day. I had no choice but to stay with my father at his house for the remainder of the summer.

My relationship with my father had remained estranged. He lived in a one-bedroom apartment in Clifton, New Jersey, with my stepmother and younger sister. My stepmother was also pregnant at the time with my youngest sister (on my father's side). My relationship with my stepmother was tense, as she would fluctuate between being kind and being cruel to me. She also had erratic mood swings, which were sometimes violent. Her personality was the exact opposite of my father, who was mostly jovial and friendly. It seemed odd that they were a couple, as they were such polar opposites.

When I stayed with my father and his family, I remained predominantly in the living room on the couch. I would spend most of the day alone, watching TV, bored out of my mind, cursing myself for getting kicked out of my grandparents' house. Occasionally, my father would feel sorry for me and drop me off for a few hours in Paterson to hang out with my cousins. Auntie Lini allowed me to spend time at my grandparents' house, but I could not spend the night, so I had to return to my father's apartment at the end of the day. Overall, the time I spent with my father that summer was uneventful, except on the Fourth of July.

That day, my father had taken me to my grandparents' house for a BBQ. I was excited to be able to return, even if it was just for the evening, as it meant I could hang out with Devin and all my other cousins. The BBQ was a magnificent party with loud music, good food, and loads of curry. Parties at my grandparents' house were always big and extravagant, with tons of family around. I hung out with my cousins and caused all kinds of trouble, including setting off illegal fireworks.

The party was awesome, but it came to an end around midnight. I was in the next-door parking lot with my cousins when my father came to get me and said it was time for me to get ready to leave. He asked me to get my stepmother and head to the car. I said goodbye to everyone and began looking for my stepmother. I looked everywhere and couldn't find her. I looked throughout the house, the front porch, the backyard, everywhere, but I couldn't locate her. I became increasingly concerned because she was pregnant, and I began worrying that something had happened to her.

I went to the backyard, where everyone was still partying and dancing to blasting music. I saw my father and shouted over the music, "Yo, I can't find her anywhere." When I said this, my father looked enraged for some reason. Perhaps he had an argument with my stepmother, as they often fought, but it really wasn't clear as to what made him so angry. I assumed he was upset that I couldn't find my stepmother, so I went back to look for her in my grandparents' huge house.

I went back to the empty front porch. It was very dark outside at this point because it was well past midnight. Actually, the only visible lights were the yellow streetlights. I turned around, and my father stood there. "I still can't find her," I said to him. He looked sinister. I wasn't sure what was going on.

"Who the fuck do you think you're talking to?" he said to me coolly.

I looked at him in confusion. I didn't understand what I had done wrong, and I was shocked to see my normally happy-go-lucky father look so cruel. A genuine fear came over me; something was wrong. "I'm sorry," I said, confused.

"Don't you ever call me no fucking 'yo.' I am your fucking father," he said, walking slowly toward me. His eyes were bloodshot, and his breath reeked of liquor. He was frightfully enraged but calm at the same time. I walked in reverse until I backed onto the porch railing. "You don't know who the fuck I am, do you?" he said.

Then he raised his hands and wrapped them around my neck, pushing me into the porch railing. "Dad, stop," I begged, struggling to speak. "I can't breathe!"

"Oh, now I'm 'Dad'?" he said in a chilling, drunken voice. "I'll fucking kill you."

The earth began to spin, and my head and eyes felt like they would explode from the pressure and the lack of oxygen. I stared at my father's face with bulging eyes. His expression remained flat and emotionless. I briefly lost consciousness and genuinely feared that I was going to die in that moment, on my grandparents' porch, at the hands of my own father.

"Stop it!" I heard someone say. "You're going to kill him!" The voice sounded muffled, as if I were underwater. But my father's grip grew tighter and firmer. He was indeed going to kill me. My body went limp as I began to close my eyes. Then his grip finally released, and I fell to the ground, gasping for air. Some family member pulled him off me and told me to run into the house, so I did.

I ran upstairs and locked myself in the guest room. I refused to come out. My entire body was shaking, my head was pounding, and my mind was racing. I was genuinely horrified. I couldn't believe that saying something as simple as "yo" would send my father over the edge like that. I could not believe that my father almost killed me. I began to wonder what would have happened if he was not discovered by a family member and pulled off me. Would I even be alive?

As I wondered what to do, my father came and knocked on the door. "I'm sorry, come out," he said. I ignored him and remained silent, and he eventually went away. I stayed in the room in shock, but eventually my shock turned to rage. I could not believe my father had choked me and almost killed me. Who the hell did he think he was to do that to me, his flesh and blood?

I started to debate whether I should call 911, tell them what happened, and get my father deported back to Guyana. I wanted revenge; I wanted my father to pay for what he had done. But I did not call 911 and instead calmed myself down and went to sleep. I did not leave the room that night.

The next day, I woke up and went downstairs to the front porch, where everyone was. My family began to laugh and taunt me for being choked by my father. I did not understand what was so funny about being choked and almost killed. Perhaps minimizing the situation through making jokes was the only way they knew how to respond to the serious and disturbing incident. Or maybe they thought that through making the situation a joke, it would take the seriousness away and make it more palatable for both them and me. Whatever the reason was, for them, my being choked by my father was a real hoot.

Enraged at my father's family's callousness and mockery, I told them I would tell my mother what had happened, and then the laughter stopped. They said I couldn't do that because then my mother would call the cops, which meant my father would be sent back to Guyana. So, after much pressure from my father's family, I decided to keep my silence and move on as if nothing had ever happened.

Following the choking incident, Auntie Lini took pity on me. She allowed me to spend the remainder of the summer at my grandparents' house. I apologized to her for being disrespectful and resumed caring for my grandparents. Auntie Lini did not formally apologize but made her regrets known for calling me such an ugly, racist name by giving me various gifts and taking me on fun outings. My father's family has a history of avoidance when it comes to apologizing. Instead of saying, "I'm sorry," my father's family will display, rather than say, their apology through kind gestures.

My father came to visit me the day after he choked me and dropped off my belongings. He tried to have a heart-to-heart with me, but I was too angry to even look at him. He told me he was sorry and that he was drunk and would never do something like that again. "I love you," he said. "You're my only son. I love you. Don't ever forget that."

I stayed silent as he talked. Then he left.

Summer ended, and I took the Greyhound back to Dover. As a final attempt to gain my forgiveness, my father drove me to the Newark bus terminal. He begged me not to tell my mother about him choking me, and he said it could get him deported if she reported it to the authorities. I told him I wouldn't tell her and that, despite my anger, I did not want him to get deported. I also knew that if I was responsible for my father being deported, no one on his side of the family would ever talk to me again.

My father decided to wait with me at the terminal until my bus left. We got McDonald's and ate in silence. After that, we waited for my bus to be announced at the bus station. Then, when it was time for me to board my bus, we said our goodbyes and parted with an awkward hug. I kept my word and never told my mother what happened that summer.

CHAPTER 17

FOURTEEN WAS QUITE A YEAR

In 2004, Mr. W was released from incarceration and began living with us again in Marydel. Being incarcerated had changed him. He stopped being physically violent toward my mother and my brother, and he started trying to be a better father to my sister and a better stepfather to my brother and me. He worked odd jobs, and my mother continued to work at Bank of America. Our landlord would go on to sell our home to my mother after he saw how well she took care of it. We even got a dog, a black Rottweiler named Boots. Things were finally starting to look up for us.

In 2004, I entered high school at the age of fourteen. During this time, I was navigating a lot of challenging milestones: puberty, trying to gain the acceptance of my peers, and identity. High school was a pivotal point in my life, as it was when I started to come out of the closet. The girl in me came back alive, and she was ready for the world to see and celebrate her—but I wasn't prepared for her to come out fully just yet.

When I entered high school, I knew deep down that I wanted to be a girl, but I had long since accepted that I could never be a girl or a woman. Since I couldn't be a girl, I figured I could at least be a bisexual boy. Perhaps emboldened by raging hormones and having an impulsive teenage brain, I started telling other students that I liked boys. I no longer cared if I was called gay or not because I wanted to find my tribe—that is, other students who accepted me.

I still was not ready to accept myself fully as a gay boy, though, so I told everyone that I was bisexual, even though I had virtually no attraction to girls. At the time, I thought I would be accepted more by the other students if I identified as bisexual rather than gay, as, in my mind, there was still a heterosexual component to being bisexual. Of course, I would soon find out that this logic was wrong and that people who were not accepting of gays were also not accepting of bisexuals.

Shortly after I started identifying as bisexual, I discovered the word "androgynous." This word resonated with me. I figured since I couldn't live as a girl and did not genuinely want to live as a boy, I could live in androgyny and be neither.

While I identified as androgynous, my appearance was more effeminate. I began growing my hair and often wore it in a beautiful, snatched ponytail. I also discovered the wonders of self-piercing and pierced about every part of my ears that I could. My clothing choices were limited, but luckily, I had a unisex jacket, which I wore every day, even when it was warm, as it made me look more feminine.

Of course, I began to be mistaken for a girl again by some of the other students and teachers. Soon enough, people started referring to me with she/her pronouns. Despite my feminine fashion choices, I was resistant to this. While I did not truly feel like a boy, I felt more comfortable with people referring to me with male pronouns. So, I corrected everyone and told them I was a boy, not a girl.

I was not ready to attempt another social transition. I remembered what happened long ago when I was in first grade and did not want to go through that type of trauma again. Also, at this point, I was convinced that it was virtually impossible for me to ever truly be a girl. Still, other students and some teachers kept mistaking me for a girl. So, I started to wonder if I could live as a girl again.

Something that often happens with trans women is that we are told by society that we are a girl; this may be done mistakenly or with malice. Meaning most trans women are often told they are girls by others before they realize for themselves that they are indeed girls. We may be mistaken for a girl or mocked for acting like a girl. Then, ironically, after we transition into women, we are told relentlessly that we are men. Actually, I have been called a man more times *after* my transition than *before* my transition (you just can't win). For all of my life, I was mocked for acting like a girl, looking like a girl, and sounding like a girl. I had been bullied and called a girl in a derogatory manner for most of my life at that point. Still, I couldn't help but wonder if I actually *was* this thing I was being taunted for.

After awkwardly navigating the high school social system, I finally found my tribe. I had become friends with some of the female students in my school, and they found it fascinating that I was a genetic male who appeared to be female. These friends were older than I was and in higher grades, and they tried to convince me to stop correcting people and to just go with the flow and to live as a girl.

These friends told me it would be more fun for me to live as a girl than a boy and told me I would make a pretty girl. I wanted to gain the acceptance of my new, cooler, and older friends more than anything, so I did it. I started living as a girl, and to my surprise, I enjoyed it. I started to identify with she/her pronouns and did not correct people when they assumed that I was born female. I was also accepted and embraced into some female spaces, including the girl's restroom.

Taking me into the girl's restroom was particularly thrilling for my new friends. I'm not sure if they enjoyed supporting me and my gender identity or if they just thought it was fun to sneak a boy into the girl's restroom, but I was getting my life. Being born male, going into the girl's restroom was like being in some forbidden utopia. My new friends would include me in various fun activities in the girl's restroom, such as putting on makeup, gossiping, and even smoking. My peers finally accepted me for the real me—a girl.

Deep down, I knew what I was. I just needed to be reminded that I could live as a girl. These new, older, and cooler friends gave me the confidence to attempt another social transition. However, this time, socially transitioning as a girl was tougher because a lot of the students in my class had experienced me previously identifying as male. So, after a while, word got around that I was not a girl, and I was forced to live as a boy again.

Once I was forced into identifying as a boy again, my cooler, older friends distanced themselves from me. I guess these so-called "friends" were not truly my friends after all, but some teenage girls looking to have a fun time exploiting a queer kid. After another failed social transition, making friends became even more of a challenge, and ultimately, I was back to being a loner.

After the failed social transition, I revisited the concept of androgyny and figured being perceived as both a boy and girl was actually quite fierce. Although, I want to be clear that I identified as androgynous, or some would now say nonbinary, because I did not know it was possible to be transgender yet, that I could, in fact, transition into a girl. In other words, I chose an androgynous identity because of my lack of knowledge at the time. I was truly confused about what my gender and sexual identity were, and puberty made matters even more confusing.

Like most teenagers, I masturbated frequently, and the first time I ejaculated during masturbation was strange for me, as it solidified that I was becoming a man. Having the ability to ejaculate meant that I was never going to be a woman. Puberty was very sobering for me, as it reminded me of how I truly wanted to be a girl, not an androgynous boy. Going through male puberty as someone who feels female is a screaming hell. I began praying and bargaining with God to make me a girl and not to allow me to go through male puberty. Every night before bed I prayed to wake up as a girl, but each morning, my prayers went unanswered, and I woke up as a boy.

I started to really hate my penis and began torturing it. I would crush it with various items, hoping it would fall off. Many times, I debated cutting it off with a pair of scissors. At one point, I even took a compass (the one with a needle) and pierced my penis with it, giving myself a Prince Albert piercing. This was an act of hate, as I wanted to punish that part of my body because I despised it. Sadly, genital hatred and mutilation are actually very common among trans youth.

I also started to grow body and facial hair. The body hair didn't bother me as much as the facial hair, which confirmed for me that I was becoming more of a man. It mainly grew on my upper lip and a little under my chin. Luckily, I did not grow much and could quickly remove it by shaving. Still, experiencing even a small amount of facial hair awakened a distressingly high level of discomfort because it symbolized manhood.

Then puberty started to take a strange turn for me. I began to develop breasts. This was genuinely confusing, as boys typically do not grow breasts. My nipples were very tender, and even the slightest touch, even from just my T-shirts, would set them aflame. I did not know how to react to having breasts.

It seemed that God was answering my prayers somewhat, even if the breasts were small. Still, I had a penis, and women do not have penises. So, what kind of sick game was God playing with me? It seemed he was making me a woman from the waist up, so why couldn't God just finish the job?

Despite my anger with God and the universe, having small breasts was the highlight of my puberty as it aided in further enhancing my femineity. Then, one day, my mother called me into her room and was mortified by what she saw: breasts! Her son had grown a set of B-cup breasts. While I had grown to love my breasts, my mom didn't. At the time, I had more of an average build, so the breasts really stuck out. So, my mom forced me to begin wearing one of her sports bras to flatten them.

At first, I resisted the notion of wearing a bra. I thought wearing one of my mother's sports bras was weird. Also, I did not want to wear a sports bra to flatten my breasts down; in fact, I wanted them to grow even bigger. Then I thought about it and realized I would be wearing my first female undergarment! I decided to take the bra and start wearing it regularly. Wearing it made me feel empowered, feminine, and beautiful. I was truly getting my life wearing that sports bra. I started to realize that maybe having breasts and a penis wasn't so bad after all.

CHAPTER 18

RELIGION, SEXUALITY, AND EVERYTHING IN BETWEEN

It was another Sunday night. I was in my bedroom, preparing for the next school day. My mother was going on about something, yelling from her bedroom. The only statement I remember her saying was "And stop spraying all that damn perfume in the morning. You're not a girl!"

My mother had her share of mental health issues. At one point she was diagnosed with bipolar disorder, but she refused treatment, so her moods were erratic. When she was kind, she was beautiful. When she was irritable, she was a nightmare. Her way of parenting was toxic as well. She would bully and shame us into doing what she wanted.

The perfume she was referring to was a Victoria's Secret body spray called Love Spell that a cousin had given to me the previous summer in Paterson. I loved spraying it in the morning before school because it made me feel more feminine. Well, I guess combined with my boobs, jewelry, ear piercings, and long hair, the perfume was the last straw for my mother. Usually, I stayed silent when my mother berated me, but that night, I had had it and felt empowered to stand up for myself.

I marched into her room and declared, "I'm bisexual!" I was still in denial about being gay, so this lie was both for my mother and myself. My mother was, and still is, a very devout Christian, and I knew she held negative views of homosexuality. Even though I was coming out, I figured saying I was bisexual, instead of saying that I was gay or a girl, would be better received, but I was wrong. My mother turned white as a ghost. Her mouth was wide open, and in confusion, she asked, "What do you mean you're bisexual? You like boys?"

"Yes!" I declared.

As I suspected, I was met with an unyielding resistance.

She began to cry but quickly regained her composure and lit a cigarette. "So, you want to be bisexual? You want to get fucked in the ass?" she asked with a chuckle.

"Yes…I guess I do," I responded meekly. I couldn't believe she would ask me such a personal and invasive question, but I had watched my fair share of straight and gay porn up to that point, and yes, I supposed that was true.

She raised her eyebrow and, at a loss for words, took another pull from her cigarette. "So you want to go to hell. Is that what you're saying?"

The thought had crossed my mind plenty of times, but I figured I had prayed to God and asked him to change me, and he never did. I mean, he did give me boobs, but I never changed into a girl, so he must have wanted me to stay the way I was. However, being faced with the question was quite sobering. "No, I don't want to go to hell, but I can't help how I feel," I said.

She responded, "Well, you're going to have to give this to God to take away from you. God can take the gay away."

I felt a sense of relief. Maybe there was something she knew that I didn't. Some special prayer or Bible verse that I didn't know about.

She pulled out another cigarette. "Pass me that Bible." She shuffled through the Bible. I thought she was looking for some magical gay reversal verse. Instead, she found a verse that confirmed God's hatred of gay people. "It's in here somewhere… Here we go. 'If a man lies with a male as with a woman, both of them have committed an abomination, they shall be put to death.'"

Abomination, I thought. *What a horrible word.* What did it mean to be an abomination? I had heard of the abominable snowman, but what did it mean to be an abominable gay man? The confidence and gusto I had when I marched into my mother's room began to quickly fade away.

My mother's relationship with Christianity was complex. When I was a child, my mother identified as an atheist, but this changed following the birth of my younger sister when I was around the age of ten. When my sister was born, my mother began experiencing auditory hallucinations telling her to kill my then-infant sister. When my mother told me this story as an adult, it was clear that she was experiencing postpartum psychosis, but she told me that what she was experiencing was something more frightening: demonic possession. Understandably, hearing a voice telling her to kill my sister scared the life out of my mother, and she turned to Mr. W's mother, Grammy, for help.

Grammy, a loyal Christian woman, immediately took her Bible and began reading scripture. Grammy and my mother presumed the voice she was hearing was the voice of the devil, and the only solution would be to pray, so that's what they did. Then, one night, when my mother was fast asleep, she said God spoke to her and called her name. When my mother heard the voice of God say her name, she felt a sense of peace and warmth come over her that she had never experienced before. Following this, the voices telling my mother to kill my sister went away, and since then, she has been a devoted Christian.

Like my mother, I, too, am a Christian, but my relationship with Christianity started at a young age. My Auntie Lini was highly religious and exposed me to both the Hindu and Catholic religions. As a child, I found Hinduism intimidating, as I found Hindu gods to look frightening. So, I gravitated toward Christianity, attending church and praying regularly with Auntie Lini. Growing up, I upheld my Christian virtues and religious practices, so being told by my mother that I may go to hell for being gay truly terrified me.

I did not want to disappoint God. I did not want to go to hell, but I had no idea what to do at this point. I had prayed to God to make me a girl, I had prayed to God to make me stop liking boys, and nothing had changed. I still liked boys, and my body was still a boy's body. I was lost.

"I don't want to go to hell," I confessed to my mother, "but I can't help how I feel; I like boys."

My mother looked at me with pity and concern. "You're going to start going to church, and you're going to give this to the Lord to fix. Don't tell anyone else about this, especially not Mr. W. He'll lose his shit. Do you know who Donnie McClurkin is? He used to be gay, but God saved him, and now he is a straight gospel singer. You can be like him."

The idea of being able to rid myself of this abnormality and "abomination" brought me relief. Maybe I could be like Donnie McClurkin and turn straight. So, I agreed and told my mother I would start going to church.

***

I hated church. I started going to this Southern Baptist church filled with really country White people. A school bus would pick me up from my Marydel home and drive me to Dover, Delaware to hear the good word. The church was so loud and filled with chaotic energy. People would yell and scream at the top of their lungs like banshees. Sometimes, the overzealous church people would run around the pulpit, falling on the floor, shouting, and crying. It was quite a spectacle.

Shortly after I started attending church, I realized that religion appeals most to individuals who struggle with higher levels of thinking. (No, I do not believe all religious people are dimwitted; actually, this would be an insult to myself as I am religious.) However, there are a lot of religious people who struggle to understand complex concepts like homosexuality, queerness, and transgender identity.

Religion takes the complexity out of life: "this bad," "this good," and whatnot. Religion provides structure, guidance, and routine, which comforts some of those who cannot navigate life of their own volition. For many, life is easy when you have a rulebook to follow. Most members of that church believed if they followed those rules, suffered accordingly, and practiced unwavering appreciation, they would be rewarded, if not in this lifetime, in the afterlife.

Everyone at church was the complete opposite of me: White, straight, and conservative. I would sit in the front row, quiet and standoffish, hoping no one would say anything to me. I just wanted to hear the preacher preach, get saved, turn straight, and then go on my way. I tried the conversion thing my mom suggested and got saved, but nothing worked.

I would go up to the pulpit, get on my knees, and pray to be turned straight. I would also put a request in the prayer book to rid me of the gay demon. I got saved maybe five times, but nothing worked. I still felt attraction toward men. Mind you, my mother left me to do all this on my own. My mother was a Christian but did not regularly attend church, for reasons unknown to me. So, while I was at church trying to pray the gay away, my mother would stay at home with Mr. W.

Eventually, I realized that the temptation would never go away. I would forever be plagued by this gay demon, and the only thing I could do was control how I responded. I didn't realize it at the time, but my attempts at gay conversion started me on my path of OCD. I had many obsessive or intrusive thoughts surrounding gay sex and would compulsively pray to get rid of the thoughts. However, I found that prayer did not stop the thoughts or the pleasure I felt from thinking about gay sex.

I started to feel so dirty and impure that, at one point, I began secretly bathing in bleach. I would usually rub bleach on myself after masturbation. I would stand in the shower and rub bleach on my genitals and the rest of my body. The bleach would burn my skin, but I welcomed the burning sensation, as it made me feel like I was punishing myself for my impure thoughts. I viewed the burning from the bleach as both a physical and spiritual cleansing. Eventually I developed excruciating chemical burns on my hands and body. Unable to continue cleansing myself with bleach, I prayed even harder for God to take the gay away. I also kept going to church.

Then, one Sunday at church, a true miracle happened. It was a Sunday morning like every other. The preacher preached the good word, and everyone screamed and shouted as usual. I sat in agony in the front row, counting the minutes. Then, the doors opened at the back of the church. Of course, everyone turned to see who dared to show up to the sermon so late.

It was a family like any other family at the church: a father, a mother, and two small children, but the person who I assumed was the father was dressed to the nines in a stunning black Sunday dress with a matching veil, hat, and heels. I don't know how the father identified, but it was apparent that they were born male. Well, I was captivated. I had never seen such a thing, and something about it resonated. I thought, *Is this person here to get straight like me?* But that didn't make sense because it was clear that the father was happy and proud of their feminine appearance.

Well, the church got mighty quiet, which was another miracle, and the family took their seats in the middle of the church. The preacher clearly saw the father dressed in women's clothing and took the opportunity to preach some real ugly hate. "You know what I can't stand? People who say it's okay to be gay!" he yelled in a frenzy. The congregation erupted into a wild cheer. Then the preacher continued and shouted, "The gays are going straight to hell!" The church attendees began to make all kinds of noise, yelling, screaming, and encouraging the preacher to continue his monologue of hate. So, the preacher continued, "The Bible says that being gay is an abomination unto the Lord! All gays will go to hell!"

I was in shock. Clearly, the message was directed toward the family that came in late, particularly the father, who was visibly male and wearing women's clothing. The preacher continued his vile sermon. He went on and on. The crowd ate up every hateful word the preacher spoke. Finally, the father and their family quietly exited the church.

The relationship between religion and queerness has always been complicated. Christianity claims that you should be Christ-like and love radically, but Christian love is often limited when it comes to queer people. We are told repeatedly that we will burn in hell. Then, when we try to go to church to get our souls saved, we are chased out. The message that this sends to queer people is that we are not wanted and we are not loved.

The church members relished their victory and celebrated as the family left the church. I recoiled in horror at the sight. It was at that moment that I said to myself, *Fuck this shit.* I did not want to belong to a church or an ideology that believed I was going to go to hell for something I could not control. If I was going to go to hell, so be it, I thought—but so was everyone else in that church who chased that family out. That day, I decided I was no longer going to lie to myself and continue to identify as bisexual. I knew at that moment that I had no choice but to accept myself as the real me: a gay teenage boy.

Chapter 19

The Cycle II

Between the ages of fourteen and fifteen, I had entirely accepted that I was gay; however, I was still a closeted gay. I pretended I was straight and did all the straight things, like going to prom with a girl. My mother seemed happy with my successful conversion. However, she continued to force me to go to church against my will, since she thought it was working. But she didn't know that I was coming to a point of self-acceptance.

I continued to struggle with my gender identity, but at this point in my life, I started to accept myself for what I was and began identifying my sexuality as gay, as I knew I was solely attracted to men. Eventually, I built up the courage to tell other kids at my school that I was gay, and to my surprise, coming out as gay at school was well received, for the most part.

Once I started to accept myself as being a gay boy, I began to accept my body as well, including my penis. For most of my life, I had detested it, but with puberty and discovering the pleasure that my penis could bring me, I started to appreciate this part of my body. My breasts stopped growing for some reason. I have no idea why my breasts started growing or why they stopped growing. Maybe somehow my body was responding to my deep desires to be a girl, or maybe it was just a part of puberty and raging hormones—I guess I'll never know.

With my breasts now being significantly smaller, I no longer needed to wear the sports bra. I also tried my best to assimilate into masculinity. I stopped shaving my face and even had a (struggling) mustache. I also swapped out my long hair for a buzz cut.

It was around this time that I started to explore my sexuality through viewing online pornography. I started out watching straight porn, but once I discovered the wonders of gay porn, I was off to the races. Watching porn was both pleasurable and educational for me; I learned a lot about sex and, more importantly, gay sex. I found gay sex to be fascinating and exciting. I started learning the lingo as well, including what it means to be a top, a bottom, or versatile. I hadn't had gay sex up to that point (at least consensual gay sex), but I identified more with the role of a bottom and started to explore that part of my body as well.

Watching pornography was initially harmless, but after a while I became obsessed with gay porn and masturbating. I would stay up until dawn, sometimes watching porn in the downstairs computer room. I would masturbate two or three times a day as well. I was starting to go down a dark hole and became addicted to pornography, but I didn't realize it. Also, the more I watched gay porn, the more desperate I was to have gay sex. This desire was so intense that I once propositioned my own brother to have sex with me.

It happened one late night when my brother and I were the only ones awake. My brother had begun spending excessive amounts of time in the bathroom; he is about two years older than me, so I figured we were both going through puberty and exploring our bodies.

That night, as I watched pornography in the computer room, which was next to the bathroom, I started to wonder if my brother would be willing to have sex with me. In my sick thinking, I wondered if my brother would be receptive to us having sex with each other instead of masturbating separately. I thought if he did not want to have sex, maybe we could masturbate together, the way I had done with my cousin in New Jersey. Then, I did something that I am deeply ashamed of. I turned off the computer, walked to the bathroom, and opened the door.

The bathroom door was unlocked. As I had suspected, I discovered my brother in the act of masturbation. Seeing his mature penis startled and intimidated me. It was much bigger than mine, and he had more pubic hair as well. He quickly pulled up his pants and asked me what I was doing. I then asked him if he wanted to touch each other, and he became upset, called me crazy, and yelled at me to leave the bathroom. Embarrassed and anxious, I left the bathroom and closed the door.

My mind was racing. What had I done? Had I really just tried to have sex with my brother? How could I do something so disgusting? I could not help but think of how I was molested when I was a child and wondered if I was like this because of what had happened to me. I wondered if I would ever be normal. Then, a thought entered my mind that scared me to my core: "What if he tells on me?" A genuine fear ran through me that my mother would find out that I was not only still gay but had stooped so low as to try to have sex with my brother. I didn't know what to do, so I went to my room and went to sleep.

***

About a week went by, and my brother hadn't told my mother or anyone else what had happened. Although we acted as if everything was normal, our relationship became estranged and awkward. I'm not sure why my brother did not tell on me or discuss with me what had happened that night. We shared a room at the time, which added to the awkwardness.

I did not have the guts to bring up what had happened or to ask for his forgiveness. Truthfully, I did not believe what I did was forgivable. Eventually, the guilt of what I had done overwhelmed me, and I knew I had to tell my mother what had happened.

It was nighttime when I came to talk with her. I sat in her room on the loveseat stationed across from her bed. We were in the room alone, with the door closed. I told her I had to talk to her about something I had done and begged her not to get upset with me. I started by confessing that I had been watching gay pornography. I told her I was even spending my allowance money on gay porn. I told her about my continued desires to have gay sex and how prayer and church were not helping. I cried as I confessed, which made my mother pity me instead of getting upset.

She told me that I would have to continue to pray and go to church and that, eventually, God would deliver me from my homosexuality. She told me that it was out of my control if the devil placed those thoughts in my head, but what mattered was what I did after I had the thoughts.

Then I felt a knot in my stomach. I told her there was something else I had done. Crying, I told her about how I had tried to have sex with my brother. I spared no details and told her that he rejected my advancements. She thanked God that we did not end up having sex and praised my brother for standing up for himself.

Then my mother asked me something that struck me to my core. "Were you ever molested?"

I was unsure what prompted my mother to ask me such a question, but I answered truthfully. "Yes."

My mother began to weep. My heart was racing.

"Who?" she asked. I was terrified to tell her what had happened to me when I was younger. I did not want to tell her what my cousin had done to me since she would probably try to keep me away from my father's family if she knew, and I did not want my cousin to get into trouble. Instead, I told her about the molestation that occurred when I was in preschool.

I recounted all the details of what had happened that day in preschool with pristine clarity, and my mother sat in silence, continuing to cry. "Why didn't you push him off of you?" she exclaimed.

"I don't know," I answered meekly, looking to the floor. Then I began to wonder, why *didn't* I push him off me? Did I want what had happened to happen to me, or was I just too weak? Did I allow myself to be molested?

I felt shame like I had never experienced in my life. My mother told me how I had to fight against the devil and this spiritual sickness that I had acquired. She told me how she was molested as well in her childhood and that she, too, had homosexual thoughts before and attributed them to the molestation she had survived. Based on her rationale, I was gay because I was molested. I had never associated my gayness with being molested, but at the time, it made sense. I began to question whether I would have been straight if I had never been molested. Who would I be in that case? Would I be a completely different person? A normal person?

My mother told me that I could not control the devil from putting homosexual thoughts in my head, but I could control how I responded to those thoughts. She told me not to tell anyone what I had told her and to ask God and my brother for forgiveness. Then, she told me I needed to fight and pray harder before my sickness worsened. Telling my mother about the molestation softened her heart to me, and she had mercy on me for violating my brother.

I did what she told me to do. I asked my brother for forgiveness and told him I had told our mother what I had done. I couldn't believe it, but he actually forgave me. He told me that I was still his brother and that he loved me but that I should never try anything like that again. I promised him I wouldn't, and I kept my promise.

I stopped watching pornography altogether. I threw myself harder into Christianity and began reading the Bible and participating more in church again. I started to make attempts to act straight again. I remembered what my mother had told me. I could not stop the gay thoughts from coming from the devil, but what mattered was that I did not act upon those thoughts. I felt clean. I had been given a second chance and wouldn't mess it up.

FALL FROM GRACE

It's hard to face

Another day

When you've fallen from grace

I can't get up

For I am stuck

Down on the ground

What wonderful luck

Deep in a black hole

I have slipped

But still I grip

And hold onto the edge

Religious images

Running through my head

I have asked for forgiveness

I have repented my sins

But He remains silent

Did He forgive me?

I wonder

But how could he forgive

For what I did

How could he forget

The pain I caused

No, he couldn't

No, he shouldn't

Forget

At any cost

The pain I caused

I must remember

The love I lost

The wounds I created

And the scars I left

If only I knew

What I would lose

I would think twice

Before ruining a life

Forgive me, Father

Forgive me, Mother

Forgive me, Brother

CHAPTER 20

LIVING ALL ALONE

The year 2005 was tumultuous for everyone in my family. My mother and Mr. W were both unemployed. The year started with my mother giving birth to my youngest sister in January. I was fourteen going on fifteen when my mother came home from the hospital with the baby. Mr. W had left her home alone with the baby, which was usual for him. It wasn't until I was an adult that I discovered that Mr. W struggled with mental health issues, as well as substance use. So, looking back, I can only presume that he was spending so much time outside of the house using substances.

It was nighttime, and no one besides me was available to assist my mother. She spent the night in her room alone with my newborn sister. I checked on her occasionally to see if she needed anything, but she insisted she was okay.

Then, later that night, I heard her screaming. I knocked on her door and asked if everything was alright. "I need help!" she screamed from behind the door. I opened the door to find her lying on the floor, fully nude. She had had a C-section and was trying to clean the stitches. I told her to calm down and I would help her. I covered her with two towels and only exposed the sutures. Then I cleaned the suture site with the gauze and a cleaning solution that my mother had been given from the hospital. Afterward, I helped her stand up and put her into bed.

I left her in the bed next to my sister, who was fast asleep. I was so upset with Mr. W, leaving my mother alone after she had returned from the hospital after giving birth. It should have been him helping her off the floor, but once again, I had to be "the man of the house," like my mother often told me that I was.

Being the man of the house came with specific responsibilities, like taking care of her and my siblings and being a source of masculine presence. I didn't want to be the man of the house—or a man in general. I was still struggling with gender identity. Besides, being the only actual man in the house, it only seemed fitting that Mr. W should be the man of the house, but then again, he was unable to fill the responsibilities of this role.

After his incarceration Mr. W had stopped being abusive toward my mother and brother, but a leopard can't change its spots, and eventually he went back to his old ways, filling the house with tension, drama, and violence. Fortunately, Mr. W was barely home, so we did not have to constantly deal with his reign of terror. So, I guess with Mr. W being absent from the home so often, it was only fitting that I was the man of the house.

***

About a year after my youngest sister was born, Mr. W was incarcerated again, which left my mom unemployed and single with four kids. Marydel, Maryland, was out in the middle of nowhere. The closest major city (Denton) was about thirty minutes away and wasn't even a city but a town. We were living off government assistance, but the state had started forcing people to attend life skills classes. If you didn't go to the classes, your help would be terminated, which is what happened to us.

Unfortunately, my mother had no gas money to travel to Denton, where the classes were held. So, they cut off all our assistance. My mother's solution was to move to South Carolina to find work. Her foster family still lived in South Carolina and vowed to help her by providing food and shelter. Unfortunately, not all of us would go to South Carolina. My mother took herself and my two younger sisters and left my brother and me in Maryland by ourselves. Since my brother and I were both close to graduating high school, my mother did not want to interrupt our schooling and thought it would be best to leave us in Maryland. As a young teen, I was petrified to be left alone like that. However, my mother had confidence that I was mature enough to run the house and look after myself and my brother. If ever there was a time for me to be the man of the house, this was it. My mother left me a debit card that I was to use to pay bills and go grocery shopping. I felt like an adult, and eventually, the fear of being left alone faded. My brother was hardly home anyway. He would stay with friends most of the time. My mother's best friend would stop by once a month to take me grocery shopping, but other than that, I did everything on my own. Although, some incidents happened that scared the life out of me.

To start, I almost burned down the entire house once trying to cook fried green beans. I had seen them advertised on a TGI Fridays commercial and figured I could make them on my own. The issue was that I used frozen green beans, and combining the frozen green beans with the cooking oil caused a colossal grease fire.

I had left the stove for a quick second; then I heard something that sounded like a campfire. I entered the kitchen to discover a roaring flame extending from the frying pan to the ceiling. Ignorantly, I tried to extinguish the fire by pouring water on it. Of course, this only made the grease fire grow more.

I ran upstairs and called 911. "My house is on fire!" I yelled in a panic to the 911 operator. I slammed down the phone and ran back downstairs to discover that the fire had gone out on its own. The kitchen was covered in soot and smelled horrible. Still in shock, I ran out of the house. Firefighters arrived shortly after. They seemed upset that the house was not on fire, as if I had wasted their time or something.

The firefighters asked me where my parents were, and I said at work. I knew that telling them my mother was in South

Carolina would open a can of worms. They told me to be more careful and left. It was snowing that day, and they had tracked snow and mud throughout the house. I couldn't believe it; the house looked like a piece of burnt toast. I knew my mother would be upset, but I called and told her what happened anyway.

She was livid and told me never to leave the stove unattended again. I thought she would be more focused on my safety, but it seemed that she was more focused on the damage done to the kitchen (which she wouldn't see until she returned to Maryland a year later). The kitchen looked awful. No matter how much I wiped, I couldn't get the soot off the walls, so I lived with the dirty and burnt kitchen. Every day was a constant reminder of my mistake, and it haunted me endlessly.

The other scary incident involved a near break-in, which occurred about a month after my mom had left. Somehow, word had gotten out that she was gone, so people started to assume the house was abandoned. Most likely, my brother told all his friends that my mother wasn't home. Likely due to his genetic condition, my brother lacked a filter and would often disclose family secrets to outsiders, which is a big taboo in Black families.

Word also got around to my nosey neighbor that my mother had left town, and she decided to file a report with DYFS. Following the report, I was harassed at school by teachers and DYFS workers about my mother's whereabouts relentlessly. I had plenty of experience with DYFS by that time and had become a master at manipulating DYFS workers.

My relationship with DYFS has been predominantly negative for most of my life. Since they entered my life, it seemed that DYFS had no real interest in protecting me— or my family—from true danger, like Mr. W. Instead, it seemed that DYFS was more interested in separating my family, which terrified me. So, I told the DYFS workers enough lies to protect my family and prevent my brother and me from being placed in foster care.

Anyway, back to the almost break-in. One day, I woke up to a freezing house. It was winter at the time, and the cold was unbearable. I went downstairs to discover that the back door screen had been slashed and the lock had been tampered with. I was horrified. Someone had tried to break into my house overnight while I was asleep. What's more, the heat wouldn't come on.

I began panicking. What would have happened if the intruders got into the house and discovered I was inside? Would they have harmed me? I became overwhelmed with anxiety. I called my mom to tell her everything, and she instructed me to leave the lights on more so that people would know that the house hadn't been abandoned. She also said she would send my dad to fix the heat.

My relationship with my father was still rocky. I was still recovering mentally from the secret choking incident. He had tried many times to bond with me, but I just couldn't forget that he almost killed me that day. I had no desire at the time to seek a relationship with my father. He had moved on with his life, and so had I. Honestly, because he was around more, I viewed Mr. W as more of a father figure than my actual father.

My dad arrived the next day from New Jersey. He discovered that the copper tubing connecting the external oil tank to the basement furnace had been stolen. Apparently, copper has some value at the junkyard.

I felt like I was under attack, being watched by some unknown thugs. What if someone tried this again? What if they actually broke in and killed me? I didn't want my dad to leave. It felt comforting to have an adult in the house again, but he left after he fixed the heat. I wished my dad had taken me with him, but I was left all alone to fend for myself.

I nailed the back door shut, always had the lights on, and played music at night. I began to stay up at night and sleep during the day. Of course, this new sleeping pattern made it difficult for me to stay awake in school, but somehow, I managed to make it through. Actually, I was so hell-bent on getting out of Marydel that I took more classes than were required so that I could graduate high school one year early.

I decided to graduate from high school one year early so I could move on to adulthood. I frequently fantasized about leaving Marydel, attending college, and getting a new start. Plus, I figured I could be my true queer self in college, as I would be miles away from my mother. After a tough final year of high school, I graduated eleventh grade when I was seventeen.

My mom and sisters finally returned to Marydel in the summer of 2007, just in time for my high school graduation. It was a memorable event. My father, stepmother, and sisters on my father's side came down from New Jersey to attend the ceremony. Grammy was there too, but Mr. W was still incarcerated. Everyone, especially my mother, was so proud of me, being the first person on my mother's side of the family to graduate from high school. I even wrote the class poem, which all the students voted on and selected, although I did not get to read it. The valedictorian read the poem, but I stood for recognition while it was read.

I had applied to numerous universities and was accepted by quite a few. Still, with my mother being absent for the final year of high school, I could only make a little progress in college enrollment. Not having my mother present made applying to college, filling out financial aid applications, and visiting colleges nearly impossible. So, despite my high school academic success, my college choices were limited. Ultimately, I decided to enroll in community college at Chesapeake College in Wye Mills, Maryland, for the summer semester.

Chesapeake College was mighty far from Marydel. I had no car, so I had to take two buses to college. I would have to be on the first bus at 4:30 a.m. I would get home sometime around 6:00 p.m. It was tough, but I managed.

I was so poor I couldn't afford to buy lunch, so I survived off rice and ketchup. My hustle was intense. My mother had drilled into my head since I was a child that the only way I could make it out of the mess of our lives was to graduate college. Well, the time was here, and I was going to graduate, come hell or high water.

MEMORIES IN A HIGH SCHOOL HALLWAY

2007

As I write down these words

And remember the years

I look back on all the laughter, yells, and tears

I reminisce on the work, kind teachers

Sad goodbyes, weary eyes

And the friends I've come to gain

The ones who were there in those moments of joy and pain

I remember the forgotten assemblies
and the thrown away pep rallies

Uncrumpled a balled-up note

Drifted on class floats

Saw another game

Reopened an old locker

Reread an old textbook

I danced again at homecoming or prom

And breathed in the warmth inside memories they brought

Played in those old childlike thoughts

K.K.

Whispered once more all those murmured library talks

Heard once more all the school bells that rang

Soared once more in the melodies I once sang

I felt those anticipated feelings of the mysteries in the first second,
of the first moment, of the first day of school…another time

Then my eyes began to fill with water

And a frown began to form

My heart sank and my joy was torn

The rapture was blown away and misery set in

Then suddenly, it quickly stopped
when I relived walking down the halls,

and feeling my fingers run down all the tiles,
and seeing all the smiles

CHAPTER 21

COCAINE
IS ONE HELL OF A DRUG

Shortly after I started college in 2007, my mother began disappearing a lot. She started hanging out with this new group of friends, acting like a teenager, and staying out all night. It was strange to see, and I knew something was wrong. My mother had always been so put together and classy. I had never seen this partying side of her before, and it was alarming.

She was working at a gas station but had stopped going to work so that she could party. It started off with her partying all night; then she would disappear for days without notice. She would come home disheveled, sometimes even malodorous. My mother's disappearances impacted us in many ways, including becoming a hindrance to my education.

Because she would leave for days, I was forced to care for my two-year-old and seven-year-old sisters. All of my time was dedicated to taking care of them. I couldn't attend class or study because I was too busy being a substitute mother. Eventually, I missed so many days of school that I had to drop all my in-person classes. But luckily, I was able to continue school with online courses. My mother didn't care. All she cared about was partying. But soon I realized this was more than just partying. One night, everything became crystal clear.

My mother had come home from partying one night and was completely out of it. She was loopy, nonsensical, and behaving bizarrely. I remember her standing on the steps, clinging to the banister, and swinging back and forth. "Are you okay?" I asked. It was midnight, the children were asleep, and my brother was out with friends, so it was just the two of us.

"I can't stop. I'm in love with cocaine," she confessed.

Cocaine, I thought. *Well, that explains it.* Her admission shocked me, but it wasn't a total surprise. I had begun to suspect that she was using crack after discovering a burned spoon hidden in a dresser in her room. I didn't know much about drugs, but I knew what a crack spoon was.

"Mom, what do you mean you love cocaine?"

"When I do crack, it's like I'm in a hot-air balloon floating in the sky. I don't want to come down."

A hot-air balloon, I thought. *She has lost her mind.* "Why don't you just try to lie down, Mom?"

"I can't," she said. "Talk to me."

Of course, she couldn't sleep; she was high on crack. "Okay, well, what do you want to talk about?" I asked sassily. Honestly, at this point, I was sick of my mother and her charades. What was there to talk about at that point? The weather? Give me a break.

"Never mind," she said. I walked past her and went upstairs to bed. Shortly after, I heard the back door close and her car back out of the driveway. She was gone again.

My mother's disappearances would become a regular thing. Each day, I would pray for her to stop using drugs, but it seemed my prayers went unanswered.

One night she came home in tears. She wouldn't tell me what happened. Finally, she told me that she was tired of using drugs and just wanted to stay home and be a mom again. I couldn't believe it. My prayers had been answered. But I was still angry with her; she had discarded us countless times at that point. I knew the Christian thing to do was forgive, so I told her it would be okay and hugged her. I told her I would run a bath for her so that she could relax.

We didn't have any hot water because we were out of gas. So I boiled some water for her on the electric stove and mixed it with the cold faucet water in the tub. "Are you hungry?" I asked her.

"Yes," she replied.

"Well, take a bath, and I'll make you something to eat," I told her. Truthfully, there wasn't much food in the house, being that most of my mother's money was being spent on drugs, but I managed to make her a sandwich. After her bath, I brought her the sandwich, and she began weeping again.

"Thank you, Boo-Boo." Her shame and guilt were palpable. I completely believed her when she told me she was done using drugs. I thought she would finally be on the straight and narrow, that I would have my old mother back. The next day, she left to use drugs again.

***

Summer and fall had passed, and winter was almost over. My mother was still leaving us for days at a time to get drugs and party. I thought with the cold weather that the drugs and the partying would stop, but they didn't. In fact, things had gotten worse. There was no more happiness, laughter, or holidays, just worry and anger.

My mother had left us on Thanksgiving, Christmas, and New Year's to get drugs and party. I tried my best to make the holidays special for the children, but it was hard, still not being an adult. I used my money from my Pell Grant to buy my sisters Christmas gifts, but it didn't help because nothing is sadder than a Christmas morning with no parents.

With our mother out using drugs and partying and Mr. W still incarcerated, I was the only consistent somewhat-adult presence in the home for my sisters. My brother was barely home as well, spending most of the time with his friends. The weight on my shoulders was tremendous, but I carried it nonetheless.

I continued online classes and immersed myself in schoolwork as a distraction. However, my mother's addiction caused her to reach new lows. Running out of her own money, she began stealing the money I had that was left over from my Pell Grant. She would do anything to get high at that point, and all of her finances went toward drugs. She even stopped paying the bills, including the mortgage, which led to an eviction.

I remember the day that she discovered we were being evicted. She got a letter in the mail informing her that we were going to be evicted. After she read the letter, she completely lost it and started smashing things in her room. She lay on the floor, screaming and kicking objects in the room. I did my best to comfort her, but she was inconsolable. She was about to lose everything that she had worked so hard for and was now facing the possibility of homelessness.

The eviction notice seemed to have scared her a little, and she started to stay home more, and even started working nights again at the gas station. But when spring came and the days became warm and inviting, the partying and drug use resumed. Perhaps the lengthy eviction process gave my mother a false sense of hope that she had more time to procrastinate, party, and use drugs.

Shortly after my mother resumed using drugs and partying, people began calling the house phone asking for "Renee," my mother's apparent new alias. I was fuming. We were facing the sobering reality of eviction, and my mother was more focused on using drugs, partying, and being Renee. I began to hate my mother. It seemed she had forgotten what really mattered. She disregarded her family, her home, and her dignity.

I had never felt more alone or angry at that point. I was given the tremendous responsibility of being an adult figure in the house, even though I was seventeen. My brother still remained relatively absent from the home, and I'm not even sure if he knew what was happening with the eviction and my mother's substance use. My sisters were still very young, so they were oblivious to what was going on.

Whenever my mother came home from partying, I would be furious and not speak to her. At the time, I had little understanding of addiction. I did not realize that my mother had lost control and was using substances to cope with the tremendous stress of being a single mother, being poor, and facing eviction. Ignorantly, I blamed my mother's addiction on a lack of morality and turned away from her when I should have given her support and freedom from judgment.

It seemed I was alone in my anger at my mother, as my little sisters would never get upset with her. Children are so forgiving. My little sisters would greet my mother with open arms and enthusiasm when she came home, like a soldier returning home from war. And that's precisely what she was, someone at war with her mental health, her trauma, her addiction, and most of all herself. I was too naïve to see this at the time. To me, my mother was making conscious decisions to leave us. I didn't realize that she was powerless to her addiction.

I only did what I could at that point: continue praying. I prayed and cried for my mother every night, but it didn't seem to make a difference. She told me my prayers went unanswered because I didn't have "faith" in her. She told me that it was my anger and resentment that stood in the way of her recovery, and I believed her.

STRANGER

Hello, stranger

Someone I used to know

Someone I used to love

Someone who used to love me

Once upon a time

You were mine

Once upon a time

You were a close friend

Shelter during a storm

A place of safety and comfort

But

Now you're a memory

A forgotten yesterday

Come in, stranger

Sit down

Tell me your name

Part III: Manhood

CHAPTER 22

JERSEY BOUND

The summer of 2008 came quickly. The spring semester was over for me, and I was on summer break, which meant it was time to go to New Jersey. At this point I had had enough of my mom's dysfunction, and I wanted out. I started planning to leave Maryland for good and move to New Jersey with my father's family. I knew that if I stayed in Maryland, my mother would continue to deteriorate, and I would be right behind her.

Once, she told me straight out that she felt comfortable leaving for days because she knew I would be there to take care of the kids. At that point, I knew what an enabler was and that I was one. So, I decided I would no longer enable my mother and force her to be the incredible mother I knew she could be again.

I planned to leave for New Jersey sometime in July. But unfortunately, it just so happened that that is when my mother became suicidal. The incident took all of us by surprise.

One night, my mother called her friend Ms. Diane and told her she was having thoughts of killing herself. Shortly after, Ms. Diane showed up around 10:00 p.m., and I opened the door for her. I wondered what Ms. Diane was doing at our house so late. She seemed to be uneasy, but I did not think much of it. She told me to tell my mom she was there and to come downstairs.

I went and knocked on my mother's door. She opened the door, crying hysterically. I didn't understand what was happening, but I told her that Ms. Diane was downstairs. She scurried past me, rushed to the door, and hugged Ms. Diane, who comforted her and told her everything would be alright. I stayed in the living room with them to make sure everything was indeed alright. My mother told Ms. Diane that she felt like she was going to kill herself. "I'm sick and tired of being sick and tired," she kept saying over and over.

Ms. Diane told me to stay with my sisters so she could take my mom to the hospital. About two hours later, she returned and informed me that my mother had been admitted to the psychiatric unit of the hospital. She took my sisters and dropped them off at Grammy's house. My brother continued to spend most of his time with his friends, so I was all alone again in the house.

My mother stayed in the psychiatric unit for about two weeks. She even spent her birthday there. When I called her to sing "Happy Birthday," she busted into tears on the phone. She was diagnosed with bipolar disorder and came home sedated on medications. For a while she took her medications; then, like most individuals with bipolar disorder, she became convinced that she had been misdiagnosed. "I'm not taking that shit anymore. I feel like a zombie," she told me one day. I begged her to take the medication, but she had her mind made up.

My mother's refusal to take medications to treat her mental health condition confused me. She was also recommended to participate in therapy and go to Narcotics Anonymous meetings, but she did not do this either. I couldn't understand at the time why she chose to admit herself to the hospital and then refused to follow the doctor's orders. However, it is actually a common occurrence for people who suffer from mental illness to be treatment noncompliant.

Once I realized that my mother was not going to adhere to her mental health treatment, I became serious about my plans to move to New Jersey. I was now eighteen and could technically live where I pleased. I contacted Auntie Lini to provide bus fare, which she did. I packed my bags and pretended to be taking another summer trip to New Jersey. My mother asked me repeatedly, "You're coming back, right?"

"Yeah, of course," I responded. But we both knew the truth: I would never return to Maryland again.

She drove me to the Greyhound bus station in Dover, Delaware to take a bus to Newark, New Jersey. Once I got on the Greyhound, I knew I was in the clear. I was finally going to leave my mother and all her drama behind me. I could enjoy being a young adult. I could go to school in New Jersey and get a college degree. But leaving was bittersweet because it meant I was also leaving my siblings behind with my mother, who was anything but stable at the time.

I thought that if I left Maryland, my mother would be forced to be the mother she previously was. In hindsight, my intuition was wrong; after I left, my mother continued to spiral. Sometime after I left Maryland, the eviction process was finalized, and my mother, brother, and younger sisters were all forced to move out of our house in Marydel. Mr. W was released after I left, which seemed to be a big help, as eventually, they moved into another house in Delaware that they rented. But still, even with them having a home, the dysfunction continued.

It would take years for my siblings to forgive me for abandoning them, especially my younger sisters, as I left without telling them I was not coming back. For a significant portion of my sisters' lives, I had an important role in raising them, so leaving them behind truly hurt them. Leaving my siblings behind was a complex decision. It was probably one of the most selfish things I have ever done in my life, but at the same time, I knew that if I stayed, I would have no future. I knew if I didn't leave Maryland, I wouldn't be able to finish college, and I would be stuck cleaning up my mother's mess for the rest of my life.

Also, I would be stuck in the closet, not being able to express my true gender or sexuality. So, I boarded the bus and took my seat. I looked out the window and waved goodbye to my mother. Then the bus pulled off. I couldn't believe it. I was finally free.

***

My grandparents' house in Paterson always felt like my home. I loved being around my father's family. They were eccentric and fascinating people who loved to have a good time. I kept all the drama of Maryland to myself. Nobody needed to know that I was running away from a disaster, and they definitely didn't need to know about my mother's addiction or Mr. W's incarceration and violent behavior. (Remember, in the Black community, it is taboo to disclose family secrets.)

I also did not disclose to anyone that I had no intention of returning to Maryland after summer was over. I knew my father's family wouldn't mind me living there, so I figured I would cross the bridge of having the conversation to stay there with them at a later time. For now, I was more focused on enjoying my newfound freedom and peace.

In New Jersey, I was able to revamp myself into something of a starlet. I was super thin then and fashioned myself as an undiscovered male model. I had no idea how to become a model. I joined a bootleg talent agency and got a few modeling gigs, but after a while, it became clear that modeling would be a lost cause. Next, I decided to try singing. I even auditioned for *American Idol*, but it was another bust. I didn't even make it past one round.

Auntie Lini caught wind of my lack of clarity and suggested I go to nursing school. I had volunteered in high school to help the school nurse for a semester, but the idea of becoming a nurse myself had never crossed my mind. Auntie Lini had been a nurse for quite some time at that point and was convinced that I would be a great nurse.

She saw how well I cared for my grandparents and was confident I had the nursing gene. I accepted her guidance and agreed to go with her to sign up for nursing school. Then, she made me an offer. She said I could continue to live with her and my grandparents for free. In addition, she would pay for my school expenses as long as I continued to care for my bed-bound grandparents. I took her up on this, and in October of 2008, at the age of eighteen, I began school to become an LPN (Licensed Practical Nurse).

Starting nursing school was exciting. I still remember my first day of class. I had gotten up early, around 6:00 a.m., as Auntie Lini agreed to drop me off at class, but she had to be at work by 7:00 a.m. I sat on the attic stairs across from Auntie Lini's room, eating a plate of rice and ketchup, as I had done many times in Maryland before my morning commute to community college. The point of eating this was to stay full for as long as possible, as I had no money to buy lunch.

When Auntie Lini came out and discovered me there with my unusual breakfast, she chuckled and asked why I was eating plain rice and ketchup. When I explained why, she told me I didn't have to do that anymore as she would provide me with pocket money for food and bus fare.

I should have known that Auntie Lini would have no issue providing me with money for food, as she had supported me in so many ways for most of my life. Still, I did not want to be a burden to her, as she had already done so much for me, but there were no limits to her love and kindness. So, Auntie Lini told me to throw away the rice and ketchup, and she would get me Dunkin' Donuts on the way to school.

Nursing school was an exciting experience. I wasn't expecting to be the youngest person in my class, but most of my classmates were in their thirties and forties. My older classmates took a liking to me and gave me the nickname "little boy," which I hated.

I excelled in school, but not without being a smart aleck and class clown. Most teachers thought I was adorable, but some grew tired of my shenanigans. Luckily, my high grades and smarts made up for my immaturity.

K.K.

It wasn't until I began clinicals that I started to understand the seriousness of what I was doing, taking care of people who could not take care of themselves. I was exposed to all sorts of interesting illnesses during my clinicals, including seeing a bedsore that I had to stick my whole fist in to clean. I began to take pride in what I was doing, and eventually, it became clear that Auntie Lini was right: I was destined to be a nurse.

CHAPTER 23

LOSING MY RELIGION

Sometime after I started nursing school, I began to explore my sexuality as a gay male. I remember feeling as if I was on a mission to lose my virginity, but I had no idea where to begin to find any fellow gay guys. I joined many dating websites but had no luck finding a man. Then, one day, I was scrolling through Myspace and came across a profile of a man who identified as bisexual.

We were both nineteen years old. His name was Josh, and he was White and average looking. Honestly, I didn't care much about how he looked; I just wanted to lose my virginity, and any consenting adult male would do at that point. We began talking online and took a liking to each other. After chatting for about four days, Josh invited me to his house to hook up. The moment was finally here. I would finally lose my virginity, and I was ecstatic.

I had done plenty of "research" on gay sex by watching porn and had decided that I would identify as versatile. Josh identified as a top, meaning I had to be a bottom with him. I didn't mind. In fact, in many ways, I preferred to bottom.

My biggest concern about bottoming was, of course, cleanliness. I did more research on how to prepare to bottom to get ready for the big day. I learned what foods to avoid before bottoming and how to give myself an enema. I also did research on what condoms and lubricants to use. I wanted to be as prepared as possible. So, when the big day finally arrived, I was a certified bottomology expert.

Josh lived in Clifton, New Jersey, and I still wasn't driving, so I took the bus to get to him. It was a warm afternoon when I boarded the bus from Paterson to Clifton. I was a nervous wreck. The bus was mostly empty, so I sat by myself, lost in my thoughts. I started questioning what I was doing; I had only talked to this man for a week. What if he turned out to be a serial killer? But I decided I was at the point of no return. Plus, I had spoken with Josh on the phone, and at least he didn't sound like a serial killer (as if I would know what a serial killer sounds like).

Josh was kind and knew I was an anal virgin and had guaranteed that he would be gentle and patient with me. He also told me that he had condoms and lube, so the only thing I needed to do was show up. I tried to calm down, but then I began wondering about something even worse. What if I pooped on him?! What if, for some reason, I got explosive diarrhea and covered Josh in poop from head to toe? I think being a messy bottom is every gay man's fear. Nobody (well, almost nobody) wants to defecate on their partner during sex.

I took a deep breath and reassured myself I was just being silly. I had given myself an enema and skipped breakfast, so being a messy bottom shouldn't be an issue. Then, I decided that I was going to go into this with a positive attitude. I had prepared myself to the fullest, and I was ready to put my practical and scholarly knowledge to the test. I looked out the bus window and realized I needed to get off at the next stop. After I got off the bus, I walked past a drugstore and decided to call Josh to see if he needed me to get anything, like lube or condoms. He told me that he didn't need anything and had all the necessary supplies.

I arrived at Josh's house and called him. He came outside and escorted me into the house. Thankfully, Josh looked better in person than he did in his pictures; not much better, but better, nonetheless. He was shorter than I thought he would be, but he smelled good and was so nice.

We went into his house, and he introduced me to his mother, who didn't seem interested in talking to me. Actually, she seemed annoyed at my presence in her home. I'm not sure if Josh had told her about his bisexuality or not, but he told her that we would be in his room playing video games. She didn't seem to want to talk anymore, so we made our way to his bedroom.

His bedroom was small and lit with red lighting. Josh said everything looked better in red lighting, and he was right, as the red lighting made him look handsome. His room was what you'd expect of a nineteen-year-old. He had posters all over his walls and laundry scattered on the floor. His mattress lay on the floor with no box spring.

I sat down on his bed, and he apologized and told me his mother was always grouchy, so I shouldn't take it personally.

"So, do I look like my pictures?" I asked him.

"Yeah, but you look better in person," Josh responded. "What about me?"

I hesitated in my response but said kindly, "I think you're cute."

Then he leaned in and kissed me. I had kissed girls before, growing up, but this was the first time I had been kissed by a boy. It felt kind of weird; I could feel his stubble scratching my face. Then he began sticking his tongue down my throat, which felt strange as well. I didn't know what to do, so I copied whatever he did.

Then he stopped and asked, "Are you nervous?" I nodded and smiled. "It's okay. I'll be really gentle," he said shyly. Then he began to grope me through my jeans. We began fondling each other over our pants and continued kissing. Then he moved his hand up and unbuttoned my jeans.

I felt a rush of adrenaline flow through me. I couldn't believe it. I was finally going to lose my virginity. Truthfully, I wasn't that into Josh, but at that point, I figured I would make the best out of the situation and go with the flow. No matter what, I was not going to leave Josh's house a virgin.

Josh leaned over and grabbed a condom. He opened the packet and placed the condom on his penis, which, like the rest of him, was average. Still, it was the perfect penis size for me to lose my virginity to. Then, he placed my legs over his shoulders in preparation to penetrate me. I was confused, as he had not applied any lubrication yet, which I knew was essential to preventing pain during anal sex.

I stopped him and asked, "Are you going to use lube?"

"Oh yeah," he said with a chuckle. He put my legs down, and then he reached for a bottle of lotion, which looked like it had come from the 99-cent store.

I became irritated with this, as I had asked him if he needed me to get anything from the drugstore, and he told me no. So, I questioned him politely, "I thought you said you have lube?"

"Don't worry, I always use this," he responded.

He began rubbing the lotion on his penis and then put some on me. He put my legs back on his shoulders and began to enter me. It hurt. It was a pain I had never experienced up to that point. It felt as if I was being torn in two. I stopped him at least three times, but he was patient with me. "Go slower," I told him, and he did.

Finally, he told me, "I'm all the way in. How does it feel?"

"A little painful," I responded meekly.

"Don't worry, it will feel good once you loosen up." He began thrusting, which made the pain worsen.

As I lay there being penetrated, I was not only experiencing physical discomfort, but mental discomfort as well. As Josh continued penetrating me, I felt myself getting lost in thought. I began questioning if I was doing the right thing—having gay sex. I couldn't help but remember all the sermons I heard and Bible verses I read saying that what I was doing was a sin, an abomination, and a betrayal unto the Lord. But at that point, what was I going to do, turn back time and take my virginity back? That would be literally impossible. So, I figured I had no choice but to continue having sex with Josh and try my best to enjoy it.

I tried to get into it, but it was virtually impossible to enjoy the sex at that point. I was still in physical discomfort, as Josh's cheap lotion lube was not doing what it needed to do. So, I couldn't help but wince in pain. Josh could see that I was in pain and told me to lie on my side, as it would hurt less, so I did. He re-entered me, but this time, he used his spit as a lubricant, which seemed to work better than the lotion.

Finally, I had begun to experience some form of physical pleasure from the sex, and I began to let go of my inhibitions and religious restraints. The pleasure had begun, and I closed my eyes in ecstasy. I stopped worrying about God and hell, as in that moment, I was in heaven.

Then Josh suddenly got off me. I was confused as to what was going on, but then he said, "I'm getting close." He then lay flat, took the condom off, and signaled me to perform oral on him, which I did. Then he positioned himself on his side, pulled my penis to his face, and began performing oral on me, which was a sensation I had never experienced. I felt a rush of pleasure come over me and said, "I'm about to cum."

"Me too," he responded. Then, in synchrony, we both ejaculated. I was shocked by the taste of his semen. It was very bitter and thick. I quickly swallowed it, and he swallowed mine. It was done. I was no longer a virgin.

We lay on his bed in silence. "So, how was it?" Josh asked.

"Amazing," I responded.

We put on our clothes, and then I headed home.

I got to the bus stop and excitedly called one of my cousins. "I lost my virginity!" I told her.

"What?!" she responded. "We have to celebrate!" She drove over and picked me up with two other cousins in the car. We went to eat pizza, and I told them all the details.

As we sat in the pizzeria, eating and laughing, I thought back on the young boy I once was and remembered all the struggles I had with my sexuality. I had come a long way. I was no longer the powerless child being forced to give someone oral sex or being held down and molested. I was no longer the same person punishing myself, bathing in bleach, for having thoughts of gay sex.

Losing my virginity was much more than a physical act; it was a spiritual awakening. By choosing to lose my virginity, I had taken my power back and accepted myself for who I was. I had conquered my demons and faced my fears. At that moment, I felt free, and more importantly, I felt like a proud gay man.

CHAPTER 24

GAY AND GUYANESE

I continued to talk to Josh here and there. We had sex a couple of other times, but it was difficult to see him and also tend to my studies. Nursing school was hard as hell, and I needed to dedicate all my attention to it. I was determined to succeed, so I studied hard every day.

One night, while I was studying, I started to have a terrible itch on my lower back. I looked in the mirror and discovered that I had developed a rash. It was about medium-sized, reddened, had fluid-filled bumps, and was incredibly painful. It was located between my right buttocks and my lower back. Immediately, I began panicking. What the hell was this rash, and why did it develop after I started having sex with Josh?

I looked into my anatomy and physiology textbook for an answer and was convinced I had developed herpes simplex 2. I couldn't believe it, I had had sex three times at that point, with only one person, and now I probably had herpes. It just couldn't be. I calmed myself down, called my cousin Samantha, and asked if she would take me to the clinic downtown in the morning. Coincidentally, she was planning to go there already, so she said she would take me with her.

I woke up the next day filled with anxiety. I decided to skip class, as going to the clinic was more important. We arrived, checked in, and sat in the waiting room for about an hour. I wanted to vomit from nervousness. Then, finally, a nurse came out behind a door and called me.

I looked at Samantha with worry. "It's going to be alright," she told me lovingly. I squeezed her hand, stood up, and began walking toward the door where the nurse was.

I was taken to an examination room, and the nurse sat down and began typing on a keyboard. She asked many questions and hardly looked at me. I tried to make small talk, but she didn't seem interested. It was clear that she just wanted to do her job as quickly as possible.

"Sexual orientation?" she asked.

"Gay," I responded with a smile.

"Race?" she asked next.

"Guyanese and Black."

"Guyanese? You're Guyanese?"

"Yes, on my dad's side."

"So, you're telling me you're Guyanese *and* you're gay?" she asked in shock.

"Yes," I responded, confused.

"I'm from Guyana, and I never heard of someone being gay and Guyanese."

I had no idea how to respond to the nurse, so I said, "Okay?" in embarrassment.

She finished the questionnaire and asked to look at the rash. I pulled my pants down to expose it. The pain had worsened to the point where even the slightest touch hurt. She touched the vesicles gently and told me to pull my pants up. "What do you think it is?" I asked her.

She took off her gloves and washed her hands. With her back turned from me, she said, "Well, you're gay. So it's probably HIV."

"HIV?" I asked in shock.

She turned around, drying her hands. "Yeah, I'm ninety-nine percent sure it's HIV, but the doctor will come to look at it." Then she started walking out of the room. "The doctor will be in shortly."

I felt the room begin to spin. I couldn't believe that I had just been told by a nurse that I could have HIV. I started hyperventilating. Could this be a punishment from God for having gay sex? I had only had sex with Josh three times, and we had used protection each time, so how could I have caught HIV from him? I tried to calm myself down. A rash can be an early sign of HIV, but it just didn't make sense that I had HIV.

After about ten minutes, the doctor came into the room and asked to see the rash. He turned the lights off in the room and held a lamp over the rash. "Yeah, it's fluid-filled. That's not a good sign," he said.

"So, I have HIV?" I asked shakily.

"I'm not sure. When was the last time you had sex?"

"About a week ago, but I've only had sex with one person in my life," I told him.

"Yeah, we're going to have to do bloodwork. The instant test might not pick up if you have HIV and can give you a false negative. You're going to have to go to another clinic to do the bloodwork there," the doctor told me. Then he left the room.

I tried my best to gather myself before I walked back into the waiting room. I felt a tremendous amount of shame and didn't want my cousin to know that I needed to do bloodwork to make sure I didn't have HIV. Then I heard my mother's voice in my head. "Abomination." I was sure that God was punishing me with HIV, and I would soon die.

I walked out into the waiting room and saw Samantha. She looked at me, smiling. "How'd it go?"

I burst into tears, crying hysterically.

She ran up and hugged me. "What's wrong?" she asked, worriedly.

"They told me I might have HIV. There's a ninety-nine percent chance!"

She calmed me down. I didn't know what to do at that point. I truly believed my life was over and I was going to die. I told her I had to go to another clinic on the other side of downtown to do bloodwork, and she said she would take me there.

We got into the car, and I called Josh, still crying. "What's wrong?" he asked me.

"You gave me HIV!"

"What? I don't have HIV. I was tested a month ago," he said.

"Well, I have a rash, and they told me at the clinic there's a ninety-nine percent chance that I have HIV!" I hung up the phone in anger.

We arrived at the building, and I was still tearful. The nurses at this clinic were all very friendly and sympathetic. They comforted me without judgment and treated me like a human. They told me that I was going to be tested for every STD. They drew my blood and told me it would take seventy-two hours for them to get the results, but they would call me as soon as they had them. They said they wouldn't read the results over the phone, whether negative or positive. How would I survive seventy-two hours being in this state of panic? But I had no choice.

I was a raw and exposed nerve waiting for those results. I couldn't focus in class. The rash still ached. It was a constant reminder of the possibility that I could have HIV. I prayed to God for forgiveness for having gay sex. Josh must have called me a million times, but I didn't want to talk to him. I texted him that I would call him once I got my results.

I didn't want to talk to anyone. I couldn't eat, and I couldn't sleep. I wanted to stay in bed and hide under the covers from the world. I wondered what I would do if the results came back positive. What would I say to my partners? Worse, how would I tell my mother? This was the mother who told me I was going to hell for being bisexual. I just couldn't do it. It would be some deep, terrifying secret that I would have to keep to myself.

Three days passed, and I got a call from the clinic saying my results were in. Of course, I asked what they were, but they explained to me again that they were not permitted to discuss results over the phone and that I would have to go to the clinic in person. I called Samantha, who drove me to the clinic as soon as she got out of class.

I arrived at the clinic full of worry. I sat by myself in an exam room again, my mind racing. I was convinced that I would be told that I had HIV, or genital herpes, or something else that I would have to live with for the rest of my life. Finally, a doctor came into the exam room.

"I have your test results, and everything came back negative," he said.

"What!" I exclaimed with joy. I couldn't believe it. "Well, what about my rash?"

"I'm not sure. Could be some sort of allergic reaction to a lotion or a detergent or something."

At that point, I didn't care what caused the allergic reaction so long as I didn't have an STD. I walked back to the waiting room and told Samantha the good news. Then I called Josh and told him. He said he had also gone to a clinic and tested negative. I was so relieved. I decided to look at the situation positively. I decided that God wasn't punishing me and that this was a sign to have more faith in God's love for me.

The rash went away eventually. It left as mysteriously as it had come. Josh moved, and we lost contact with each other.

***

I began dating other men and was having a ball, being an out gay man. I remember dating this guy named David, who was a little older than I was.

One day, when I was at David's apartment in the Bronx, we started watching the first season of *RuPaul's Drag Race*. It was the first time I had watched a drag show in my life. I had no idea what I was looking at, but the show spoke to me for some reason. Watching the contestants transform from handsome men into the image of beautiful women was amazing. I remember binge-watching the entire season with David that day. I asked him all kinds of questions about drag and even began considering doing drag myself. He saw the fascination in my eyes and told me, "Whatever you do, just don't become a girl."

CHAPTER 25

THE BATHHOUSE

I was still nineteen and figuring out my new life. I was having a blast dating but struggled with feelings of guilt for leaving my siblings back in Maryland with my mother. I limited my contact with her and spoke with her only rarely on the telephone, but I was friends with her on Facebook, and after she saw my posts proudly proclaiming I was a gay man, she called me hysterically and told me I was going to hell and spouted all the usual homophobic rhetoric that conservative Christians say.

My mother really had some nerve judging me after everything she had done in Maryland. I continued to be friends with her on Facebook and rebelled against her homophobia by posting even more provocative posts and images of myself. I was nineteen, meaning I was an adult and free to do whatever I pleased, including dating men.

Online dating was all the rage, and I had a lot of success with the website Craigslist. You have to understand that back in those days, there weren't too many online dating websites for gay people. I know the stigma and taboo associated with Craigslist now because of the Craigslist killer, but it really aided me in developing socially and sexually. I met all types of exciting men on Craigslist. I often posted under the casual encounters section and got responses from men from all different backgrounds.

For a while I dated a man named Howie, who was fifty-nine years old (yes, that is forty years older than me). Howie was an

Italian man from New York. Everything about him was pretty average: height, weight, looks. But what made Howie so likable was his personality. He was happy-go-lucky, positive, and very kind.

He often told me how handsome I was and how fortunate he was to be with a guy like me. I was insecure about my looks. I thought I was too thin and lacked muscles. I also struggled with facial acne and even started wearing a foundation to cover up the acne scarring. So, getting praised by Howie for my looks meant a lot and made me feel better about myself.

Howie was a very wealthy man. I don't think he ever disclosed what he did for work, but he would take me to fancy restaurants and buy me gifts. I joked with my cousins that he was my sugar daddy, even though he never gave me money.

Once, we went on a date together to the beach. I found it odd being out in public with Howie. Not because I was insecure about being out in public on a date with another man but because of our visible and dramatic age difference. So, I usually dated Howie mainly during the evening hours. I still wasn't driving then, so I would take the bus to New York to go on our dates.

One day, Howie told me he had planned something different and exciting. He was going to take me to a gay bathhouse in New York City. I had never heard of a bathhouse, so I asked him to explain it. He told me it was basically an underground spa where gay men go to have sex. He said we could go there to relax and have fun. Before, we had only had sex in hotels; I never visited his home, and I'm not sure why. But I was bored of meeting in hotels, so I agreed to go to the bathhouse to spice it up.

I met him in front of a seedy-looking building that looked nothing like a spa. We went inside to check in. The whole room was dark, aside from some red lighting.

We walked up to a booth. "Name?" the man in the booth asked. Howie told him his name. A membership was required to get into the bathhouse. You would think I would be intimidated by the process, but I was intrigued. Howie gave the man all his information; then he opened a door, and we entered the bathhouse. Unlike the front entrance, the inside of the bathhouse was well lit.

Howie told me he had his own room, and we could go in there and drop our stuff off and get naked. "Get naked?" I asked him.

"Yes, everyone will be naked," Howie explained. Suddenly, I got nervous; I did not want to walk around naked in front of everyone! I was very slim at the time and insecure about my penis size.

On our walk to the rooms, we passed some attractive guys who were walking around with towels wrapped around them. I breathed a sigh of relief seeing this as I realized I could at least walk around with a towel.

We made it to the private rooms section. The area was also dark with red lighting. We went inside, and I noticed the rooms had no ceilings. This meant that if you really wanted to, you could peek over the top of the wall and see what was happening in the room next to you, which fascinated me. I could hear men having sex, as there was loud moaning and even some cracking of whips and jingling of chains. I didn't know what was going on, but I was intrigued, to say the least.

"Come on," Howie said, "let's go to the sauna." We went back into the hallway and returned to a fully lit area. I couldn't believe what I was seeing. As we walked through the bathhouse, there were televisions everywhere, and they were all playing gay pornography. I thought this was as racy as it could get, that is, until we passed a huge indoor pool. Men were surrounding the pool, most of them fully nude, and some of them were having sex right there in public. Howie saw the shock on my face and started giggling. "Cool, right?" he said to me with a big smile on his face.

We continued our walk. Howie was fully nude, but I had wrapped a towel around my waist. As we walked through the hall and passed other men, they all looked at me with excitement and lust. I was initially confused, but then I realized that all these men were looking at me because they found me attractive. I had never thought of myself as handsome or attractive. I was bony and considered myself goofy looking. I looked nothing like the hot men in gay porn. *Am I hot?* I thought. Then I decided to take the towel off and match Howie. "Now you're getting into it!" he said with excitement.

We finally made it to the sauna and sat down on a bench. There was another couple in the room with us, having oral sex. Howie and I watched the couple and began groping each other. We started making out. His kisses tasted salty. We were very wet because of all the steam and sweat. Then Howie started to perform oral on me. As Howie serviced me, I kept my eyes on the other couple in the room. This was quite the experience.

After about thirty minutes of fooling around in the sauna, Howie and I returned to his private room. "Do you come here a lot?" I asked as we walked back.

"Not that often; most of the time, I come alone," Howie responded.

We continued our walk, both of us fully nude still. We continued to pass other men who all continued to look at me lustfully, which made me feel more confident about my naked body.

When we got back to the room, Howie started groping me all over and laid me down on something similar to an examination table or a massage table. We began being intimate with each other.

Afterward, we lay on the padded table, wrapped in each other's arms, and fell asleep for a couple of hours. Eventually, we woke up, got dressed, and left the bathhouse.

Going to the bathhouse with Howie was a memorable experience for me because I had been so vulnerable and exposed myself fully. Walking around in the nude and getting positive feedback from the other men gave me confidence in my body and looks. I left the bathhouse that night feeling a sense of pride and happiness with myself for being so brave and submerging myself into the unique situation.

"So? How was it?" Howie asked me as we left the building. With glee, I responded, "Incredible!"

CHAPTER 26

SHAKING THE TABLE

It was New Year's Eve, and everyone in my family was excited to welcome in 2010. My family loved throwing huge parties, and today was no exception. My family booked a big, beautiful hall to host the celebration. It would be a night to remember filled with laughter, joy, music, and plenty of delicious Guyanese food and liquor. I knew I would have to make a statement and create an outfit that was worthy of *Vogue* for the big New Year's Eve celebration.

I continued modeling and started dabbling in design. Truthfully, my creations were ugly as sin. I tried my best to combine feminine and masculine fashions and construct androgynous creations. I was particularly drawn to curtains as a material for some odd reason. However, when you think about curtains, they are the perfect material: They're cheap, beautiful, flowy, and have a good amount of material. I started going to furniture stores and 99-cent stores to obtain the chic curtains that I used to create my dramatic fashions, but sometimes I would nab some of my aunt's curtains when she wasn't looking.

For my New Year's Eve ensemble, I came up with the design of combining and pinning two curtains together to create a sash, which I would wear over my torso with no undershirt, but my bare chest. I pinned a fake rose onto the sash and figured I would combine everything with a pair of black jeans to make an outfit worth bringing in 2010. I knew my outfit would turn heads and make my family gag.

The whole house was vibrating with chaotic energy on the night of New Year's Eve. Everyone was getting ready and dressing to the nines to welcome the new year. I was in my room, still pinning together my sash made of curtains, when one of my cousins came to check in on me to see if I was almost ready to leave to go to the hall with her. I opened my room door and showed her the outfit I was still working on, and she looked shocked.

"You're going to wear what?" she exclaimed. I did not understand her response and was appalled, as I had put so much thought and work into creating my outfit. "You can't wear that. Curtains? People are going to think you're crazy!" my cousin said. I told her I would wear the outfit, regardless of what she thought, which caused a huge argument.

My aunts came to see the fuss and began also shouting at me that I could not wear the outfit. But I protested and told them I was going to wear that outfit come hell or high water. They then pleaded for me to at least wear a tank top with the outfit to cover my chest, and I agreed. Agreeing to wear the tank top appeased my family, and we left for the hall.

The hall was big, beautiful, well-decorated, dark, and filled with strobe lighting. I said hello to everyone, and they all looked shocked and asked me what in the hell I was wearing. "It's couture!" I responded with sass. They clearly knew nothing about fashion.

The room was filled with noise: booming music, laughter, people talking. I really was enjoying myself and decided to have a drink. Well, one drink turned into a few, and a few turned into several until I was completely inebriated. I was a wasted mess and was living for every moment. My family seemed to like seeing me get wasted, as they kept giving me shots and drinks, which I gladly guzzled.

After I became highly intoxicated, I made my way to the dance floor to show off my moves and, of course, my custom-made couture curtain creation. The music was bumping, and I was getting my life dancing to the Indian, Reggae, and Soca music.

Then, the liquor really kicked in, and I became completely uninhibited. I took the tank top off, began waving it in the air, and threw it into the abyss. I kept the sash on, however. My family didn't seem to mind my unique outfit anymore and cheered me on as I continued to dance feverishly. Of course, everyone was pretty wasted at that point. So, my family gave me more drinks and continued to encourage me to have a good time.

I felt myself quickly losing control of my behavior. I was obnoxiously drunk and began running up to everyone, forcing them to dance with me. Then, I saw a table with a lot of people sitting at it, talking and eating. I had no idea who these people were. Not everyone at the party was family; some people were family members' friends. Regardless of not knowing who the people were at the table, I decided that they needed to loosen up and party with the rest of us.

I approached them and jumped onto their table. I began dancing wildly, knocking over their drinks and stepping on their food. I took my sash off and started swinging it in the air, screaming and singing along to the music. The people at the table did not appreciate my chaotic behavior and began yelling at me.

Suddenly, the men at the table started shouting and approached me as if they were going to fight me. I had no idea what was happening, and I continued dancing, knocking over drinks and waving my sash. Then, I was suddenly grabbed by three of my guy cousins, escorted down from the table, and taken outside the hall. There was a lot of commotion going on, but I was so drunk that I paid it no mind.

Once outside, my cousins told me to sit on a bench and wait for them. It was cold and snowing, and my chest was completely exposed. However, the cold felt good, as I was so hot from all the dancing and liquor. The last thing I remember was passing out and lying down on the ground in the snow.

***

The next day, I woke up in my room. I had no idea how I got there, but I figured my family watched over me, took me home, and placed me in bed. I had little recollection of the night before. I did not even remember doing the countdown to welcome in the new year. I looked for my sash, but it was gone. I was still shirtless but had on my jeans. *It must have been a good night*, I thought. I got myself together and went downstairs to have breakfast with my family.

"You up?" one of my aunts said to me with glee. "Ya rass was drunk!" she continued with laughter. I told everyone I didn't remember what had happened the night before. They all gladly told me how much of a drunk mess I was: going up to people, forcing them to dance, passing out in the snow, and, of course, table dancing.

I told them I couldn't remember most of what had happened the night before, as I had eventually blacked out from all the liquor. "You don't remember? They were going to fight you!" one of my guy cousins told me. "We stopped them."

My cousins told me how upset the people sitting at the table were that I had disrespectfully kicked their drinks on them and stepped in their food, and they wanted to fight me as a result. My guy cousins then told me how they stepped in to protect me and told the people at the table that no one was going to put a finger on me because I was family.

Family, I thought. I was overcome with emotion. I couldn't believe that these guy cousins of mine—the same ones who terrorized me most of my life for being gay—stood up for me. I knew at that moment that despite everything, they loved me. My father's family rarely showed their emotions, but I knew that protecting me was an act of affection.

I didn't say it, but I was grateful for their protection and watching over me. It was a memorable moment for me because it was the first time that I felt accepted and loved by the men in my father's family. In some sick way, I guess they can bully me, but no one else can!

CHAPTER 27

LOVE FOR SALE

My dad's family occasionally had movie nights, when we watched all kinds of fascinating Bollywood films. One night, we watched a movie about a glamorous woman who was a high-paid escort. After watching it, I became fascinated with escorting. It seemed like the best of both worlds: sex and money.

I want to be clear: Many queer people escort for survival, but this was not the case for me. I tried escorting simply for the thrill of it all. I didn't really need money. I was still in nursing school, and Auntie Lini was paying for everything. She still gave me a weekly allowance, covering my meals and bus fare, which was more than enough to cover my needs. But the money Auntie Lini gave me didn't cover my wants, and I wanted nice things like fancy clothes and jewelry. Escorting seemed like a solution to what in the grand scheme of things was a very minuscule problem.

I did research online and came across a website dedicated to advertising for male escorts. I couldn't believe such a site existed or was even legal. I took pictures of me in my boxers and created a profile. My tagline was "Satisfaction guaranteed or your money back." It sounds stupid now, but I thought it was brilliant advertising then. I didn't know what to expect from the website, but I figured it was worth trying.

After about two hours of creating the profile, I got a text message from some guy looking for my "services." *My services*, I thought. *How exciting!* I told him I was free for the evening. He asked me my rates and what I was willing to do. I told him it would be $350 plus taxi fare, and I would do anything he wanted. Then he texted me his address and told me to meet him in an hour. He was staying at a hotel in Secaucus, New Jersey.

I arrived at the hotel dressed plainly. The hotel was very fancy and expensive looking. I called the man and told him I had arrived. He told me his room number, and I walked to his suite. I couldn't believe it. Here I was, nineteen years old and escorting. I was no longer that boring, closeted gay guy stuck in Marydel, Maryland. I was a vivacious and well-paid escort in a fancy hotel, going to sleep with some wealthy man. I walked into the hotel, went to the man's room, and knocked on the door. He opened the door and ushered me in.

He was a White male of average height and appeared to be in his fifties. We began chatting, and he told me all about himself. He told me he was from New Zealand and was in the U.S. for business. He also told me he owned a large cattle farm in Texas. I started kicking myself for not charging him more. Then he said to me that my money was on the dresser. I took the money and counted it very quickly. I turned around and looked at him. "Do you want a receipt?" We laughed. Then, we both began undressing.

He hopped on the bed and positioned himself lying flat on his back, signaling for me to perform oral on him, which I reluctantly did. I was not attracted to the man but felt an obligation to have sex with him. I mean, I did agree to have sex with him, in exchange for money, and also had advertised "satisfaction guaranteed." So I fought through my revulsion and proceeded to have sex with the man.

After we were done, things got quiet and awkward. The man thanked me for my services and offered his restroom to me to wash up. I seized the offer. I felt filthy, physically and mentally, and wanted desperately to take a shower. After my shower I came out and got dressed, and he told me he would call me again the next time he was in town, but I never heard from him again. I thanked him and left.

The taxi ride home was somber. This was nothing like the Bollywood movie. I was not a glamorous escort but a pitiable man who just sold himself for money. I felt dirty.

I debated if I would do this again. Maybe I would go home and delete my profile from the escorting website. But then I began counting the money and felt some sense of comfort in knowing that I could go shopping and buy something nice for myself.

I had somehow managed to convince myself that I needed to escort, but the reality is I wanted to escort, as I enjoyed spoiling myself with luxurious purchases. Despite the damaging after-effects of escorting, I could not stop. I became addicted to the rush of meeting a new client and getting paid.

Eventually, I stopped feeling dirty, and I began to feel emboldened. Somehow, having men pay to sleep with me made me feel empowered. It made me feel as if, for once, I was in control of what happened to me sexually. Perhaps the money made me feel like I was worth something, literally and metaphorically. Ultimately, I decided that I would continue escorting until I graduated from nursing school.

I remained in control of my clients. I stayed away from obvious weirdos and psychos and managed to have a pretty regular clientele. There was one client, however, who creeped me out. His name was Bill, and he was a White man in his late forties. He was what we call in the queer community a "bear" (a large, hairy man). He contacted me and asked if we could role play in which he would be a dad, and I would be his child. It seemed strange, but I agreed to do it and met with him.

Bill lived in New York City in a lovely one-bedroom apartment. Of course, we had some small talk before we got into the action. He told me he was a teacher of some sort and always had a fantasy of molesting a child. This sickened and shocked me, but I made sure to conceal my disgust.

He told me he would pretend to be my dad, and I would be his four-year-old son. He detailed the scenario to ensure that I was dedicated to the character. We were home alone, as "Mother" was on a work trip. It was bath time, and Bill would help me get washed up. Bill ran a bathtub for me and filled it with bubbles. He helped me to take my clothes off and gave me a bath.

After Bill finished bathing me, he dried me off and guided me to his bedroom. He placed me on the bed, threw my legs in the air, and began to perform oral on me. I didn't know how to feel. I felt grossed out at the concept that this man was getting off to a pedophilic fantasy. Still, at the same time, I was physically turned on. I began to feel like that toddler on the naptime mat again. I couldn't believe it. I had worked so hard to never feel like that again, and this man managed to awaken that scared little child inside of me.

He climbed up on top of me and entered me without a condom. I had not agreed to unprotected sex, but I was so scared that I didn't know what to do or say. I felt powerless. I was in mental anguish and wanted him to stop.

"Daddy's going to cum," he said. Then he pulled out of me quickly and ejaculated all over my face. It was finally done. I felt sick. I quickly cleaned up, got my money, and left. I never saw Bill again.

After the incident with Bill, I decided I needed a break from escorting completely. What had happened was a lot for me to process. Also, classes were coming to an end, and I had to get ready to take the nursing boards. So, I threw myself back into my studies.

HARD CASH

Have you ever thought

How much you would cost

If you could be bought?

Every day I sold a piece of myself

To the highest bidder

Just the thought alone could make me shiver

Isn't it strange?

The things we do for some change

I sold my soul

But the price I paid

The debt I owe

You'll never know

Isn't it funny

The things we do for money

Once a man told me he loved me

As he thrusted in and out

A liar, no doubt

Once a man told me I was beautiful

As he spit in my mouth

Revolting, I know

The things I've done for some dough

Why, you ask

Would I do such things just for some cash?

But when you have no wealth

You'll do anything

You'll even sell yourself

CHAPTER 28

MAN OR WOMAN?

It bears repeating that nursing school is hard as hell, but I made it through the fire and graduated with honors at the age of twenty. It was time for me to find employment. I had a naturally androgynous look at the time and was constantly mistaken for a female, and I was also flamboyant in my appearance. Auntie Lini observed this and knew that this would not be tolerated in professional nursing.

So, one day, she sat me down to have a serious conversation about professionalism and how to present myself in the workplace. She instructed me to dress plainly and in a masculine way when going on interviews. She also told me that once I secured a job, I should show up with my hair pulled back and wear men's scrubs (I had worn unisex scrubs up until that point).

The reason why Auntie Lini instructed me to butch it up was because she wanted me to avoid discrimination and bigotry. Surprisingly, the thought of someone mistreating me at work because of my appearance or sexuality had never crossed my mind up until that point. From my perspective, everyone at the time loved me. Nursing school was a completely different experience for me than grade school and high school. I was out as a gay man, and for the most part, everyone accepted me (classmates, teachers, patients, etc.). I mean, I was a cute, sassy, gay queen; what was there not to like?

Since she had over ten years of nursing experience at that point, I trusted that Auntie Lini knew what she was talking about. She had guided me all my life, so I knew she wasn't steering me in the wrong direction. I decided that I would listen to Auntie Lini and butch it up.

I made myself as masculine-presenting as I could for interviews but was still mistaken for female. After a few interviews, I didn't hear back from anyone. As a new graduate with no experience, my employment options were slim. But somehow, I managed to land a job working with a pediatric home care agency. Auntie Lini also pulled some strings and got me a per diem job working at a drug detox and rehab in downtown Paterson.

More than anything, I wanted to be the best nurse I could be. I continued escorting occasionally when the money was good enough, but my main focus was nursing. I worked the pediatric home care gig during the week. Then, I would work at the drug detox and rehab center on the weekends, when needed. My first home care job involved providing nursing care for an eight-year-old child. She was non-mobile and on a ventilator with a tracheostomy. Working with such a sick child was a rewarding experience for me. I loved home care and felt proud to be a nurse.

I came to work presenting as my Auntie Lini had instructed, hair pulled back, in men's scrubs. I tried to make myself small and go unnoticed, but I started garnering negative attention from the child's father. There was a lot of tension coming from him, and I could tell he felt uncomfortable around me. I knew the father's discomfort had to do with my appearance and sexuality; I don't know how to explain it, but I just knew. When you're queer, you develop a sixth sense of these things.

The child lived with her father, and he was the only parent in the home. The father didn't speak much English, so conversation was limited. He was a constant presence, always hovering over me. I'm sure he was being protective because he was fearful that I would harm his child, as some cis-het people ignorantly believe queer people are child predators.

Another nurse who worked the case told me the father asked her if I was a man or a woman. She thought it was funny, but I found it offensive, and it struck a fear within me. The father had told the nurse that I looked like a woman, but I didn't have breasts. I couldn't believe it. I did not understand the father's curiosity about my gender, my absence of breasts, or the relevance of any of it to my nursing experience. Also, the father talking about me behind my back to another nurse made me uncomfortable. I began to feel unwanted and out of place. I started to question if I had made the right decision to become a nurse and whether there was a place for queer people in nursing.

One night, when I came to work, the front door to the home was locked. I was working a night shift, so it was pitch dark outside, aside from some minor light from the streetlights. I was in Paterson, a city with high crime rates, so understandably I became concerned for my safety.

I called the agency I worked for to ask the father to let me into the home. What the agency representative told me blew my mind. They told me that the child's father requested that I no longer return to his house. He said to them that he felt "uncomfortable" with me being in his home and around his daughter. So, I was taken off the case. I could not believe it. I was fired.

I had provided the best care possible and had tried to make the father realize I wasn't a threat. I did what Auntie Lini told me to do, pulled my hair back and wore men's scrubs, but that did not matter. I was shocked; I had done everything I could to prevent it and was still fired.

I left the patient's house and took a taxi home. Sitting in the taxi, I kept replaying what happened to me. I was in shock. Fired for being gay. This was my first taste of professional discrimination, and it was very bitter. I wondered if there was a place for someone like me in nursing. Would I ever be able to fully be my gay self and be a nurse?

I started to contemplate how I could avoid being discriminated against. Then it hit me. Since my appearance was so feminine and people kept questioning if I was a woman, maybe I could just go ahead and be a woman.

Then another epiphany struck. I could be like the men I watched on *RuPaul's Drag Race*. I could do both: dress as a man or a woman. I did not have to dress as a woman 24/7, and I could still dress like a man when I wanted to. But at least at work, I could dress like a woman and let people think I'm a woman, just as I had done in first grade. I decided this was going to solve the problem. *If the world thinks I'm a woman, then I'll be the best damn woman you've ever seen*, I thought. It was time to let the girl out again.

CHAPTER 29

ARMANI

Androgyny had made its way back into my life. Modeling also reentered my life, between nursing jobs. I was now an androgynous model signed to two agencies, one in Clifton, New Jersey, and one in New York, New York. At the time, being androgynous seemed like the perfect solution to my gender dilemma. I viewed androgyny as being neither man nor woman but something in between, or a little bit of both.

I decided I would need a unisex name to go with my new androgynous identity. My name given to me at birth was a traditionally Indian male name, so I knew that wouldn't do. Then, one day, while in a waiting room for a go-see, I saw a picture of a beautiful girl on the wall with her name written under the picture: Imani. It had a nice ring to it. But it needed to be more high fashion and androgynous. Then it hit me: Armani! This became my new name for my new androgynous and high-fashion identity.

To go along with my new androgynous name, I started to dress in gender-bending ensembles. Still exploring my gender identity (and being ignorant of the nuances of some of the terminology around this), I started identifying as an androgynous drag queen: a part-time woman and a part-time man. Of course, this is not what a drag queen is, but at the time, that was what I thought it was. (To clarify, generally, a drag queen is someone, traditionally male, who temporarily presents in feminine attire and makeup for entertainment purposes.)

I was loving every second of exploring my gender identity. I started dressing as a woman to go to work as a nurse, but I also dressed as a woman to go on modeling gigs sometimes. I began escorting dressed as a woman occasionally as well. I soon found that I made more money escorting in drag as a woman than as a man. In my escorting advertisements, I would have pictures of me dressed as a man and pictures of me dressed as a woman. My clients could tell me how they wanted me to show up, and most preferred me to show up as a woman.

In my off-hours, that is, hours not working as a nurse or escort, I typically dressed as a man. I would wear an outfit that I thought was masculine, such as a white men's tank top, tight pants, and boots, and pair it with wild, curly hair. Despite wanting to look like a man during these times, I was still read as a woman, which was frustrating because I was sincerely attempting to look like a man.

Being read as a woman also caused confusion among straight men who found me attractive. Most men who I encountered did not read me as a man or even androgynous; they read me as a woman. I would correct these men and clarify that I was a man. (Though at the time, I ignorantly used the terms "man" and "male" interchangeably—one is a gender identity, one is a sex.) While I identified as androgynous, or as what would now be called nonbinary, I thought it was more comprehensible to these cis-het men to simply tell them I was a man.

Revealing this garnered mixed results. Some of these straight men would thank me for my honesty and go about their way, but most still wanted to pursue me. Once, a man told me he didn't care that I was a man. He told me, "I don't care…I could still fuck you from the back." As enticing as his offer was, I politely declined. I heard all kinds of rationales from men who identified as straight but did not mind having secret sex with a gay man ("A hole is a hole"…"We can have sex as long as I don't see your dick"…"If *you* give *me* head then *you're* gay, not *me*"…"You're still pretty, though"…"I just want to bust a nut. I don't care how").

There was one situation with a straight man that I could never forget. The man was Hispanic and handsome. He catcalled me from his car, wanting my phone number. He asked me to talk in his car. I found him attractive and agreed. At this point, I was used to men reading me as female, so once in the car, I asked the man if he knew that I was a man. "Stop lying," he said.

I told him I was telling the truth and apologized for the confusion. Still, he accused me of lying and demanded to see my penis, so I showed it to him. Even with my penis on full display, the man continued to say that I was being dishonest and that I was really a woman. He said my penis wasn't real and accused me of having a dildo between my legs! "If you didn't want to give me your number, you could have just said that," he said to me. At a loss for words, I put my penis away and swiftly exited the car.

***

After a while, I began dressing less and less like a man and started spending more time dressed as a woman, as I had more fun that way. I felt most beautiful and most comfortable when I was a woman, and I enjoyed being passable as a woman. I also liked telling people I was a man and the shock and awe that followed this disclosure. However, I continued to run into situations where men became enraged at me revealing that I was not a woman, and I began fearing for my safety. So, I stopped disclosing to people that I was a man and let them presume I was a woman.

When I was dressed as a woman, I experienced a sense of normalcy as people read me as a cisgender woman, which was a new and fascinating experience for me. Simply put, when I presented as a woman, people treated me differently than when I presented as a man. I received a level of kindness that I never had experienced before. People sincerely wanted to interact with me. Suddenly, men wanted to protect me, and women wanted to be me. People found me fascinating and beautiful for the first time in my life and wanted to be my friend. The newfound positive attention I received gave me a natural high, and I wanted more of it.

I decided that I would start living full time in "drag" and threw out all of my men's clothing. I decided that I needed to find my tribe and be around other drag queens, so I began to go out to gay nightclubs. I would get all dolled up and ride the dollar bus from Paterson to New York City, which quickly became my second home.

New York City was like something out of a fairy tale: I was Cinderella transforming into this stunning creature, and New York City was my ball. I became what is known as a "club kid." I would wear extravagant, eccentric, and sparkling outfits and go to all the gay clubs that would allow me in (I was twenty at the time, and my options were quite limited). I particularly gravitated toward a club called "La Escuelita," close to Times Square.

The club was set underground in a basement. It was always very dark but had plenty of strobe lighting, and the primary light source came from the stage. In the middle of the dance floor was a stage with two levels. Behind the stage was a curtain, and behind that curtain was a dressing room for all the performers. To the stage's right was a DJ booth, and behind the booth was a separate section dedicated to coat checking. It was a decent-sized club, and it even had a disco ball.

I mingled with people and continued developing my social skills. I was a queen, honey, meaning I had to "sparkle, Neely, sparkle!" I studied all the other queer folk and learned their mannerisms, slang, dialect, and wit. It was as if I was enrolled in Faggotry 101, and I was the star pupil. My life had become a lesson in queer social studies. I spent a lot of time watching queer cinema, and I would also listen to all the essential queer music like RuPaul, Madonna, and Cher. I wanted to know all the references that I could.

My fascination with *RuPaul's Drag Race* continued, and I even considered auditioning for the show. Sadly, I never got the courage to do it, but the show inspired me to start doing professional drag part time.

La Escuelita would often host competitions and give out cash prizes. One night, I garnered the balls (pun intended) and signed myself up for the La Escuelita talent show. In my mind, this was my big moment. I would hit that stage, and all of New York would adore me. I would win the contest and become the next drag superstar. Well, the reality was quite different!

I began putting my act together about a week before the show, and finally it was the big night. My cousin Samantha had donated all her old clothes to me. She was pregnant at the time and couldn't fit them anymore. I dug through the bag to find my perfect ensemble. I wore high-waisted shorts, a pink lace bra, and five-inch nude pumps. My hair was shoulder-length, so I skipped the wig of it all. Instead, I simply bedazzled my hair with gel and barrettes. I beat my face to the gods, threw on a white fur coat, and headed to New York to hit that stage!

It was showtime, and the pressure was on. I was surrounded by a crowd of shady queens ready to read me for filth. I began the performance by singing a short tune from *Carmen Jones*, starring Dorothy Dandridge, called "Dat Love." Holding a microphone, I came from behind the curtain, covered in my white fur coat. I held the microphone to my mouth and began singing the operatic tune.

Well, talk about knowing your audience! The crowd was dead silent and confused. They clearly didn't know the reference. I began to get nervous but quickly calmed down and channeled my inner fierceness. Then I went behind the curtain, threw off my coat to reveal my scandalous pink shorts and bra ensemble, and told the DJ to hit it!

I returned to the stage, and Lady Gaga's "Love Game" began playing, and the crowd livened up. I had bought a disco stick and taught myself my own choreography. I killed it, bitch. I was popping and dropping so hard I broke the damn disco stick (talk about iconic).

Unfortunately, I didn't win, but it was clear that I had made a good impression with the club promoters and the other talent because I was invited back to perform. I was even offered to join Riggz Entertainment, a talent agency that worked closely with La Escuelita. So, this was me now, Armani: a nurse, a drag queen, a model, and one fierce bitch.

I loved the nightlife, and I certainly loved to boogie on the disco, round, baby! La Escuelita quickly became my stomping grounds. In between working as a nurse and model, I would go there all the time by myself at all hours of the night. My only rule was to never make it home before 7:00 a.m. I was in gay heaven.

ANDROGYNOUS

If I had my way
I'd be him
And I'd be her
The best of both worlds
A boy and a girl
Truly, if I had my way
I'd be neither
I'd be something more fascinating
Something more special and unique
Unisex
Queer
Nonbinary
Something in between
Something that defies gender norms
The very reason for which I was born
Androgynous
Is what I would be
Androgynously beautiful
That's me

CHAPTER 30

BUTCH QUEEN
FIRST TIME IN DRAGS AT A BALL

One Sunday, I randomly found myself at an event called "Rumble Ball." On one of my various outings at La Escuelita, I saw a flyer that said there would be a runway competition, and the prize was $100. I was a model, so I figured I had this one in the bag. Well, Ms. Thing, I gagged when the competition began.

I wanted to compete in the runway category called "animal realness" and took hours getting dressed. I wore red fishnet stockings with a red corset, a leopard coat, and a blond wig, and I painted a massive butterfly on my face. I arrived at La Escuelita around 11:00 p.m. and was surprised to see the club was still empty, so I stood around awkwardly for a while. But after midnight more people came in, and the ball started.

The first event was something called LSS (legends, statements, and stars), consisting of the commentator calling names over the speaker, people voguing and runway walking in something similar to a *Soul Train* line. LSS is an opportunity to honor and acknowledge individuals in ballroom who are recognized for their contributions and status within their category.

Individuals allowed to walk LSS have been deemed a star, statement, legend, or icon. Stars are new competitors who have begun making a name for themselves and are still relatively new to their category (usually less than two years). Statements are also

192

relatively new to their category (usually two to five years) and have the clear potential to become a legend or an icon. Legends have typically competed in their category for over five years and won multiple times. An icon typically has spent ten years or more competing and winning in their category.

Once LSS was over, the ball started. I watched in sheer amazement. I had watched *Paris Is Burning* about a million times at that point and was somewhat familiar with ballroom culture, but seeing it in person was a completely different experience.

I tried to enjoy watching the ball but was nervous waiting for the runway category to be announced. Then, finally, around 2:00 a.m., the runway competition began. I was surprised that only I and one other queen were competing in the category. We walked in front of the judges individually and got "tens across the boards." Then, we competed against each other to determine who had the better runway walk. I tried my best, but I lost to her. I was disappointed by the loss but felt relief that the runway competition was over. Now, I could truly enjoy the ball and mingle.

After the runway category came voguing. There were all types of queens in amazing costumes. I had not seen voguing in person before, and I was entranced. Every time someone dipped, the crowd went crazy and screamed, "HA!" The excitement in the air was infectious. I was thrilled to witness the show, and my mind was blown by the sheer talent. I saw many great voguing legends that night, including (now icon) Leiomy Maldonado.

People kept coming up to me asking what house I was in and if I would consider joining theirs. Then, this very kind woman came up to me. She was plus-sized, beautiful, and warm, with the most charming southern accent. "I'm Abbey St. Clair," she said gracefully. "You're beautiful. What house are you in?"

Then, stupidly, I said, "I'm not in a house, and I'm really a drag queen," and she said, "Me too!"

My mind was blown. How could this gorgeous creature have a penis? I had never met someone like me and wanted to know everything about her. "My mother wants to meet you," she said as she grabbed my hand and walked me over to the queen I had competed against earlier that night in the runway category.

Her name was Aaliyah St. Clair, and she was beautiful, but her voice was handsome (no shade). Immediately after meeting Abbey and Aaliyah, I knew I wanted to join their house. However, truth be told, I wasn't that picky when choosing a house. I figured these people came up to me, so it must have been destiny for me to be in this house. Aaliyah invited me to a St. Clair house meeting the next day, and I accepted the invitation.

***

The next day it was warm and summery when I went to the House of St. Clair meeting in Newark, New Jersey. I was wearing a navy-blue jumpsuit from H&M, with a pair of ruby-red sparkling five-inch pumps. I was greeted by Aaliyah out of drag. The transformation was incredible. I couldn't believe that this good-looking man was the same gorgeous woman from the night before.

I met with all the house members. Everyone was so kind and inviting. We all had dinner and kiki'ed and got to know each other. Everyone had their own category in which they competed. Some categories included runway, realness, labels, sex siren, and face. Shortly after I met everyone, the house took a vote to decide whether I could join. It was unanimously declared that I was an official member of the House of St. Clair, and from that moment forward, I was known as Armani St. Clair.

Ballroom was pure magic. I was truly getting my life. I was the new girl on the scene, and everyone was living for me. I walked face briefly, but my main category quickly became drag's female figure realness. Female figure realness is a category in which contestants compete against one another to determine who is the most passable. Female figure realness is divided into two subcategories: femqueen realness and drags realness.

A femqueen is basically a transgender woman who has socially and medically transitioned (hormones, surgery, etc.). Being that I had not fully socially transitioned yet and was not on hormones or had any surgeries done, I was considered a drag queen by ballroom standards. Also, I still identified as a drag queen and did drag, so competing in drag realness was appropriate for me at the time.

A realness battle entailed "selling" your realness, meaning advertising what made you more passable than your contender. For example, if you were battling (competing against) a girl with masculine hands and you had small hands, you would walk up to the judges, put your hands out, point at them, and then point at your competitor's hands to show that your hands were more feminine. If your competitor had on a wig and you had your own natural hair, you would make that a point and encourage the judges to rub your scalp.

One of the fiercest moves in realness was competing without makeup. If two girls battled each other, one with makeup on and the other without, the girl without makeup would win the category nine times out of ten (although for drags realness, it was acceptable to wear makeup). The point was to be passable, effortless, and natural.

I remember the first drags realness ball that I walked. The ball was themed "cook-out," and the drags realness category that night was based on a luau. I wore a short, flowy, pink flower dress with a pink pump. I straightened my curly hair and placed a fake yellow flower in it. I was in a secluded corner of the club with the rest of my house members. The commentator called out the category over the microphone: "Drags realness, drags realness, anyone for drags realness?"

Once I heard the category announced, I headed to the stage. The other contestants then lined up on the stage, and we all got ready to battle each other. I battled a lot of beautiful girls that night. I had taken the advice of my house father, who told me to "just stand there and be pretty." After about ten minutes, the competition ended, and I won a trophy and $100. I couldn't believe it. All I did was walk to the stage, stand there, and I won, just like that.

I returned to the corner where my house members were. They were all so happy and proud of me, especially Mother Aaliyah, who was now my gay mother. Mother Aaliyah explained that I had sat down a legend. From that night forward, I slayed the realness category. I won so many realness battles that I went on to win the highly regarded "of the Year Drags Realness" award one year. I was on my way to becoming a ballroom legend, and it was everything.

CHAPTER 31

BITCH
YOU AIN'T NO DRAG QUEEN

I continued competing in and dominating the drags realness category. The more I won, the more my competition began complaining to the judges that I was not a drag queen. They couldn't believe that I lived life as a man, or that I had not taken any steps to medically transition. Because I looked so passable, a lot of people began suspecting that I was taking hormones.

I was no longer living part time as a man, as I felt more comfortable living as a woman, though I still identified as a drag queen. The reason I was a controversial figure at the balls was because I had not done anything to medically transition into a woman. But at that point in my life, I was presenting and living full time as a woman. It was a confusing situation for most people, me included. How could I live as a woman but not have done anything to medically become a woman?

I did not understand the difference between social and medical transition and ignorantly concluded that since I had not medically transitioned yet, I was still a drag queen. However, like my competitors, I had started questioning whether I was truly a drag queen. Something deep within me never felt right identifying as a man, even part time. I had known I wanted to be a girl since childhood, that much was clear.

Before I entered ballroom, I had no idea that a man could become a woman. For most of my life, I thought I was just stuck in the body of a man. I had come to accept that I could never be a woman. I would never be able to get a period, get pregnant, or give birth to a child; at the time, I thought this is what defined a woman. I had been forced by my family, religion, and society to believe that I was not and could not ever be a woman.

Since I couldn't be a woman, I figured I could at least dress as a woman. Being a drag queen seemed like a solution to my predicament; I would still be a man, but I could express myself as a woman. Being a drag queen to me meant being neither a man nor a woman but something else that didn't need a gender label. But the more I surrounded myself with all the gorgeous ballroom femqueens, the more I realized that I was more than a drag queen. I had heard the term "transsexual" thrown around at balls, but I knew I was not a transexual, at least not the way I had been introduced to the concept in nursing school.

When doing my mental health rotation in nursing school, I learned the concepts of transvestite, transgender, and transsexual. Nursing school taught me that a transvestite is someone who dresses in clothing traditionally associated with a gender different than the gender that they were assigned at birth, such as a man dressing in women's clothing. Drag queens were once referred to as transvestites, but now the term "transvestite" is considered derogatory and has been replaced with the term "cross-dresser."

Some cross-dressing men experience sexual arousal when they don opposite-gender clothing, which is a condition currently known as a transvestic disorder. Similarly, autogynephilia is a condition in which a man experiences sexual arousal by the thought or image of himself being a woman. It is thought that some individuals who regret transitioning their gender and de-transition have underlying transvestic disorder or autogynephilia.

In nursing school, I also learned that someone transgender is someone who has transitioned from one gender to another (in my case, man to woman). Lastly, I was taught that someone transsexual is someone who has undergone sexual reassignment surgery (SRS), i.e., to go from having a penis to a neovagina. Of course, now the term transsexual is considered outdated because you can never truly transition your "sex," as that is chromosomal and physiological. However, some individuals still identify as transexual and consider the term "transexual" to fall under the transgender umbrella.

I identified more with being transgender than transsexual. I wanted to live as a woman, but I didn't want to have any type of bottom surgery. In fact, I had come to love and appreciate my penis. A concept that often confuses most cis-het people is a trans woman not wanting to have SRS (now known as gender-affirming surgery). When you tell someone you are trans, most likely, they will assume that you've had "the surgery." They assume that all trans women hate their penis and want to "chop it off".

For some trans women, bottom surgery is a necessity for their gender dysphoria treatment. However, many trans women do not wish to have SRS, as they are not dysphoric about their penis. For me, having the aesthetic of a man caused me dysphoria. So, treating my gender dysphoria mostly involved expressing myself with the aesthetic of a woman. Some trans women are dysphoric about their faces and have facial feminization surgery. Some trans women are dysphoric about not having breasts, so they have top surgery (breast implants). That's the key to a gender transition, treating what causes gender dysphoria, not simply having SRS.

For a long time, society did not view trans women as women unless they had SRS. It was because of this societal pressure that most trans women pursued having SRS despite not having dysphoria about their penis. However, having SRS in this situation can result in catastrophic psychological effects, including feelings of shame, regret, and suicidality. For this reason, trans women should never be pressured into having SRS. Society must come to realize that being a woman does not require you to have a vagina, as genitals do not define gender.

While sex is biological, gender is a social construct and varies significantly from culture to culture and person to person. It took me a while to realize it, but being a woman is much more than having a vagina, getting a period, or even giving birth. Instead, being a woman is living one's life guided by social constructs of womanhood, defined by one's culture.

"What is a woman?" you ask. Well, a woman is me, my mother, and my Auntie Lini; cisgender or transgender, it does not matter. We are still women. Yes, a woman is an adult human female, but a woman is also a chosen gender identity that is not bound to sex (male or female). In other words, one can choose to live as a woman, a man, or neither, regardless of sex. It is not up to society, the medical industry, or your parents to decide what your gender is. The decision is yours and yours alone.

Once I discovered the wonders of being transgender, I began to seek treatment to medically transition into a woman. I was living full time as a woman, so I had already unknowingly socially transitioned. Now I wanted to medically transition to enhance my aesthetic as a woman. I wanted breasts, butt, and hips. I didn't have much facial hair growth, but I wanted the little bit I had gone. I knew that I would have to start hormones to attain my goals, so I searched for a local endocrinologist (a hormone doctor) to start me on hormone replacement therapy (HRT).

HRT usually encompasses taking an estrogen supplement and an androgen (or testosterone) blocker for someone born male transitioning to female. The rationale behind HRT for trans women is to suppress testosterone and increase estrogen levels. Transgender women who decide to go on HRT will experience feminization as the hormones will suppress facial and body hair growth and promote breast growth as well as the distribution of fat in areas like the buttocks and hips. I didn't have insurance at the time, so I knew I would have to pay out of pocket for the hormones.

I found a local endocrinologist and set up an appointment. I told the receptionist over the phone that I was seeking HRT, and she assured me that the doctor prescribes HRT for transgender women. I arrived at the doctor's office and was immediately confused. I saw posters on the walls for thyroid disease and diabetes, and the waiting room was filled with elderly cisgender people. *Where are all the beautiful trans women?* I thought. I began to feel uneasy; it was becoming clear that this doctor did not see many transgender women. Then they called my name, and I went to see the doctor.

The doctor seemed cold and stern. "How can I help you?" he asked.

"Can you make me into a woman?" I jokingly said and chuckled. He did not laugh. Instead, his face was emotionless. After a moment of awkward silence, I clarified, "I want to start hormone replacement therapy to become a woman. Have you done that before?"

"Of course I have," he said. "I just give you estrogen and testosterone suppressors, but I need you to get a psychiatric evaluation and bloodwork done first."

"I don't have insurance," I said. "How will I pay for all of that?"

"I don't know, but when you can, call me," the doctor said dismissively.

I walked out of his office feeling hopeless and defeated. How was I to become a woman with no insurance?

I had already paid $300 for the office visit; God knows how much a psychiatrist visit and bloodwork would cost. I went into my car and wept. Then, an idea came to me. What if there was a way to get hormones from off the street? Surely I could not be the only transgender woman without insurance. So, I reached out to one of my house mothers to see if she had any connections for street hormones. Her name was Mother Erica St. Clair, and she was legendary femqueen realness. She told me she had a hormone connection and that I could take the pills or the shots, but that I should take both if I wanted quick results. I learned all the secrets and steps to becoming a trans woman from Mother Erica.

I met up with her that same night to get the hormones. We drove to someplace in Newark. She told me to stay in the car and to give her $150. She left and returned about thirty minutes later and handed me a Ziploc bag full of yellow Premarin pills, one vial of estrogen, and two syringes with needles. I couldn't believe it. I was actually going to start hormones! Mother Erica told me to take one Premarin pill a day and an estrogen shot every two weeks. I dropped her off and headed home.

When I got home, I ran into my room and took a Premarin pill immediately. I could not believe it; I would finally be a woman! Next, I drew up one shot of estrogen into one of the syringes. The solution was highly viscous, so it took a while to get the medicine in the syringe, but once I did, I put the cap back on the needle and placed it onto my dresser. My heart began racing. I had given countless injections at that point as a nurse, but I hate receiving needles, and the thought of giving myself an injection caused me severe anxiety.

I pulled down my pants, wiped the upper right corner of my buttocks with an alcohol pad, and let it dry. *Alright, here we go*, I thought. I uncapped the needle and held it by my buttocks. Then I dropped it. "Oh shit!" I said. I wiped the needle with the alcohol pad and then tried to give myself the injection again. I had all kinds of thoughts racing in my head. Taking the shot seemed so much more real to me than taking a pill. Was this what I really wanted? *Screw it,* I thought. Then I took a deep breath, stabbed myself with the needle, and pushed the estrogen into me. I withdrew the needle with my hands shaking and pulled up my pants. I felt a rush of euphoria flow through me. I had done it. I had finally started my hormones.

I was around the age of twenty-one or twenty-two when I started taking street hormones. Once I started taking hormones, I began to feel more comfortable identifying as a transgender woman. Of course, you don't need to medically transition to be trans, but for me, taking hormones solidified that I was no longer a gay man but a straight transgender woman. (I considered myself "straight" because I was now a woman who was sexually attracted to men.)

I took my hormones religiously, but being a nurse, I knew that I would need to have bloodwork done eventually. I learned about Callen-Lorde from some of the ballroom girls. It's a clinic in NYC that provides healthcare to those in the LGBTQIA+ community. Their prices were reasonable, and they even had payment plans for people without insurance. I had my first appointment there with a therapist to evaluate me to see if I had gender dysphoria or not.

The therapist was a kind, short, and stocky man. I sat on his couch for about an hour, going over my life and how I had always felt like a girl. He asked me all about my life, including past traumas, and asked me if I was sure that I wanted to start hormones, to which I replied I was already on street hormones. The session was unremarkable for the most part until we got to the end of the evaluation, where the therapist revealed that he was a trans man. I was shocked! I had spent over an hour with this man, and the thought of him being trans never crossed my mind. I was truly inspired and thanked him for his positive self-disclosure, as it was therapeutic for me to see someone trans in his position.

The therapist gave me the gender dysphoria (or Gender Identity Disorder) diagnosis, which gave me the green light to meet with the facility's nurse practitioner to start prescribing me HRT. The nurse practitioner was named Rudy, and he specialized in HRT. Rudy ordered bloodwork for me, and once that was back, he prescribed me legitimate HRT, which was a relief. I was prescribed estradiol and spironolactone to start with. My prescriber recommended estradiol over Premarin and told me there was no significant difference between injectable estrogen and oral estrogen. Meaning I could stop giving myself injections and continue with the pill. I love Mother Erica and will forever be grateful for her help, but it felt good knowing that I was getting my HRT under the care of a medical professional.

Shortly after I started HRT, I stopped escorting for good. The decision came after the wife of a regular client of mine started calling me, asking me if I knew "Louis." Finally, I became fed up and answered her with, "Bitch, the only Louis I know is Louis Vuitton!" and hung up. I was not here for the drama, so I decided I was done with escorting. I decided that starting HRT meant starting a new chapter in my life, a life without prostitution.

Entering womanhood and taking hormones changed how I viewed the world in so many ways. It was as if my eyes were finally open. I finally felt at ease in my body. Taking hormones was such an exciting journey for me. Seeing my butt, hips, and breasts grow was miraculous. I even started electrolysis on my face, significantly reducing my facial hair growth. I looked so damn good that Auntie Lini started stealing my hormones in hopes of looking as good as I did! I was a budding flower, and it was simply beautiful.

PART IV: WOMANHOOD

CHAPTER 32

HEART OF A NURSE

In my early twenties, my main focus was ballroom and work. I continued working with the pediatric home care agency on a variety of cases, working different cases each week until I finally landed an ongoing case.

I got a call one night from the home care agency. There was a callout, and they needed someone to cover a case only three blocks from my house. The agency was so desperate that they gave me an extra $5 per hour. I had nothing else to do, so I agreed to work the 11:00 p.m. – 7:00 a.m. shift.

I arrived at the house a couple of minutes early. The place seemed small from the outside and was in a quiet part of town. I walked up the steps, and the front door was wide open. I didn't want to walk inside, so I knocked on the open door. "Come on in, mami!" I heard a voice yell from up the stairs. I knew the family lived on the house's second floor, so I walked up the stairs.

I opened a second door to discover a woman sitting at a kitchen table. I figured she was the child's mother, so I introduced myself. "Hello, you must be Jennifer. I'm from the nursing agency."

The lady smiled and said, "I no Jennifer."

"Oh, I'm sorry," I responded. "Do you know where she's at?" I always introduced myself to the parents before meeting with the child.

Then I saw a woman run by me, wrapped in a towel. The lady sitting at the table pointed to the woman running around in the towel, indicating that she was Jennifer. I turned to the woman and tried to introduce myself again. "Hi, I'm—"

She interrupted me. "Hey, mami! I'm Jennifer! It's my birthday, so I'm about to get fucked up! The baby is in his room sleeping. Everything you need is in the room." Then she ran into the bathroom and shut the door.

Well, alright then, I thought.

I went into the bedroom to check on the baby. He was so cute and tiny. He was a nine-month-old Hispanic baby who had a tracheostomy, a gastric tube, and a ventilator. He was connected to a pulse oximeter, and a feeding machine pumped formula into the gastric tube. The room was pitch dark aside from the light from the machinery. He was fast asleep. I checked his vital signs very quickly and delicately so I wouldn't wake him. Then, I headed back to the kitchen.

Jennifer ran out of the bathroom and up the stairs into the attic, where her room was. About twenty minutes later, she ran back down the stairs and said, "All right, mami, I'll be back around 5:00 a.m. My number is on the fridge if you need me."

Jennifer was a beautiful woman. She was Hispanic, about average height, curvy, light-skinned, with dark black hair. She was a young single mother and had three kids in the house. My patient came from a set of twins, and she also had a daughter. The woman I met earlier stayed with the other children; we didn't talk much as she didn't speak much English. I wished Jennifer a happy birthday and told her to have fun. Then Jennifer closed the door and ran out of the house.

The night was pretty quiet. I didn't have much to do except ensure the child remained safe. Jennifer returned home around 6:30 a.m., just in time for me to leave. She came into the house and ran straight into the bathroom. I heard her vomiting, and she left the bathroom door open, so I went inside, held her hair, and rubbed her back. *What the hell is going on?* I thought.

I never knew what to expect with home care. It's one of the most intimate settings to provide nursing care because you're in someone's private home. For the most part, all the other houses I had been in were quiet and boring. But I honestly enjoyed Jennifer's chaos. It was refreshing and somehow reminded me of my mother.

She thanked me and got up from the toilet. "You're coming back tonight again, right?" she said to me.

"I'm not sure. I was just filling in, I think."

"Fuck that other nurse," Jennifer said. "I like you better." And just like that, I began working full time on the case.

I fell in love with the baby. His name was Liam, and he was so adorable. He really took a liking to me as well. When he got older and learned to walk, he would run around the house excitedly when I arrived. He stayed up until about 1:00 a.m. to spend time with me. We would play together and watch all types of movies. He was obsessed with the movie *How the Grinch Stole Christmas*, starring Jim Carrey. I watched that video at least a hundred times with that child. I really developed a bond with Liam and him with me. I began to feel my maternal instincts develop.

I treated Liam as if he were my own child. With Jennifer's permission, I would take him to meet my family and even take him shopping for clothes and toys. I loved that kid fully. I would give him baths and feed him, and I would take him on walks when the weather was nice.

He was nonverbal due to the tracheostomy, so we developed our own way of communicating. I always knew exactly what he was trying to say, even though he couldn't talk. It was one of the few times I experienced pure and innocent love. It was amazing having someone love me like that.

I stayed on the case for a few years, watching Liam grow from an infant to a toddler to a preschooler. I was privileged to witness him come off the ventilator and begin eating by mouth. I even went to the hospital when he had surgery to take out the tracheostomy. Once his trach was out, he was able to talk. I remember hearing his little voice for the first time. It was so cute.

He sounded so gentle and husky when he spoke due to years of having the trach in place.

I'm not sure as to what happened to make Liam so ill. Jennifer was always evasive about what happened to Liam when he was a baby. The most she ever told me was that she was overwhelmed with being a single mother caring for twins. She said she forgot to feed him, and basically, he became so dehydrated that he went into kidney failure. He had minimal kidney functioning when I started the case. However, I never knew what happened to make him need a tracheostomy and a ventilator.

The case was coming to an end. Liam was finally getting to a healthy state and getting ready to begin preschool. This meant the day nurse, Ralph, would need to accompany him to school. Ralph was a miserable person; he was always so cranky and rude. Ralph and Jennifer would argue like husband and wife. Still, he was an outstanding nurse and provided excellent care to Liam.

When it was time for Liam to start preschool, Ralph fought to change our hours. I wanted to work Monday through Friday 11:00 p.m. - 7:00 a.m., which would allow me time to go clubbing on the weekends. Ralph was fine with the Monday through Friday schedule, but he wanted me to work 11:00 p.m. – 6:00 a.m. instead of 11:00 p.m. – 7:00 a.m., and he would work 6:00 a.m. – 3:00 p.m., because he wanted to be there an hour earlier to prepare Liam for school. However, this would mean that I would work seven hours instead of eight. Ralph wanted me to work an hour less because Liam's insurance would only allow sixteen hours of nursing time per day.

I wasn't about to give up an hour of my schedule just to please Ralph. So, instead, I suggested I get Liam ready for school and have him all dressed and ready to go by the time Ralph arrived at his usual time, which was 7:00 a.m. Well, Ralph resisted the suggestion. We couldn't agree on resolving the matter, so a supervisor had to step in to mediate.

The supervisor came to the house one morning, and immediately, Ralph started fussing with the supervisor. "I'm not going to trust that she did everything she was supposed to do before I take him to school for six hours," he said.

Of course, I felt insulted. "You don't think I know how to prepare a child for school?" I asked calmly.

"I'm sorry, but I prefer to do it myself," he said.

The nursing supervisor heard both of our arguments and decided that I would be the one to prepare Liam for school, as it just made the most sense.

Well, Ralph went utterly ballistic. "So you're taking her side?" he asked the supervisor. "I've been on this case longer than she has! Doesn't that mean anything?" he barked.

"Ralph, calm down," I said.

"Don't tell me to calm down. I'm not going to just trust that you do everything correctly."

I realized there was no getting through to Ralph, so I excused myself and started walking out of the house.

Ralph continued arguing and yelling at the supervisor. As I was walking down the stairs, I heard him make a comment along the lines of "Fuck her and her empty bra!" I was shocked. I was still flat-chested at the time and highly dysphoric about it. I began questioning if he had known if I was trans or not; this is something that I would often wonder about at work.

I had started my medical transition shortly before I started the case, and I wasn't as passable at the time. I often felt insecure about my appearance at work and would try my best to sink into the background. The less attention I brought to myself, the better. Less attention meant less time for people to interact with me and pick up on my tells, such as my large hands, broad shoulders, and height (5'10").

Ralph's comment about my flat chest invoked a sense of paranoia that really distressed me. I began wondering if Ralph or Jennifer knew that I was trans. I had already dealt with discrimination at work. I started fearing that I would be terminated from the case for being trans. However, I knew that Jennifer loved me and saw what excellent care I had provided to her son for those few years, so this was unlikely.

As I continued walking down the stairs to exit the house, I became enraged at Ralph's comment. I stopped mid-step and began debating whether I should go back and confront Ralph about his stupid comment. However, after I gave it some thought, I realized this would most likely lead to a heated argument, which would be unprofessional, especially in front of the nursing supervisor. So, I decided to take the high road, ignore him, and resume walking down the stairs. Still, something deep inside of me couldn't help but wonder if someone like me could ever be accepted as a nurse.

CHAPTER 33

I AM WOMAN

Shortly after Liam began school, the case closed. I was happy and grateful that I had gotten to see Liam grow and get healthy, but it was time for me to move on. I didn't have the heart to take on another case. Luckily, a full-time Monday through Friday 3:00 p.m. – 11:00 p.m. position had become available at the drug rehab where I worked per diem. I was offered the position and took it. I thrived in addiction nursing. Of course, with all my experience with my mother, I felt right at home.

Another reason I enjoyed working at the drug rehab was because there were other nurses my age who I quickly became friends with. I gravitated toward two Black cisgender nurses, Kim and Nicole, in particular. They were so pretty. We would spend almost the entire shift laughing and kiki-ing. Working with them was so much fun that I would show up to work on my days off just to hang out with them.

I had become so comfortable around Kim and Nicole that I decided to tell them my tea, that I was trans. I don't know what magic they put on me because I had never done such a thing at work. I had learned to fly under the radar after being let go from my first home care case, but I was so caught up in having fun with my new friends that I threw caution to the wind. I was excited to brag about my life doing drag and competing in balls. It seemed that they were accepting of me being trans and enjoyed hearing all my stories about my nightlife outings.

I really thought that Kim and Nicole were my friends until another nurse, Nan, approached me one day and told me that those two were telling everyone I was a "man." I was in disbelief. It was the ultimate form of betrayal. I mean, I had told them my tea in secrecy. I made sure to tell them that my being trans wasn't something that was shared carelessly or with everyone. Not only were they misgendering me, but they were outing me. How could they do such a thing? I told Nan that she must be mistaken. Then she told me that Nicole and Kim were taking their phones, going on social media, and showing my pictures to my coworkers, saying, "Can you believe that's a man?" I was dumbfounded, humiliated—and enraged.

The next time I saw Nicole and Kim, I asked them if they were going around telling people that I was a man. Of course, they denied it. "We were only showing them your pictures and saying, look how pretty she is," Kim said.

"Yeah," Nicole chimed in. "Why would Nan say such a thing? She's just a hater."

"Anyway, what difference does it make?" Kim said jokingly. "You still a nigga, right?"

I was at a loss for words. *Still a nigga?* I thought. At that moment, I knew I could trust no one with my tea and would begin living in stealth at work from that point forward. I have never been so betrayed in my life. I thought they were my friends, but they were anything but.

Situations like this are why most trans women prefer to live in the shadows. Luckily, I am passable, so I can blend into the background. Being passable is a privilege because many trans women are not fortunate enough to pass. Non-passable trans women often avoid coming out during daytime hours due to fears of being discriminated against or physically harmed. Nicole and Kim didn't realize it, but telling my tea like that was reckless and potentially put me in harm's way.

I wanted to quit, but I still had bills to pay. So, I stuck it out through the fire and continued to work at the rehab. I stopped interacting with Kim and Nicole, but I kept it professional around them.

After this, rumors spread around the rehab that there was a nurse who was a "man" in disguise. Even the patients were talking about it. I felt like a magnifying glass was on me, paranoid that everyone was talking about me and looking at me, wondering if I was a "man." I became even more self-conscious about my tells and overcompensated. I found myself raising my voice, putting on too much makeup, and wearing too much perfume. Once, a patient told me flat-out that I was "trying too hard." I felt like everyone was against me, including the nurses, the doctors, the patients, and even the janitors. I didn't know who to trust. I became standoffish and pushed people away from me, even being mean to my coworkers to distract them from my tells.

I dreaded going to work and would spend hours in the mirror looking at myself before leaving the house, making sure I looked my best and did not look like a "man." It was exhausting. Then, one day, Nicole approached me and tried to extend an olive branch. "Are you okay?" she asked. "You don't seem like yourself."

It was as if I was waiting for someone to reach out to me because I began crying immediately. "I'm tired of wondering if people are calling me a man behind my back," I told her. "I feel like everyone is talking about me, and I don't know who to trust anymore."

Then the strangest thing happened. Nicole also began to tear up. "I know what you mean. A patient asked me if I was a man," she said.

"What?" I responded.

"Yeah, a patient came up to me and said, 'Ms. Nicole, there's a rumor going around that one of the nurses used to be a man. Is it you?'" She took a shaky breath. "I was so embarrassed. I know I have a deep voice and short hair, but I can't believe people are wondering if I'm a man."

I stopped crying and consoled her. "You're so pretty. They're just being ignorant."

"You're pretty too. I don't think anyone would ever think you're a man," she told me.

I still did not trust Nicole, but I could not help but feel sorry for her. Black cisgender women are often misgendered due to them not meeting Eurocentric beauty standards. This means that because they do not carry the features of White women, Black women are often called men. Worse, many Black cis women often fall victim to gender identity discrimination by perception, in which they face prejudice and violence, including murder, for people believing they are trans. This type of discrimination is based on incorrect assumptions about someone's gender identity rather than their actual identity. It is for this reason that one of my trans role models, Ts Madison, says that transphobia affects *all* women, trans and cis.

I decided I would forgive her and Kim for outing me and accepted that they did it out of ignorance. Also, at that point, I had begun to realize that if someone as pretty as Nicole could be called a man, then any woman, trans or cis, could be called a man. Furthermore, I began to understand that so-called "realness" and being passable was a façade. Stating that you're passable is stating that you're pretending to be something you're not, and if there is one thing I know, it's that I am a woman. A trans woman, but a woman, nonetheless.

I also realized that every woman has things they are insecure about, but that doesn't make them less of a woman. I discovered it's okay that I have big hands, big feet, and broad shoulders. So do many women, cisgender and transgender alike. It's okay that I'm tall, or sometimes my voice sounds deep, as this does not define my womanhood. After that day, I began to embrace my so-called tells because they are a part of me and make me the unique woman I am. I decided to stand in my womanhood fully from that day forward, for I am a woman. Hear me roar!

ROYAL

I am worth
My weight in gold
I am diamonds
I am pearls
The entirety of this world

Made of magic
A divine creation
A dream come true
A sweet and intoxicating drink
Perfection, don't you think?

My beauty blinds
My touch heals
My voice, a symphony
The great awakening
An epiphany

Heaven lies
Between my thighs
Paradise, in my bosoms
My presence, an orgasm
My absence, the deepest chasm

I am queen
I am king
The most sacred of all things
Worship me

CHAPTER 34

AGONY AND ECSTASY

I was blooming into womanhood and began exploring having sex as a woman. I had long since discovered the wonders of Craigslist and its casual encounters section as a gay man, but now I was exploring the wonders of casual sex and the men who like to have it with trans women.

Many of the men I slept with lived double lives, sleeping with me in secrecy during the wee hours of the night and being in monogamous heterosexual relationships during the day. Many of these men found sleeping with me to be an experiment, a fetish, or a fantasy. However, I did not mind being objectified in this manner at the time, as I just wanted to have fun and explore my sexuality.

One man sticks out in my mind from this time in my life. His name was John. My time with him was perhaps the first time I really observed the psyche of a man attracted to trans women. He was a stunning Puerto Rican man. We had the best sex. But, after we had sex, John would become a completely different person.

John was married and experienced a lot of guilt and shame for sleeping with me and cheating on his wife. It was as if once he ejaculated, all his underlying feelings of guilt and shame began to surface. Men typically are not thinking clearly when they are horned up. The focus for them at that point is purely seeking orgasm. I coined this phenomenon Post-Orgasm Distress Syndrome (PODS). I define PODS as a state of mental distress and disequilibrium that occurs after a man reaches orgasm.

It was apparent to me that John was struggling with PODS, as after we had sex, he would often tell me about how he felt horrible for being unfaithful to his wife. "I love my wife," he would say. "I just wish she had a dick." It was a tale I heard over and over again with these trans-attracted men. Yet, despite John's guilt and shame, he continued to see me.

Like most of the men I slept with, John would also tell me about his insecurities about being able to pleasure a cisgender woman. For most trans-attracted men, being with a trans woman is familiar and reassuring because both parties typically have penises. Some trans-attracted men feel more comfortable sleeping with trans women with a penis because they feel more confident having sex with someone with a penis than a vagina. These men think there is less chance of them not knowing the pleasure zones of a trans woman than a cis woman because they have firsthand experience with how a penis works.

Furthermore, these men find security in seeing an erect penis of a trans woman, which symbolizes many things to them: desire, pleasure, and attraction. Also, when a trans-attracted man sees a trans woman ejaculating, he gets an undeniable confirmation that he was able to please his partner to orgasm. In short, men like John enjoy sleeping with trans women because they get a woman's aesthetic with the comfort and familiarity of a penis. But, of course, this is not the case with all trans-attracted men, as some want nothing to do with a trans woman's penis.

Some men have told me that they choose to sleep with trans women simply because they prefer anal sex versus vaginal sex, and these men claim that cisgender women are more reluctant to have anal sex when compared to trans women. On the other hand, some men have told me they like to be penetrated anally (the male G-spot is the prostate), but they do not want to be penetrated by a cisgender woman wearing a strap-on or by someone who identifies as or looks like a man.

A concept that often confuses cis-het people is the sexual orientation of trans-attracted men: are they gay, straight, or bi?

The answer is complicated, but it is clear that they are neither gay nor bisexual because, unlike gay and bisexual men, they are not attracted to a man's aesthetic. However, calling them straight doesn't seem quite right either.

There is the term pansexual, which means the attraction is more about the person than their gender, so a pansexual person could be attracted to men, women, or nonbinary people. But again, this encompasses an attraction to men, and most trans-attracted men are not attracted to men. There is a scientific term for men attracted to trans women with breasts and penises called gynandromorphophilia (GAMP), but who can even pronounce that?

The answer, I guess, is that they are simply "trans-attracted," a sexuality that appears to be poorly explored. Although as the visibility of trans women increases, I suspect clarity on this matter will also increase. I hope we will eventually reach a point in society where everyone, including men like John, can love whoever they want freely and openly without judgment or shame.

John really struggled to come to terms with his sexuality. He identified as straight but had an internal conflict because he liked sleeping with trans women and loved the penis of trans women. John seemed to always need reassurance from me that he was not gay. Some cis-het people would categorize John as gay because he slept with trans women (who used to be boys/men). These cis-het people still view trans women as men ("once a man, always a man"); thus, they view trans-attraction as gay.

The potential of being labeled gay by most trans-attracted men puts them in a state of identity crisis. It is this state of crisis that often leads to the murder of trans women by trans-attracted men. Fueled by confusion and shame, these men rationalize that killing a trans woman they've slept with eliminates the possibility of them being outed and subsequentially labeled as gay.

John, like most trans-attracted men, struggled severely with the possibility of being labeled gay. I don't think I've ever witnessed such shame and fear before. However, I truly felt compassion and empathy for John as I, too, once struggled with my identity and sexuality and knew the horrible war that was going on in his mind.

***

One day, while walking, I received a call from John. He was crying hysterically, saying that he didn't know if he could go on like this. He told me he wanted to kill himself. He had been in his car for about two hours, contemplating a plan to kill himself.

As a nurse, I had been trained to respond to crises like this, but I had never been in this situation. So, I did the best I could with the knowledge I had. I kept him on the phone and instructed him to stay where he was, and I would locate him. He was nearby, and I managed to speedwalk to his car in about ten to fifteen minutes.

I got into his car and witnessed his hysteria. He was covered in tears, and his face was beet red. He told me that he had felt a tremendous amount of guilt for cheating on his wife with me. He also disclosed his shame surrounding his sexuality and attraction to trans women. "She deserves better than me," he cried.

I knew that John struggled with his sexuality, but I had no idea that it could drive him to the point of wanting to end his life. I consoled him and told him that I would need to call 911 for his safety. However, he begged me not to call as he feared that if I did, his wife would find out about the affair somehow.

I began questioning how I would handle the very serious situation. I did not want John to take his life, but I also could not force him to call 911. I thought about calling 911 against John's will, but I knew that would only make matters worse, as he was in a very delicate state.

Running out of options, I pleaded with John to go to a local psychiatric hospital for his safety. I told him to think of his wife and kids and how devastated they would be if he were to take his own life. Fortunately, John agreed to go to the hospital.

I did not trust him to drive himself to the hospital, and I knew he wouldn't allow me to drive him. So, I instructed him to call his wife and have her take him to the hospital. "How will I explain this to my wife?" he questioned. I instructed him to call her and say that he wanted to kill himself and not tell her about anything else. He agreed to call her.

I remained in the car, silent, as he made the phone call on his cellphone. He told her he was struggling and felt like he couldn't go on and would kill himself if she didn't take him to the hospital. She sounded terrified and urged him to come home so that she could drive him to the hospital. He thankfully agreed. He hung up the phone and gave me a big hug. He was so frightened and was still crying hysterically. I told him everything would be alright and that he was not alone.

I got out of the car and told him to begin driving home. Then I called him and remained on the phone until he arrived home. I instructed him to call me once he was admitted, and he told me he would. A few hours later, I got a text from him saying he would be admitted to the hospital. He thanked me for my help but wouldn't be able to contact me again. Of course, I understood and wished him and his family the best.

Many years later, I saw John and his family at a Kmart. Our eyes met, but we both stayed silent. He looked frightened as if he had seen a ghost. I'm sure he thought I would out him, though I would never do such a thing. Still, it was rewarding seeing him with his family. His wife was beautiful, and they had the cutest kids.

I felt proud that I had helped John that day and was grateful that he didn't take his life. I wanted to run up to him, hug him, and congratulate him for making it through the storm. But, of course, this would mean that I would have to explain who I was to his family, which would likely open a can of worms. So, instead, I stayed silent and continued shopping. John resumed laughing and smiling and shopping with his family. I was so happy for him.

CHAPTER 35

AND ALL THAT ASS

I continued to compete in balls and figured it was time to step my game up; it was time for me to start bodywork. My face had always been feminine, but my body significantly lacked curves. I had been on hormones for less than a year. The hormones had given me some extra fat on my hips and butt, but I was still dysphoric about my body. I began searching for illegal silicone injections (also known as "pumping"). I asked around at the balls and got the contact information for a renowned pumping doctor, who was also a trans woman, but it was difficult for us to coordinate our schedules.

I had told Mother Aaliyah that I was looking to get pumped, and initially, she tried to talk me out of it. She suggested I allow more time for the hormones to work, but I was impatient and wanted to have a bigger butt as soon as possible. Mother Aaliyah then told me about a pumping doctor named Dr. Gucci in Newark, New Jersey, who she could hook me up with. I knew I could trust Mother Aaliyah's judgment and told her to contact Dr. Gucci to see when she was available.

When Mother Aaliyah called Dr. Gucci, she stressed that I was her daughter so that Dr. Gucci would give me the best product (pure medical-grade silicone) at the best price possible. We set a date for an upcoming weekend. I was so excited to finally start my bodywork.

I had always been insecure about my butt, and I was encouraged by many queens at the balls to "fill in" my boy pockets. At the time, I was still competing in the female-figure realness category and needed to look as passable as possible. I sometimes padded my butt and hips when I competed in balls, but I wanted to elevate my realness and get pumped. This seemed like the only solution to filling out my small buttocks, as Brazilian butt lifts (BBLs) were not common at the time.

The day had finally come for me to get pumped. I was really nervous and asked Mother Aaliyah to come with me, and she agreed. So, I drove to Mother Aaliyah's apartment to pick her up so she could accompany me to Dr Gucci's. Once I got to Mother Aaliyah's apartment, she told me we would have to wait a while as Dr. Gucci was waiting for the silicone to be delivered from Mexico via FedEx. Apparently, Mexican silicone is of high quality.

I did not communicate with Dr. Gucci directly. Instead, all communication went through Mother Aaliyah. We waited at her apartment for about two hours before we got the green light from Dr. Gucci to come over. Once we got the okay to head over, we got into my hunk of junk 1999 Mercedes Benz C280 and drove to Newark.

We arrived at Dr. Gucci's apartment midafternoon. She opened the door and ushered us in. She was a tall, average-looking, but voluptuous Black trans woman. She told us she was finishing up with someone and would be with us in a second but to come into the living room.

We followed her in, and a cis woman was standing in the middle of the living room, nude from the waist down. She must have just finished getting pumped because Dr. Gucci covered her in cotton balls, and she was getting "bandaged" up in Saran Wrap. She didn't seem to mind exposing herself to everyone in the room, which made me nervous as I began wondering if I would be required to do the same.

Seeing a cisgender woman getting pumped was shocking to me because, at the time, I thought pumping was primarily exclusive to trans women. The woman who had just gotten pumped started to get dressed and put on a pair of scrubs. She shared that she worked as a CNA (certified nurse's assistant), which further shocked me because I, too, worked in healthcare, and like her, I knew better than to be doing a procedure as risky as getting pumped. However, it provided an odd sense of comfort knowing I wasn't the only person crazy enough to risk my life to get pumped, and if she was okay, then maybe I would be okay too.

Another cisgender woman was sitting on the couch, talking to the woman who just got pumped, and I presumed they were friends. The woman on the couch started bragging about how she had gotten pumped before, and no one could tell, and how her husband loved it. Then the woman who just got pumped gasped as she said, "My husband! How am I going to hide this from him?" Everyone in the room laughed. I wondered if this woman was genuine and had only just considered her husband now.

Dr. Gucci said, "Don't worry, once he sees that ass, he won't care!" Everyone laughed again. Then the two ladies left, leaving me and Mother Aaliyah alone in the room with Dr. Gucci.

My heart started racing. It was my turn to get pumped. "Have a seat. I'll be with you in a second, baby; I just got to clean up," Dr. Gucci said to me, and she went over to the other couch and started disinfecting it. My mind was all over the place. At the time, some cases had come out in the news about women getting pumped and dying. Some were even passing away from getting pumped with products other than silicone, like Fix-a-Flat.

What the hell am I doing? I thought. *What if I die?* However, my desperation to fix my flat ass outweighed all my fears. I remembered that Mother Aaliyah was there to protect me, and she and Dr. Gucci were friends, and she vouched for her work. Also, I just saw Dr. Gucci's work in person, fresh off the couch, which also eased my nerves. So, I threw caution to the wind and stuck to my guns: I would get pumped that day no matter what.

Dr. Gucci finished cleaning the operating couch and covered it with Saran Wrap, which seemed pointless as it was already covered in plastic. She instructed me to get fully nude, which embarrassed me as Mother Aaliyah was still in the room, but I did as instructed. Then Dr. Gucci told me to lie face down on the operating couch, which I did. She assured me she would use 100 percent medical-grade silicone and poured some loose silicone from a big bottle into a Dixie cup.

Next, Dr. Gucci cleansed my butt with rubbing alcohol. After the rubbing alcohol dried, she took twenty wide-bore needles that looked like little funnels and forced them into my buttocks, ten on each side. Dr. Gucci instructed me to take a deep breath each time before she put in a needle. The pain from those large needles going into my butt was excruciating, but I remained silent. She then took a syringe and aspirated the loose silicone from the Dixie cup.

Once the syringe was full of silicone, she would attach it to the needles and force the fluid into my buttocks. When she pushed the silicone into the buttocks, I felt a tremendous amount of pressure and pain. The first pump caused my head to spin, but I remained silent and started to pray to God for me not to die right then and there. I began to spiral about what could happen. What if the silicone got into my bloodstream, and I got an embolism and died of a heart attack, stroke, or pulmonary embolism? I distracted myself by watching the television.

Dr. Gucci had put on videos of her competing in pageants for us all to watch as she did the procedure. As I lay on the operating couch in severe pain, Dr. Gucci and Mother Aaliyah were both pageant queens. They talked endlessly about pageants and commented on the video playing. Their casual conversation made me feel at ease, and every now and then, I would chip in and comment on the video as well.

"Alright, baby. I'm done," Dr. Gucci said. I let out a big sigh of relief. "I just got to close you up," she said. Once she was done, she took out the needles and sealed the open wounds with Krazy Glue and cotton balls. She then guided me to a standing position.

I was still nude, which meant my penis was on display, which made me feel embarrassed, but the embarrassment quickly dissipated once I realized that I had just finished getting pumped.

"Turn around and let me see that ass," Mother Aaliyah said giddily. "Yes, daughter!"

Hearing Mother Aaliyah praise the work made me even more happy and excited.

"It looks good, right?" Dr. Gucci chimed in. "I put a little in your hips too, for free."

I glanced at myself in the living room mirror and was pleased to see my new, bigger ass that no longer had those dreaded boy pockets. Still, something in me wondered if my ass was big enough. I asked Dr. Gucci about a second procedure, and she said it would be best to wait a full month before getting pumped again. I told her I would definitely reach out to her in a month.

The procedure had taken about an hour to complete. My ass was sore as hell, and I was exhausted from the adrenaline rush. Dr. Gucci began wrapping me in Saran Wrap and gave me aftercare instructions. She said I was to not sit down on my butt for three days and try to lie flat for the next twenty-four hours. I could remove the Saran Wrap and cotton balls and shower tomorrow morning. After she finished wrapping me in Saran Wrap, I put on my clothes and got my purse to pay her. The procedure cost $500, and I was given a discount being Aaliyah's daughter.

***

As I look back, I still cannot believe I was so stupid to have that procedure done. I would not recommend anyone get injected with loose silicone. It is an extremely dangerous procedure. Being injected anywhere in the body with loose silicone can cause fatal complications. If the loose silicone enters the bloodstream, it can create a deadly embolism. As a nurse, I was fully aware of the possibility that I could have died on the operating couch that day, but I didn't care. I was so dysphoric at the time that I was willing to do anything, including risking my life, to get the look I wanted.

The procedure enhanced my buttocks, but not by much. I didn't follow Dr. Gucci's instructions. Mother Aaliyah drove us back to her apartment, but I drove myself home from there. I tried hovering over the seat while driving to avoid sitting down, but a lot of the silicone drained out of me while driving home. Silicone was all over the driver's seat when I exited the car. Luckily, the seat was leather, so I could wipe up the silicone, but I was pissed that so much silicone came out of me. It felt like I not only wasted money but endured so much pain in vain.

Fortunately, I was able to follow Dr. Gucci's instructions after the ride home. I lay flat for twenty-four hours, avoided sitting down for three days, and ultimately ended up retaining a good amount of silicone. Initially, I experienced some nerve pain and pins and needles shooting down my legs after being pumped, but this went away with time. I realize how fortunate I am that I am still alive and have no permanent complications.

I told no one that I had been pumped except my gay family. My gay sister Abbey was very upset that I had the procedure done and said that our gay mom, Mother Aaliyah, should not have helped me. Still, I explained to her that my decision to get pumped was mine and mine alone. No one forced me to get pumped; I was an adult at the time, and I made the choice to have the procedure done. If something were to have happened to me, I would have had no one to blame but myself.

In the beginning, I was satisfied with the results because my boy pockets were finally gone, but I still wanted to get pumped again, as I felt like my butt was not as large as I wanted it to be. I have come to realize that body dysmorphia is something that I will always struggle with and that I am not the most reliable judge of my own image. My butt looked perfectly fine and big, but I could not see or accept this.

Many trans women who struggle with body dysmorphia end up getting pumped excessively. I had seen trans women at the balls who were excessively pumped to the point that they were deformed, and I vowed that I would never allow myself to be cosmetically altered to such an extreme. I had also seen some videos online showing people losing limbs, becoming paralyzed, and dying from infections and embolisms after getting pumped, which terrified me. Nevertheless, regardless of being afraid of the complications, I still wanted to get pumped again.

I continued to search for alternative pumping doctors until I discovered some shocking information about Dr Gucci that finally scared me straight. Some years after I got pumped, Dr. Gucci was incarcerated for manslaughter after one of her clients died following getting pumped. After discovering this shocking information, I realized how truly fortunate I was to be alive after I got pumped. I then decided that risking my life and my health like that once was enough. I never got pumped again.

CHAPTER 36

RED FLAGS

Fall had come, and the air was brisk and crisp. I was going to California Pizza Kitchen at the Garden State Plaza mall in Paramus, New Jersey, to meet a man named Blake, whom I had invited to go on a date. I met Blake on Craigslist under the "miscellaneous romance" section. I had grown tired of one-night stands and wanted a long-term relationship. So far, I'd had no luck finding love. Something felt different about this man, though. He was White, tall, and muscular. Despite his solid build, he had a tenderness and insecurity that I found charming. He was also eight years older than I was, which did not deter me from him, as I preferred to date older men.

I arrived at the mall plainly dressed in jeans and a black-and-white striped T-shirt. Blake was dressed plainly as well. He was awestruck when he saw me. I could tell he really thought I was beautiful, which made him very nervous. However, I tried my best to make him feel comfortable, hugging and kissing him on the cheek. Then we sat down at our table to eat our pizza.

Blake told me he would soon take a test to become a police officer. He had just moved back home to New Jersey after living in California, where he had worked as a border patrol agent. He told me he quit border patrol because he missed all his family and friends in New Jersey. At the time, he was unemployed, and he told me that he was living with his parents temporarily until he got on his feet. He planned to continue working in law enforcement in New Jersey, hence the upcoming test. He said he was guaranteed to get a job as a police officer because his uncle was a retired cop who had connections. The idea of dating a handsome police officer really enticed me and added an extra layer of masculinity to Blake, making him even more attractive.

We finished our meal, and the check came. I took the bill and took out my wallet to pay. Blake looked at me with wide eyes. "You're going to pay?" he said.

"Of course," I said. "I invited you out." He seemed impressed that I was willing to pay, and I even left the tip. (This was when I, like many trans women, often felt obligated to pay for love, affection, and even time.) I would later find out this was a huge red flag.

Blake and I quickly fell quite hard for each other. Within a week of our meeting, he invited me over to his house to meet his family. I was taken aback by the offer but accepted it, nonetheless. I arrived around 8:00 p.m. The house was a gorgeous, large, two-story home in a quiet and quaint neighborhood. Blake escorted me inside to meet his family in the living room.

There were about eight other people there. Blake had three siblings, and they all had their partners there. Blake's elderly parents were also present, and they seemed very kind. His father was an eccentric character and really gravitated toward me. It appeared that they had just had dinner and were ending the night with some drinks. I felt awkward at first, being the only person of color in the room, and I also wondered if anyone knew or guessed that I was trans. (At that point, I had become quite passable and begun living my life in stealth, which means not disclosing one's transness. A trans woman who lives in stealth has completely assimilated into society as a woman.) Although, I was not completely living in stealth, as I would disclose my tea on Craigslist and, of course, to the men I was dating.

Everyone commented on how pretty I was, so I assumed that no one knew my tea. I was offered food but declined, so I had a few drinks instead. After those drinks, I began to relax and enjoy myself.

About two hours into the soiree, Blake excused us and took me upstairs to his room. It was average-sized and dimly lit, with no overhead lighting, only lamps. He closed the door, reached under his bed, and pulled out a massive black case. He opened up the case, and there was a large gun inside of it. I began feeling sheer terror. "I wanted to show you this," he said to me. "It's pretty cool." I begged him to put the gun away as it was scaring me. "It's okay," he responded. "There are no bullets in it, so it can't hurt you."

"Just put it away, please," I asked again. Finally, he returned the gun to the case and placed it back under his bed.

He then began kissing me. He slowly started taking my clothes off. He tried to take my bra off, but I stopped him. I was still flat-chested for the most part and very insecure about it. I had a set of small B-cup breasts from the hormones, but I still always wore padded bras to give the illusion of having bigger breasts, so if he took off the bra, the illusion would be shattered. He left the bra on but took everything else off. He continued kissing me, guided me onto the bed, and gently laid me down.

"I have condoms," I said to him.

He just looked at me. "We don't need that. Don't worry, I don't have anything. I get tested all the time."

I was in quite a predicament. I didn't want to turn him off and risk him rejecting me, but I also didn't want to risk my health. I decided that I wanted him, all of him. So, I allowed him to enter me unprotected.

He began thrusting. He smiled, closed his eyes, and leaned his head back as he penetrated me, which I found to be endearing. Then he opened his eyes and said, "You're beautiful," which melted my heart. Suddenly, I began to leak precum all over myself. I had never done such a thing before with the other men I slept with. Being that Blake was the only man, so far, to cause my body to react that way, I began wondering if he was meant for me. That is, I started questioning if we were soulmates.

He looked down and saw the precum, got excited, and began pushing even harder until he finished inside of me. Afterward, he lay down next to me. I lay on his chest. I felt so womanly, so feminine, and so protected. Finally, he turned the lights off, and we fell asleep.

We woke up about an hour later to a knock on the door. It was one of Blake's brothers. He sounded drunk and was asking Blake to borrow the gun under his bed. Blake told him to go away, and he left. Then, about five minutes later, he came back. This time, he pried the door open with a knife.

"Get the hell out," Blake said. The lights were still off. I began panicking as I was still in the nude, even though I was covered by the blanket.

Blake's brother was highly intoxicated and started crawling around on the floor, looking for Blake's gun under the bed. Then he began talking in a Yoda voice. The whole time my heart was racing. I thought for sure that he would remove the covers and discover that I was trans, but luckily he didn't. He grabbed the gun from under Blake's bed, crawled back out of the room, and closed the door.

I'm not sure what Blake was doing with the large gun, nor was I sure what his brother wanted with it, but the whole situation was bizarre, to say the least. This was another red flag that I chose to ignore.

I decided to stay the night, but I was filled with anxiety from all the commotion. I barely got any sleep, but it was nice sleeping in Blake's warm, muscular arms. I was falling in love.

I was in my early twenties, still reasonably new to womanhood, and quite insecure about my femininity. Being with someone as masculine as Blake made me feel validated as a woman somehow. I needed him, and I didn't know it, but he needed me too.

CHAPTER 37

DENIAL

I ignored all the red flags and quickly became monogamous with Blake shortly after we started dating. Soon after we started our relationship, I was excited to show him the queer side of my life, so I began trying to take him with me to queer nightlife events. I'm not sure why I thought he would enjoy this, as he identified as a heterosexual man. Typically, heterosexual men do not enjoy queer outings. But he went along with it. Soon, it became obvious that Blake was uncomfortable around queer people, in particular gay men.

I never talked to Blake much about his sexual identity. He upheld very traditional views on masculinity. I had never dated a man like him who was so chauvinistic and macho. But honestly, I found Blake's traits of toxic masculinity attractive. It made me feel more feminine being with someone so masculine, toxic or not.

It became apparent that Blake was struggling with sexual identity. For some reason, being in queer settings made him question himself in a way he never had before. I picked up on this but thought maybe if I exposed Blake to enough queer culture, he would get more comfortable being around queer people. However, his discomfort never dissipated.

I wanted to introduce Blake to the world of drag, so one night, we went to a club called The Monster in New York City which had a drag show. Though I no longer did professional stage drag myself, I liked to admire it from afar. Drag has always been, and will always be, a vital part of my life and journey. Through drag, I discovered myself and my womanhood, and I will forever be grateful to and appreciative of the craft.

I was wearing a short red silk dress that night. I paired it with stunning jewelry, a red pump, and a long drawstring ponytail. I had managed to get my hands on some Molly as well, which was very popular at the time. Molly is a stimulant that is thought to be a purer form of ecstasy or MDMA. In my experience, the drug intensified all of my feelings: happiness, sadness, anger, etc.

Blake didn't take any Molly; he never did any type of drugs. Blake said that if he became a police officer again, he would be required to take a lie detector test and would be questioned about any history of drug use. If he did drugs, he would be required to either tell the truth or lie, but either way, he would likely not get the job. For this reason, he stayed away from illicit substances.

The club was packed that night. The show was excellent, and I got all of my life. I mingled with the queens as per usual. Also as per usual, Blake stayed close behind me and remained standoffish with everyone in the club. I don't know why I kept taking him out with me. He was such a stick in the mud.

I radiated an inviting energy back then, so people would always come up to me to chat and kiki, but there was a flamboyant guy, who I presumed to be gay, who really gravitated toward me. He was fascinated with my look and assumed I was a performer. He was very chatty, but it was hard for us to hear each other. The music in the club was booming, and the only way you could listen to anyone was to communicate ear-to-mouth. So, the flamboyant, presumably gay guy started talking to me with his mouth against my ear and then decided to stick his tongue in my ear. He was obviously wasted, so I didn't make a big deal out of it. However, after he did that, I stopped talking to him.

It was about 3:00 a.m., and I was ready to go home. A crowd of people walked out to their cars and the train stations with us. I began recapping the night for Blake, playfully telling him about my interactions with the drunk, flamboyant guy. "He was so wasted, he stuck his tongue in my ear!" I told Blake.

He stopped walking. "He did what?! Why didn't you tell me? I would have fucked him up!"

"It's not a big deal," I said. "He was drunk. Anyway, he's gay. It's not like he was a straight guy that licked my ear."

Blake became enraged. "But you're my fucking girlfriend! I don't want some faggot licking you!"

I gasped in shock. My mouth was wide open; I could not believe he would say such a thing. The word "faggot" rang in my ear. I had heard the homophobic slur most of my life but never thought I would hear it come out of the mouth of a man in a relationship with me, a trans woman, someone part of the LGBTQIA+ community.

The crowd around us gasped in shock as well and began distancing themselves from us in fear. I was never so humiliated in my life. "We're going back!" Blake declared as he turned around, heading back to the club. "I'm going to fuck him up."

"No!" I begged. "Are you crazy?" I pulled him back, and he pushed my hand off him. I began crying. I was afraid Blake would hurt the guy. I knew the guy had meant no harm and was just drunk and having a good time. Blake saw me crying and stopped walking to the club. Instead, he turned around and walked me to the car. I kept crying uncontrollably. I was still high off the Molly, and the sadness I felt was intense. I was hysterical; I couldn't even catch my breath.

I got into the car and sat in the passenger seat. Blake calmed me down. He began driving back to his house. My mind was still racing and replaying what had happened. I was in disbelief. *Blake is homophobic*, I thought. *I can't be with someone like that, can I?* I'm sure Blake's apparent struggles with internalized homophobia were rooted in his fears of being labeled as gay, but this was irrelevant to me. Being queer myself, how could I be with someone anti-gay?

"I can't do this anymore," I said to Blake. "I can't continue to see you."

"Why?" Blake asked in shock.

"You scare me," I told him.

Blake became choked up and appeared as if he was going to cry. "I'm sorry. I fucked up! It won't happen again. I'm sorry! I don't want to keep going to these gay clubs. I just want to stay home with you and watch TV. We don't have to go out every night," he said. "I love you."

I was shocked. We had only been together for a few months, but he said he loved me, and I believed him. My heart was pounding out of my chest. "I love you too," I told him. "I'll give you one more chance, but that's it. And no more homophobic shit."

"Alright, babe," he said sheepishly.

Despite Blake's shocking display of homophobia, I continued the relationship with him. We stopped going to gay clubs together after that night, although I would continue to go to balls and other queer functions without him. We began going to cis-het bars, lounges, and clubs together, as Blake was obviously more comfortable in those settings.

Honestly, I found that going to straight clubs with Blake was more fun than going to gay clubs. I was passable, so I blended right in with all the cis-het people. I was young, entertaining, and pretty, so all the straights loved me. Also, partying with Blake in a straight setting made him less tense and uncomfortable, which was much more enjoyable for both of us. I was so caught up in having fun with Blake at the straight outings that I didn't realize he was isolating me from the queer community, and I was slowly losing a part of myself.

CHAPTER 38

ORAL FIXATION

A year passed, and Blake and I continued our relationship. He exposed me to all sorts of fascinating aspects of both the cis-het and White cultures. We continued to distance ourselves from the queer community, and I assimilated into the cis-het world. I stopped disclosing my tea to anyone and even began distancing myself from my biological family.

While my family accepted that I was queer and trans, they struggled to use my preferred pronouns and called me by my birth name, which really upset Blake. He was still struggling with his sexuality, and hearing my family call me "he" and "him" and my deadname made him visibly uncomfortable. I realized that I had only transitioned for two years at that point, and it wasn't enough time for my family to fully adjust to my transition and new identity. So, I accepted that I had to be patient with them.

Transgender individuals often realize that, in many ways, our family has to "transition" with us. For parents, this process is even more challenging. Parents who have a transgender child often say that they have to go through a period of grief. They usually feel in many ways that they have lost a child. Parents of trans women often feel they have to grieve the metaphorical death of their son. When these parents can mourn the loss of their son, they can accept that they have gained a daughter.

I didn't mind being called my birth name, but it did frustrate me that my family still called me he/him. Blake had argued countless times to stand up for myself and demand that my family call me "Armani" and use she/her pronouns. So, I started asking family members to use my preferred pronouns, but I didn't push them on the name; I figured one thing at a time. Surprisingly, no one in my family objected to using she/her pronouns, but they struggled to remember to use my preferred pronouns, as for over twenty years, they were referring to me with he/him pronouns. Of course, I understood that it would take some time for my family to fully adjust to the change, but Blake wanted them to make the change immediately, which wasn't realistic. Then, one day, during a family BBQ, the pronoun struggle with my family reached its height.

Blake and I were socializing outside with my family when one of my aunts used he/him pronouns to refer to me, and Blake exploded. "Don't you know she's a damn woman by now?" he exclaimed. I was ashamed of Blake's behavior and did not know how to respond. I remained silent, in fear, and my eyes darted to the floor as Blake continued to yell at my aunt.

My aunt and the family surrounding us were dumbfounded, and everyone was silent as Blake continued his rant. Finally he was done, but the conversation was far from over. My aunt calmly took a breath and said to Blake, "Well, you're still gay, so what does it matter?" My heart began racing with fear, as I knew Blake's being called gay could possibly result in violence; his internalized homophobia was that strong.

Blake was stunned and at a loss for words, but he turned bright red with anger and started gritting his teeth. His silence was terrifying, and I knew it was best to leave altogether. So quickly, before he could utter a word, I grabbed him by the hand and escorted him inside the house to my room.

"Who the hell does that bitch think she is?" Blake yelled at me. "And you didn't say anything!"

I stared at the floor as Blake continued to scold me. Truly, I felt ashamed of not sticking up for him or myself. "I'm sorry...I didn't know what to do," I said softly. Then Blake looked at me, let out a long sigh, and hugged me.

I didn't know how to get my family to remember to consistently use she/her pronouns when referring to me, so I did what I usually did when faced with confrontation: I practiced the art of avoidance. I avoided my family, and I started spending most of my time with Blake and his family instead.

Blake's family were all very kind to me. They had no clue that I was trans, and I preferred to keep it that way, to be honest. They called me Armani and used she/her pronouns when they referred to me. I became more familiar with the White lifestyle and assimilated into their culture, leaving behind yet again another piece of myself to make my relationship with Blake work.

I grew close to Blake's father, who clearly struggled with alcoholism but was a kind man who enjoyed the company of a young, attractive woman. I would spend hours hanging out with Blake's father, sometimes making Blake jealous. "What, do you like him more than me?" Blake asked me one day; I chuckled in amusement and assured him I loved him and only him.

Blake was truly my first love. I had been in short and failed relationships before him, but I don't believe I had ever loved someone so strongly at that point in my life. We were sincerely crazy about each other and planned to spend the rest of our lives together. However, our relationship was not perfect, especially when it came to being intimate. Our sex life was a major struggle.

Blake played football for most of his life, in high school and college, and his knees had been badly damaged. He was told once by a physician that his knees were unsalvageable and that he would need to have knee replacement surgery. He objected to this recommendation, as he had an uncle who had an unsuccessful knee replacement surgery, and Blake feared he would end up in the same situation. So, he bore the chronic, severe pain of living with badly damaged knees, and though he tried his best, he struggled with mobility issues.

This impacted his ability to have sex. Initially, our sex life was an enjoyable experience, but it soon turned mundane and boring. Due to Blake's issues with his knees, he was unable to do the majority of sexual positions. Actually, there was really only one position that he could do, which involved him lying flat while I went on top, in reverse cowgirl.

Although, the reason we did reverse cowgirl instead of regular cowgirl had nothing to do with Blake's knees, more so with the fact that Blake did not want to see my penis. In the reverse cowgirl position, Blake only saw me from behind. I would only reach climax by touching myself, as Blake also felt uncomfortable touching my penis. Of course, this caused a sense of disconnect, and being intimate with Blake started to feel more like a chore than a pleasure.

I began seriously considering getting SRS, as it seemed Blake despised my penis. I thought if I had a neovagina, maybe Blake would feel more comfortable with my body. Of course, one should never get SRS for anyone but themselves, but it seemed like a solution at the time. However, when I brought up the idea and told him that it may help our sex life, he firmly told me that he did not want me to get SRS. He thought it would cause psychological harm, as I wouldn't be getting it for myself but for him.

After we had that conversation, he made an effort to become more comfortable and accepting of my penis. He slowly began to warm up to the idea of at least touching my penis, and sometimes he would permit me to do regular cowgirl, facing him, instead of our usual reverse cowgirl. Eventually, Blake would masturbate me until I reached climax.

I was pleased with the efforts Blake made at looking at and touching my penis, but I realized it would be plenty more baby steps until Blake would be able to perform oral sex on me.

I knew what Blake struggled with most was being labeled gay, so I assured him that because I was a woman, he shouldn't view performing oral sex on me as a gay act. I told Blake that my penis was a part of me, and I was still a woman, regardless of having a penis, as my penis did not define my womanhood. After explaining this to Blake, he began performing oral sex on me. Still, it was never a regular occurrence, and our sex life continued to be monotonous.

***

Blake and I had a regular date night, which involved dinner and a movie. Of course, I paid for everything, as usual, but I didn't mind as long as I got to spend time with Blake. After one of our date nights, I had to work the following day, so I could not spend the night at his house. So, once our date was over, he drove me home to my grandparents' house in Paterson, where I still lived.

When Blake dropped me off, it was around midnight. He drove into the fenced-in parking lot next to my grandparents' house. Although the parking lot was part of a busy doctor's office, it was completely empty at that time of night.

I had gotten into all sorts of mischief in that parking lot, having various romantic escapades with different men over the years who I did not want to bring into my grandparents' house. It was pretty adventurous to have car sex, and I thought it would be the perfect way to spice things up with Blake.

We were sitting in his car (or should I say his parents' car), talking and laughing, when I began to rub his leg and grope his penis. Blake smiled and asked me what I was doing. I looked him in the eyes mischievously, then I unbuttoned his pants and pulled his penis out. I then began performing oral on him as he slowly reclined his car seat and closed his eyes.

After about fifteen minutes of performing oral, I realized Blake was not going to climax, as he rarely climaxed from oral. So, I put my head up and gave him another mischievous look. "I think it's my turn," I said with a coy smile. Blake looked at me, paused, and then reluctantly agreed. I couldn't believe it; Blake was not only daring to have sex in public but was also going to perform oral sex on me, something he rarely did at that point in our relationship.

This time I reclined my seat, unbuttoned my pants, and gestured for Blake to begin performing oral on me. I closed my eyes in pleasure. I was so close to climax when something instinctively told me to open my eyes. I looked to the left and was mortified. A man was standing next to the car, with his phone out recording us!

"Babe!" I said with fear, tapping Blake on the head, but he continued to perform oral on me. "Babe!" I said again. "Someone's watching us!" I pushed Blake up and quickly buttoned my pants.

Blake realized what was going on and sat upright, enraged. "What the fuck are you doing?" Blake screamed to the man recording us.

The strange man was dressed in all black, wearing a hoodie. It was hard to see him in the dark, even with the shine of the streetlights. His dark skin blended into the shades of black of his clothing, and it was hard to see his face. Still, I could see the whites of the man's eyes expand in fear, and it was clear that he was frightened once we discovered what he was doing.

The man didn't know it, but he saw Blake doing something he deeply struggled with. Unfortunately, he was going to have to pay for peeking into Blake's secret world of having sex with a trans woman.

Blake swiftly opened the car door and began yelling at the man. I remained in the car, watching in shock and terror. Blake pushed the man to the ground and began struggling to take his phone out of his hands. "Eh, man! You crazy!" the man yelled. Blake began shaking the man and commanding him to let go of the phone. This struggle went on for a few minutes until Blake successfully acquired the man's phone, threw it on the ground, and began stomping on it.

The man stood there yelling at Blake to stop, but he continued to break the phone. Then the man grabbed Blake, which, he would soon find out, was a huge mistake. The man was about 5'8" and slender, and Blake stood over six feet and was broad and muscular. In one swift motion, Blake picked up the man and held him above his head like a WWE wrestler. I had no idea what Blake planned to do, and I began to fear for the man's life.

Blake then ran to the end of the parking lot and threw the man over the fence. The man screamed in horror as Blake propelled him through the air like a rag doll. "Now get out of here!" Blake barked at the man.

The man lay on the ground for a fearful five seconds in silence. *Oh my God! He's dead!* I thought. My fear intensified, and I began wondering if Blake actually murdered the man. But, by the grace of God, the man finally got up and ran away into the night.

Blake returned to the car and picked up the man's battered phone off the ground. He walked back to the car and slammed the door shut. I stayed silent; I knew better than to say anything at that point. Blake's rage had not yet subsided, and he began directing it toward me. Still, I remained quiet with my head down like a child in trouble as Blake scolded me for pressuring him to have public sex, blaming me for the whole ordeal.

In the Dark

You said you love me
But it was a whisper

You said you love me
Without exclaim

You said you love me
With guilt and shame

You said you love me
But it was in the dark
Where no one could see

You said you love me
Without care or intimacy

Walk behind you in crowds
Talk to you
But not too loud
Look at you
But not in the eyes

Give you the truth
While you give me lies

You said you love me
But it was a whisper

You said you love me
But it was a whisper

CHAPTER 39

CALIFORNIA LOVE

Craigslist unfairly gets a bad reputation. It has been the catalyst for most of my major life events. One night, I was on Craigslist looking for modeling gigs, and out of sheer boredom, I did a search for "transgender model." To my surprise I discovered there was an advertisement looking for a trans model/actress for an upcoming movie. I decided to reply to the ad. What did I have to lose? I kept my response brief. I simply said, "Pick me. I'm pretty," and attached pictures of myself.

Well, within twenty-four hours, I had heard back from the people who posted the ad. They sought a trans woman to star in an autobiographical short film. Being self-absorbed at the time, I gladly accepted the offer. The company wanted to capture the life of a trans woman, all the ups and downs and in-betweens. I mentioned that I competed in balls, and the producers were very interested in capturing my ballroom life.

I met with the two men who were the producers one day in New York City to do a photoshoot and film. The shoot went well. I showed up with no makeup. My hair was freshly washed and wrapped up in a towel. I wore nothing but a robe and my bra and panties. The producers wanted to see me get dressed as if I was going out and talking about my life while I did it. So, I took off the robe and got started. I began the shoot by saying, "Well, my real name is…but I don't know where that fucking Armani came from. Can I curse?" The producers started laughing, and I knew then that this movie would be a hit.

They continued to film me while I got dressed and asked me questions about my family, work, school, ballroom, and transition. I remember lying and saying that I wasn't on hormones. I have no idea why I lied about being on hormones. It seems silly now that I think about it. From being in ballroom, I had learned that "natural" was superior. So, I guess I wanted to impress them by making them think I was "naturally" beautiful.

We continued the shoot for about two hours, and then I left. I remember being pissed when I got back to my car because I had gotten a parking ticket; that's New York for you. I did the shoot for free, so having a parking ticket made me feel like I had paid to be in the film. I didn't mind that I wasn't paid, though; I was just grateful to have been immortalized in film (I was really feeling the fantasy).

Eventually, the producers turned the short film into a full-length movie. They added other trans women to the roster and meshed our stories together. I had allowed the producers to follow and film me competing at balls, and they caught all sides of the ballroom: the good, the bad, and the ugly. Don't get me wrong—ballroom has its pros and its cons.

For example, competing in realness gave me the confidence to live my life as a woman full time. Winning many realness battles confirmed that I was passable and could assimilate into society. Also, I got an invaluable sense of community and camaraderie from the ballroom that I had never gotten anywhere else.

Though balls are fun and festive, there is a negative side to them. There is a lot of illegal activity and violence at balls, including physical fighting, prostitution, and substance use and distribution. Ballroom is often whitewashed in the media, and I was glad that the producers decided to show a fully rounded view of the ballroom scene in the movie.

The producers began promoting the movie on various platforms. There were so many film festivals that I couldn't keep up. I tried my best to attend them all, but I was not getting paid for it, so I did what I could. I was still working as an LPN, so I wasn't making much money, and I couldn't afford to travel all over the place to promote the movie for free, Ms. Thing. However, I made sure that I made it to the official movie premiere, come hell or high water. The premiere was set to be in San Francisco. I decided to take Blake with me; what a huge mistake.

It was the morning of the flight to California, and Blake and I were headed to Newark airport. We were behind schedule, which made him on edge. We arrived at the airport about one hour before the flight. I had never flown before, so I had no idea what to do and was grateful that Blake was there to guide me along the way.

We got to the airport and checked in. Then, we had to go through the whole circus of baggage checks, body scans, and boarding. We barely made it on time to the flight, and Blake became very upset and scolded me about my poor time management skills. I didn't care at that point. I was on my way to California for a whole week, and I was going to enjoy myself.

While I had my own agenda, Blake apparently had one of his own. About a year before, Blake was contacted by an ex-girlfriend who told him she had given birth to his baby. The news came as a total surprise to me when Blake told me about it three months into our dating. He wanted to go to California to essentially kidnap the baby and bring her back to New Jersey to raise. He also expected me to fall into the role of being the baby's mother. His plan took me aback when he told me about a month prior. I told him that I wanted no part of any type of kidnapping and that he was to do all of that on his own. So, we agreed that I would travel back to New Jersey after a week, and Blake would remain in California to see and possibly abduct his child.

The flight was long as hell and highly uncomfortable. We sat in coach, so it was very cramped. I slept for most of the flight, but Blake remained wide awake. Apparently, he gets anxious when flying and cannot sleep, which is unfortunate on a twelve-plus-hour flight.

We had to change planes at some point and went to get a bite to eat at the airport. We decided to go to Pizza Hut and get personalized pizzas. Blake was still on edge, so it was like walking on eggshells around him. Since he was such a huge guy in height and stock, when he was angry, it was an utterly terrifying scene. He would scream, curse, and name-call. And whenever Blake got angry, it was guaranteed that he would have an outburst, whether it was in public or in private.

We got our food, and I hoped it would calm him down. Then Blake dropped his pizza on the ground as we walked out of Pizza Hut. I knew all hell was about to break loose, so I quickly walked to the other side of the restaurant. Blake began shouting at the top of his voice, "Fuck! This is fucking bullshit. Are you fucking kidding me?" Everyone in the restaurant started staring at him. "What the fuck are you looking at?" he shouted at them. "I'm fucking starving, and I just dropped my fucking pizza on the floor!"

I walked back over to him. "It's okay," I said. "I'll buy you another one."

"No," he responded. "We're not paying for another fucking pizza!" Then, he walked over to the register and began yelling at the cashier, telling them what happened. The cashier and the other staff were so frightened that they gave him another pizza for free. I was grateful that the scene was over. We boarded the second plane and continued our trip to California in silence.

We finally arrived in California at nighttime. We made it to the hotel and quickly fell asleep.

The next day we started fresh. There was no more anger, and I didn't feel like I was walking on eggshells. We were invited to brunch by the producers, and I accepted the invitation. We began to get dressed. I was doing my makeup in the bathroom, and Blake was ironing his shirt in the bedroom. Then, all of a sudden, I heard him yelling and cursing. "Shit!" I heard him yell. I came out of the bathroom.

"What's wrong?" I said.

"This fucking shitty iron just burned my fucking shirt!" he yelled at me. Then he spat on the iron and threw it across the room. For some reason, I found the scene to be comical, and I chuckled. "You think this is fucking funny?" he barked at me.

I felt an intense fear wash over me. "No, babe, but I think you're overreacting," I said.

"Overreacting? I just ruined a fucking shirt. Are you going to buy me a new one?"

I became silent and wondered if he was serious since I had paid for everything else until then. Finally, I managed to calm him down and convinced him to wear another shirt.

After that we left to meet with the producers to have brunch. I managed to slip away and have a private conversation with one of the producers.

"How's it going? You don't seem like yourself," he said.

I began telling him about Blake and the pizza and iron incidents. I told him I felt scared around him when he was angry.

I had been dating Blake for six months then and didn't know if I wanted to continue. The producer consoled me, saying, "Look, vacations are the ultimate test for a relationship. If you can make it through this week, that's a good sign that it might work. On the other hand, if you guys keep fighting, you may want to think about calling it quits." His advice made sense, so I decided that the rest of the trip would determine whether I would stay with Blake.

***

It was the night of the movie premiere. I looked stunning, as per usual. My gay mother, Aaliyah, allowed me to borrow one of her green gowns and a pair of emerald heels. She had also done my hair before I left Jersey and snatched it back into a sickening ponytail with a bang. My face was beat for the gods and the deities, and I had on loads of jewels and was simply dazzling. Blake looked very handsome. He wore a blue suit that hugged all his muscles just right. We looked great together; that was undeniable.

I arrived at the red carpet and took pictures. Blake seemed so proud watching me mingle on the red carpet. It was fun, and I felt like a starlet. Soon, the movie began. Seeing myself on the big screen was amazing. The audience seemed to laugh and enjoy my movie segments as well. Once the film was done, we did a question-and-answer session, and the audience lived for me. After that, we ended the night with more mingling, and I even gave out some autographs. I felt like a true movie star.

The next day, I had a photoshoot with all the girls from the movie. Blake accompanied me to the shoot, and we stayed secluded in a corner. It was the final day of my trip. I thought back to what the producer had said to me, and whether I should stay with Blake or not. He was well-behaved after the iron incident, so I decided to continue the relationship.

We discussed his plans once I left to head back to New Jersey. He told me that he planned to drive about an hour outside of San Francisco, to where he had previously lived. He said he had his car in storage there and wanted to get it. Also, that's where his ex and his baby lived. I was having so much fun with the movie premiere that I had completely forgotten about Blake's plan to kidnap his child and drive her back to New Jersey. I tried to convince him not to go through with it and just come back with me, but he had made up his mind.

I left for New Jersey the next day by myself. I hugged Blake goodbye and felt my heart break as I left him. I knew that nothing good was to come of his plans, but I also knew there was nothing I could do to stop him. I feared that he would be arrested and be incarcerated in California. I was a nervous wreck.

CHAPTER 40

TRANSPARENT

I left California at nighttime and arrived back in New Jersey in the morning. I remember the sadness; it was intense. I missed Blake severely, and I was also filled with anxiety regarding his plans to take his baby.

I called him when I landed, and he updated me on his plan. He could not contact his ex, Maria, but he was able to contact her cousin. He had managed to get his Chevy out of storage as well. He was happy to have his car back, as he had been borrowing his parents' car to get around.

I was feeling increasingly concerned about the possibility of Blake seeing his ex without me there. I had read some of her messages to him, and it was evident that she still had feelings for him. On top of that, the fact that Blake and Maria had a child together made the possibility of him dumping me and getting back with her very likely.

I never trusted that ex of his. She always seemed shady, and something in my gut told me there was more to the story than she was telling. Who gets pregnant and gives birth and doesn't reach out to the child's father until the child is over a year old? I mean, I guess it happens, but something about it did not sit right in my spirit.

I had also heard Blake speak on the phone with her before, and she seemed more interested in convincing him to get back together than discussing the child. In one of her messages, she even insulted me. Blake had sent her a picture of me after she asked to see what his new girlfriend looked like, and Maria said something along the lines that I was Black and ugly. The racist insult was random and unwarranted and indicated Maria was jealous of my relationship with Blake.

I had seen pictures of her as well. She was an average-looking Hispanic woman, but I did not feel the need to insult her appearance the way she did mine. Something was definitely up, but I couldn't put my finger on it just yet.

Blake called me maybe a day later and told me he had been staying with Maria's cousin. He couldn't get in contact with Maria at all. The cousin also had difficulty reaching her. She said she had called Maria several times with no response, and she had texted Maria that Blake was there and wanted to see the baby. Maria's cousin invited Blake to stay with her for a few more days.

Finally, about two days later, Maria called her cousin and told her she didn't want to see Blake. He took the phone from the cousin and told Maria he had a right to see the child. She gave in and said she would be there the next day with the child.

Meanwhile, back in New Jersey, I continued to be a nervous wreck. I became insecure and felt sure that Blake would cheat on me with Maria. Still, he promised me that he was not attracted to her anymore. He told me he hated her for stringing him along and ignoring all his attempts to see the child. I had no choice but to believe him; I was on the other side of the country.

I became so paranoid that Blake would cheat on me that I offered to fly back to California to meet Maria with him. Blake told me that would be a bad idea because it would make Maria upset and jealous. He was trying his best to appease her. She had his child and had taunted him by sending him pictures of the babe and saying he'd never see her.

Maria knew that Blake wanted to see the child at all costs. She also wanted to get back together with him. So, he thought my being there would only worsen matters. He told me he had lied to Maria and told her he was there to get back together with her and become a happy family—he told me it was a lie, but deep down, I thought it was the truth.

I couldn't sleep the night when Blake was supposed to see Maria and the baby. I was engulfed with worry that he would leave me. Unable to sleep, I decided to look for Maria's social media; I wanted to see the pictures of the baby. I decided to look on the bright side and mentally prepare myself to be the child's stepmother.

Due to my insecurities, I had never looked at Maria's social media before that night. To my surprise, I began scrolling through her profile and saw no pictures of the baby. I thought this was really weird. One would think that a new mother would have countless pictures of her baby all over her social media. I then began to look at her friends' profiles to see if I could find a photo of the baby. I found nothing. Something was wrong, and the math did not add up.

I contacted Blake and told him to send me the picture of the baby that Maria had sent him. He became angry and told me to just stay out of it. I told him to trust me and send me the picture, and he did. I did a reverse image web search on the picture. Then, the unimaginable happened.

I discovered the original source of the picture, and it wasn't from Maria but from one of her listed friends. I clicked on the link and found multiple images of the baby, but none were with Maria, only the friend. Then it hit me. The baby was not Maria's! She had been lying the whole time; there was no baby! I began texting Blake all the evidence. He was shocked. He texted me back and told me he couldn't believe that Maria had strung him along for almost a year and had lied to him about being a father.

Maria had finally arrived. She came alone without a baby, of course. She told Blake that she had left the baby with her mother. Blake then told Maria that he knew everything; he knew there was no baby, and he questioned why she would do this to him. Maria began weeping and confessed to Blake that she had actually been pregnant with his child but had suffered a miscarriage.

We were all in shock. I could not believe the news when Blake told me. He was distraught. He had really thought that he was a father. He had put so much thought and care into his plan to bring the child back to New Jersey to live. He had thought that he, the baby, and I would become a family. His dreams were shattered. He left for New Jersey the next day.

I began to feel a strange sense of pity for Maria. I felt terrible for her because she truly loved Blake. I also felt horrible knowing that she had a miscarriage, which must have been devastating. Blake was depressed when he returned to New Jersey, and angry that he was not a father anymore. He told me that the prospect of being a father had felt like the only chance at success he had in his life, as he was still unemployed and living at home. But then he directed his anger at me and began to make me feel guilty that I could not bear a child.

Not being able to bear a child is a struggle that almost all trans women have to deal with. It always made me feel less than a woman. I wanted to have children, and more importantly, I wanted to have Blake's children, but I simply could not due to my anatomy.

Blake's resentment toward me for not being able to have a child made me feel a sense of shame and inadequacy. He told me it was my responsibility to make him a father again. He said that he felt like a new man when he believed he was a father, and now he felt like nothing. I began to think of ways I could give him a child. He said he did not want to adopt, so that option was gone. But he was receptive to surrogacy, so that became the plan.

Looking back on this incident makes me so angry. I feel upset with Blake for making me feel so small, and angry at myself for allowing him to manipulate and control me in such a manner. I truly loved him, and I would do anything for him. He knew this and exploited it. I wish I knew at the time that this was not love; it was abuse. As time passed, Blake stopped talking about wanting to be a father, but I would always feel guilt and sadness for not being able to bear a child for him.

Chapter 41

Where the Fuck Are My Tits?

After years of dysphoria about my chest, I finally decided to have top surgery around the age of twenty-three. I had grown a set of B-cup breasts from hormones, but I wanted to go up to at least a D-cup. What worried me most was the cost. I did some research and found a financing service specifically for cosmetic procedures. I completed the application and was approved for a credit of ten grand, but you have to use surgeons who work with the financing company to use this credit. I decided to use a surgeon close to me named Dr. Henderson. I did some research on him and liked his work, and accordingly, I set a consultation appointment with him.

On the day of my consultation, Blake accompanied me to the doctor. He encouraged me not to tell the doctor that I was trans. He assured me it was unnecessary to disclose my tea to the doctor, as it would serve no purpose and would likely be embarrassing for us both. So, I listened to him and did not disclose to Dr. Henderson that I was trans.

The consultation was overall unremarkable. Dr. Henderson discussed the different types of breast implants I could get, including material, size, shape, and placement. I told Dr. Henderson I wanted to have my breasts as big as possible, without looking fake, and as "natural" as possible. Ultimately, I decided I would get 350cc silicone, or "gummy bear," implants. Dr. Henderson assured me that the 350cc gummy bear implants would give a C/D cup and feel more realistic than saline implants. We also agreed to place the implants "under the muscle" instead of "above the muscle," which would further give me the "natural" look I desired. The procedure was scheduled for a month later.

On the night before my procedure, I was so nervous that I could not sleep and stayed awake the entire night. On the morning of the procedure, I dressed very plain with sweatpants, a T-shirt, and no makeup. Blake drove me to the hospital, which was about thirty minutes away from my home. I was a bundle of nerves. I began worrying that I would die on the operating table, but I quickly dispelled these thoughts; I needed my D-cup breasts. Plus I figured if I could survive being pumped by Dr. Gucci, I could survive being operated on by Dr. H, a real doctor.

I checked in at the hospital and went to some sort of waiting area, where an admission nurse instructed me to take everything off and put on a hospital gown. Well, I didn't listen and left on my gaff panties at the instruction of Blake. Then, the admission nurse came and inserted an IV into my arm. She asked me if I had taken off my undergarments, and I lied and said yes. A little later, Dr. Henderson greeted me and drew all kinds of shapes on my chest with a Sharpie. After this, Dr. Henderson left, and shortly after, I was placed on a stretcher and rolled to the operating room.

The operating room was cold as ice. I began shivering and was then covered by a warm blanket. Dr. Henderson was there in his blue gown, mask, and gloves. "Ready?" he said.

"I guess!" I replied nervously.

"You're going to count backward from ten, and when you wake up, you'll have a new set of breasts," he said to me. I began counting and was unconscious by the time I reached seven.

I woke up in a hospital bed, surrounded by draw curtains. I was surprised because I did not have any pain at all. I then touched my chest to feel my new breasts, but nothing was there. Confused, I peeked down into the hospital gown and saw my regular B-cup breast, still covered in all the Sharpie markings from earlier that morning. I did not have the breast implants inserted. The surgery was not done. I was bewildered as to what was going on. I began wondering if there was a financial issue or something, but then I realized that my gaff panties had been removed.

My heart began racing. *What the fuck is going on?* I thought. "Hello?" I yelled out.

A short nurse came and opened the draw curtains. "Oh good, you're up," she said with annoyance.

"What is going on?" I asked. "Why wasn't my surgery done?"

"Your doctor will be in to talk to you soon," she said and walked away.

I began panicking. Did they see my genitals and find out I was trans? What in the actual hell was going on?

I was taken to another floor shortly after. Finally, Dr. Henderson entered the room, accompanied by someone who later introduced themselves as one of the hospital's lawyers. "So, you didn't tell me that you're transgender," he said to me sternly.

"I didn't think I had to," I responded. "What were you guys doing down there anyway?"

He ignored my question and continued. "You gave me quite the scare. I could not do the procedure because I need proof that you are mentally stable."

"Mentally stable?" I asked in anger. "What does that mean?"

"I need at least a letter from your doctor saying you're taking hormones and have had a psychiatric evaluation."

I began weeping uncontrollably. "I can't believe this is happening."

Then Blake showed up. "Hey, babe, why are you crying?" he asked, confused.

"They canceled my surgery because they found out I'm trans!" I wept.

Blake then turned in anger toward Dr. Henderson and began interrogating why my panties were removed; we never got a clear answer. We were told that my panties were removed in case an "emergency" happened, which made no sense at all. Dr. Henderson then excused himself and returned shortly after with the hospital lawyer and other people whose titles I do not know.

Blake started screaming at Dr. Henderson, and Dr. Henderson shouted back at him. "He needs a letter from his doctor before I can do the surgery!"

"'He'?" Blake screamed. "Are you fucking kidding me? She's a girl!" Everyone in the room began talking and shouting at once. Blake threatened to sue the hospital, which only made the arguments heighten. I started to feel the room spin.

Finally, I composed myself and said to everyone, "Look, I don't want to sue anyone." I turned to Dr. Henderson. "I'll get the letter from my doctor. Can I go home?" Everyone calmed down. Dr. Henderson told me he would reschedule my surgery a week later, but I would need to acquire the letter from my HRT doctor before then.

I called Callen-Lorde the next day and told them I would need a letter saying I'd been psychiatrically evaluated, had been living as a woman, and had been on HRT so that I could get top surgery. They told me they usually require a week to write letters. I informed them of everything that had happened, and they told me they understood and would rush the letter. I got the letter about three days later and had my surgery as scheduled.

I dressed to the nines on the day of my rescheduled surgery. I returned to the same hospital and was greeted by the same admission nurse. I guess word had gotten around about what had happened because the nurse kindly said to me, "…and this time take your panties off."

Dr. Henderson came in and drew all over my chest again, and then I was rolled back into the operating room on a stretcher. It was the same as before; I was taken to the operating room, counted backward from ten, and was asleep by the time I reached seven.

This time when I woke up, surrounded by the draw curtain, I was in excruciating pain. It felt as if an elephant was sitting on my chest, and every breath felt like a struggle. I began screaming for a nurse, and the same mean, short nurse came in. "It's a ten out of ten on the pain scale!" I screamed at her. "I need pain medicine!" I began thrashing about the bed from side to side in agony.

"If you do not calm down, you will have to go back to the operating room!" she told me.

"Fuck you, bitch! Give me my pain medicine!" I yelled at her.

She shook her head in judgment. Then she took a syringe, connected it to my IV, and pushed it in. I fell back asleep.

I woke up again in another room. Blake was by my side. "You're awake," he said. "I'll get the nurse." This time, I was greeted by a new nurse, and she was very nice. She walked me to the restroom and got me ready to be discharged. I left the hospital in a wheelchair. We drove to a local hotel, where I stayed for seven days while I recovered. I decided to stay at a hotel to allow myself some privacy from my father's family while I recovered.

Blake stayed with me and tended to my every need. I remember the next day that I took the bandages off. I gawked at my breasts in amazement. I could not believe how great they looked; it was worth all the pain, drama, and embarrassment. I paid about eight grand for my breasts, but they were worth every penny.

The recovery was rough, but I made it through. During my post-op consultation, Dr. Henderson told me he had placed a 350cc silicone implant under my right breast and a 325cc silicone implant under my left breast to make them look more "natural," as per my previous request, as breasts are typically asymmetrical. My incisions healed nicely, but I did have a decrease in sensation in my left nipple. I told Dr. Henderson about the nerve damage, and he assured me the sensation would fully return with time, but it never did.

Still, I loved my new breasts. After I healed fully and the implants fell into place, I ended up with a pair of lovely D-cups. I never thought I would feel comfortable in my skin, but after I had my top surgery, I finally felt complete in my physical transition.

CHAPTER 42

LOVE IS A BATTLEFIELD

Blake convinced me to return to school to become a Registered Nurse (RN) in 2014. He wanted me to make more money (which meant more money for him to mooch off). He was still in the same situation as when we met: unemployed, living with his parents, still aspiring to get into law enforcement. I wanted us to move in together, but I knew I could not afford to pay for rent, Blake's expenses, and my living expenses with an LPN's salary, so I agreed that I would enter nursing school again to become an RN.

I began classes at Passaic County Community College. Nursing school to become an LPN was tough, but nursing school to become an RN was even tougher, as the curriculum was more advanced. I knew I had to do well in school, so I devoted most of my time to my studies. I was swamped studying and attending clinicals and had little time to see Blake. Luckily, he was understanding. I tried my best to see him at least once a week and on holidays.

Easter was always a big deal for Blake's family. They would all gather and celebrate at Blake's house. I had arrived at Blake's early in the morning. Blake seemed to be in a bad mood. He had been arguing with his parents about God knows what. I came in and kissed him. He told me to stay in the den with him and not to talk to his parents because he was upset with them. I told him I was uncomfortable doing that, as it was rude. So, I said hello to his parents and returned to the den, where Blake was.

He was visibly upset that I defied him, but I didn't care. I liked his parents, and I wasn't going to be impolite to them just because he was upset with them. Then, his mother called me and asked me to come into the kitchen to help her with something. "Ignore her," Blake commanded me. But I ignored him instead and went to see what his mother wanted.

When I went in the kitchen, his mother told me she needed help figuring out how to use the camera on her phone. I was helping her when suddenly I felt Blake standing behind me. He grabbed me by the shoulders and started forcefully shoving me back into the den. "What are you doing?" I exclaimed. I was shocked. Blake had never become physically aggressive like that with me before.

"Get off of her!" Blake's mother yelled.

"She's my girlfriend, and she's coming with me!" Blake barked at her. Then he pushed me into the den, shoved me down onto the couch, and said, "Stay."

I knew at that moment that I needed to stand up for myself. I refused to be like my mother and allow a man to put his hands on me. I told him I was leaving and to never contact me again. I grabbed my belongings.

"And don't come back!" Blake yelled at me, as I walked out the door.

"Gladly," I responded.

I went home and cried my eyes out. Deep down, I wanted to stay with Blake, but logically, I knew that he had crossed a line and there would be no going back. I had vowed long ago that I would never date a man like Mr. W, but here I was with Mr. W 2.0.

About two months passed, and I had yet to hear from Blake. I made no attempt to contact him, and he made no attempt to contact me. I was heartbroken. I knew we had broken up, but I just couldn't let go of him for some reason. I tried to date other guys, but I had no interest in them. All I wanted was Blake, but I fought my feelings and did not contact him.

Around June 2016, I finished RN nursing school, and it was the day of graduation. In my heart, I wanted Blake to be there. Despite everything, he had been a vital part of my decision to return to school. He was actually the one who signed me up for classes. So, I decided to text him. "Today is my graduation. I wouldn't have been able to do this without your help and encouragement to return to school. I just want to say thank you." I held my phone in my hands and debated on sending the text. After about five minutes, I pressed send and went on to graduation.

I was happy to be graduating, but it was also a little depressing. I hadn't told anyone in my family about the ceremony as I had grown distant from them after I started dating Blake. He didn't get along with my family, and they did not care for him either. I didn't have anyone in the crowd cheering for me, no family or friends. I still went to graduation despite not having anyone there to support me. I needed to walk across that stage and become a college graduate. It was a pivotal moment in my life.

They called my name to walk across the stage, and I heard someone in the audience yell, "Yeah, babe!"

That sounded like Blake, I thought. Then I looked out into the crowd, and there he was, holding a bouquet of flowers. I couldn't believe it. It had been at least two months since we spoke. *What is he doing here?* I felt a sense of happiness rush through me. Blake was here. He was back in my life.

After the ceremony, Blake came up to me and congratulated me. "It's been a while since I've heard from you," I told him.

"I figured you were busy with school," he responded. "I have a surprise for you. Come on, let's go to my car." So, we got in the car, and then he started driving. It was as if we had never separated or stopped talking. We just picked right up where we left off.

We arrived at an expensive steakhouse. "This is my gift to you," Blake told me. No one had ever done such a romantic thing for me. He even paid the bill, which was about $200. We drank champagne and ate steak and had a perfect time. I felt our flame reignite, and it was magic. I didn't care about any of the bad things he had done in the past. I desperately needed this man in my life. I did not want to live without him, and he knew it. Our love had become a disease, and it took over my mind, body, and soul.

We left the steakhouse and returned to Blake's house for a nightcap. Once we arrived at his house, we went to his room. He began kissing me passionately. I was still trying to guard my heart, so I begged him to stop. He took off my clothes. "Stop," I said. I knew I was emotionally vulnerable, and I did not want to make a decision that I would regret later. Of course, I longed for Blake physically, but I was wary of what it would mean to sleep together.

"Oh, come on," he said with anger.

"Fine," I said.

We got on his bed and resumed kissing. Then he shoved his penis inside of me and finished in ten minutes, and just like that, I was in love again.

BUT I LOVE HIM

Yes, I know he ain't no good
He lies
He cheats
He beats me too
But I love him

When I met the man
He was so gentle and kind
Making me laugh
Like a pantomime
Then he changed
At the flip of a dime
To something cold
Something cruel
But I love him

I said I would leave
More times than I can count
But each time I tried
He'd beg and plead
He'd tell me he would change
But still he remained the same
I know it's strange
But I love him

I couldn't leave him
Even if I wanted
He'd kill me if I tried

Some say it's control
Some say it's power
Some say I should cower
But they don't get
What he gives to me
But I'm not dumb
And I'm not dim
It's just that
I love him

CHAPTER 43

CLOCKED

One day, Blake invited me to a wedding for a distant family member at the Jersey Shore. I was wary of accepting the invitation. I was still living in stealth, and Blake's family still had no idea that I was trans. Even though I spent most of my time at Blake's house, I kept all interactions with his family to a minimum to avoid getting clocked. Initially, I said no, as I did not want to risk being in a situation where a lot of attention was on me, but Blake convinced me to go. "I want to show off my beautiful girlfriend," he told me. He always knew what to say.

The day of the wedding was here, and I looked stunning. My hair was straightened and down to half of my back, and I wore a black dress with quarter sleeves and a sensible pump. It took us over an hour to drive down to the shore.

We finally arrived at the Jersey Shore to attend the wedding, which was on a huge boat. I had never been on a yacht before and had no idea they could be so vast and elegant. It was basically like a mansion on the water.

Being one of the few non-White people at the wedding, I garnered a lot of attention, and I'm sure everyone there was thinking, *Who's the colored girl?* I stuck out like a sore thumb, and I grew very uncomfortable. I was mainly gawked at but not spoken to, except for one kind woman who approached me to initiate a conversation. Her name was Nancy, and she said she was one of Blake's cousins. She asked me my name, and I said, "Armani."

270

"That's an unusual name," she replied.

I told her, "Well, my real name is... Armani is like a nickname."

She began telling me about her business and her family. She sold sporting equipment and was very wealthy. She asked me how I had met Blake. I told her we met online but did not dare mention that it was Craigslist. We continued our conversation with small talk for about ten minutes. It ended with her inviting Blake and me to her home. She seemed like a charming lady.

Later, I had a few drinks and loosened up. Then, Blake and I went to the dance floor and had a ball. I had never been to a White party, which was fascinating. Everyone went crazy over the most obscure songs. Songs like "Come On Eileen" and "More Than a Feeling" brought everyone into a feverish frenzy. I didn't know most of the songs they played, but I pretended like I did.

Then, it came time for the bride to throw the bouquet. I stood in line with all the other girls, waiting for the chance to grab the bouquet, when Blake suddenly pulled me back. "Are you crazy?" he whispered. "Do you know what happens if you catch the bouquet?"

"No," I replied. "Don't you just take the flowers home?"

"No," he said. "You put on a garter belt, and the groom takes it off with his teeth!"

I was extremely grateful that he told me. The last thing I needed was for the groom to look up my dress; he would have been in for quite the surprise! I'm a lady, but if you lift up my dress, it will poke you right in the eye!

We stayed at the wedding late into the night. Finally, we made it home around 1:00 a.m. I remember feeling proud of myself when I got home. I had done it. I attended the wedding, had a good time, and no one clocked me. It could not have gone any better than that, or so I thought.

A week later, Blake called me in a panic. "They know," he said. "They know you're trans. All of my family knows!"

"How?" I asked. I began panicking as well. My head started spinning, and I crouched down on the floor. "What are you talking about?"

"It was fucking Nancy!"

"Nancy?" I asked. Then it hit me. That was the cousin who was so kind to me and struck up a conversation. It all became crystal clear. "I know what happened," I told Blake. "I told her my name. My real name."

"What? Why would you do that?" Blake responded. "Now everyone knows. They know about the movie too!"

Nancy completely fooled me. The same woman I thought was so kind, whom I spoke to at the wedding and disclosed my legal name, went home and decided to Google me. The movie I was in, which detailed my trans experience, was the first thing that popped up when my name was Googled. I also had a YouTube channel at the time, which came up when you Googled my name as well. The YouTube channel had numerous videos of me disclosing my tea and queer experience.

Nancy clearly watched every online video there was to watch and discovered I was trans. To take it a step further, she decided to email the videos to people in the family. It was quite the scandal. I was mortified, as I had been living in stealth for the most part. I did not want to disclose that I was trans to anyone, let alone Blake's entire family. Also, Blake did not want his family to know I was trans either, so we had always kept this information to ourselves. This was a disaster.

To take it a step further, Nancy decided to take the information from Google and publish it in the family newspaper! I had never heard of a family newspaper, but apparently, it's an email that is sent out once a month to update everyone in the family on pertinent family events. So, she put my transness on full display and played it off like it was something to celebrate. I felt like I was living in a nightmare. My most intimate and personal information had been fully exposed to a group of strangers.

Exposing someone as trans is not just rude; it is dangerous. Outing a trans person places them at risk for many negative consequences, including job loss, stigma, violence, and even death. What Nancy did was inhumane and an extreme violation of my privacy and my basic human right to dignity and respect. Being trans is not a spectacle, it is not a scandal, and it sure as hell is not entertainment. I still cannot believe Nancy exposed me like that.

The cat was out of the bag, and Blake and I were in a crisis. I met with him at a diner to review our damage control plan. He told me he was shocked when his mother approached him and asked, "Is it true that Armani is a man?" I felt as if I was going to vomit. What did this mean for our relationship? I asked Blake if he was going to break up with me. That would make the most sense. Get rid of me and get rid of the scandal. But instead, he assured me that he would not break up with me and that he loved me.

He told me we had two options. The first option included confirming the truth, being out, proud, and open with my transness. Blake said, "Of course, this would mean people would think I'm gay. Which would kill me." The second option included denying that I was trans and lying and saying that I was an actress just acting and pretending to be trans. By denying I was trans, we could resume our everyday life, more or less. Admittedly, it seemed hard to believe that anyone would believe this lie, but Blake convinced me it would work.

So, I didn't have to think about it for a second. I knew exactly what to do. I loved Blake and felt tremendous guilt for putting him in this situation; he was clocked by proxy. I knew that I could no longer hold back on being stealth. I would need to dedicate myself fully to living in stealth, meaning no more balls, drag shows, gay family, or being in movies.

From that moment forward, I would be an ordinary, cis-het-passing woman. Blake was happy with my decision. He encouraged me to go back into the closet and never disclose my transness to anyone ever again. Blake worked tirelessly to sweep the internet of anything that associated me with being trans. He reinforced that if anyone asked about the movie or YouTube videos, I should tell them I'm an actor. Luckily, no one from his family dared to approach me and ask me if I was trans, so I did not have to use this ridiculous lie.

Months passed, and the scandal faded. Some of Blake's family members forgot all about it. Still, some, including one of Blake's brothers, would not let it go, which resulted in a full-blown physical fight. The fight happened one night when one of Blake's brothers got into an argument with him and told him to go suck my dick. Luckily, I wasn't present for this fight, but Blake told me he punched his brother in the mouth and knocked one of his teeth out. Shortly after, his brother moved out and stopped speaking to Blake and the rest of the family for some reason. With his troublemaking brother out of the picture, we had a fighting chance of moving on with the rest of the family.

I tried my best to move forward, but I couldn't help but feel uncomfortable around Blake's family. I struggled with paranoia, not knowing who I could trust, wondering if people were observing me, looking for my tells, or talking about me behind my back. How could I pretend that everything was normal? His family knew I was trans, even though they pretended they didn't. Nothing could be the same ever again.

CHAPTER 44

REVELATIONS

It was the summer of 2016, I was twenty-six, and the world was my oyster. I looked great and had just graduated with an associate's degree in nursing. I started the process of studying for the boards to get my RN license but quickly turned my attention back to modeling.

One evening I was doing a photoshoot in NYC until about 11:00 p.m. at night. I decided to surprise Blake and drop by his house after the shoot. I called him several times on my way to his home, but he didn't answer. It was late, so I figured he must have been asleep. Regardless, I thought I would still surprise him.

I pulled into the driveway and noticed an unfamiliar car parked there. *Whose car is this?* I wondered. Then I thought maybe Blake had family visiting. His family always kept the front door open, so I let myself in and walked upstairs to his room. His door was locked, which was strange, so I knocked, but there was no answer. I began to wonder where the guest was. Both of the guest rooms in the house were empty.

Something felt wrong, and my womanly intuition told me that there was something going on in that room. I knocked again on Blake's door. Silence. I started getting angry. I knew that he could hear me knocking. I didn't want to make too much noise, because I didn't want to wake up his parents. It was around midnight by then, and everyone was sleeping.

I debated if I should go home, but something told me another woman was in the room with Blake. I had suspected him of being unfaithful multiple times. Still, he always reassured me that he was faithful, and I believed him. Deep down in my gut, though, I knew another woman was in that room. I was going to wait right there to confront both of them. After all, he couldn't stay locked in that room forever. So, I went downstairs and stayed in the living room until the morning. I was wide awake, thinking about what was happening in that room.

The morning finally came, and Blake's parents came downstairs. "What are you doing here, Armani?" his father asked me.

"Blake locked the door, and he wouldn't open it."

Blake's father's face looked like he knew something that I didn't. He offered to make me breakfast, but I declined. I loved Blake's parents. They were always very kind and hospitable, but I couldn't eat. My stomach was in knots with anticipation.

Finally, I heard Blake's door creak. I knew I had to play it coy and pretend I didn't know what was happening. Blake came downstairs. "Good morning, sleepyhead," I said to him. "You were sleeping hard last night. I was knocking on the door. Didn't you hear me?"

"I'm in a rush," he responded. "Can you take me to class?"

"Sure," I replied. "I'll be in the car waiting."

After many failed attempts at getting employment in law enforcement, Blake decided he would try for medical school. He had an MBA (but didn't use it) and was now working toward a Bachelor of Science degree. He had just started the program and was struggling to keep a C.

I began acting like I was heading to the car. I grabbed my purse and keys and walked toward the front door. Blake then went into the downstairs bathroom and closed the door. I immediately ran up the stairs to his room, taking the steps two at a time. Finally, I reached the top of the steps and opened Blake's bedroom door to discover a woman sitting on his bed.

I was in shock. The woman was plus-sized, White, plain looking, and cisgender. I instantly felt rage flow through my body. My initial reaction was to fight her, but I decided to act rationally. I coolly began walking toward her. She looked confused as to who I was or what was going on. I said, "Hi, I'm Armani, Blake's girlfriend. Who are you?"

The girl looked confused and frightened. "Oh my God," she said, "I'm so sorry. I had no idea that he had a girlfriend. I would never do this to another woman."

I felt my anger release and turn into deep sadness. I began crying and sat down next to her, and she consoled me. "It's going to be okay," she said as she rubbed my back.

Then, I turned around, and Blake was at the door. My anger returned. I stood up and asked, "Who is this?"

He looked dumbfounded and replied, "Why don't you ask her?"

At that point, I experienced pure rage for the first time in my life. I yelled at him, "Why don't I ask her?" Then, in one swift motion, I threw everything off his dresser next to me. I began screaming and punching him. My rage was so catastrophic that I didn't even notice that the girl managed to escape the room.

"I'm sorry," Blake pleaded.

Then I just fell to the floor, weeping. "How could you do this to me?" I asked. The pain was unbearable; it was like nothing I had ever experienced. It was as if someone was squeezing my heart. Blake began crying. I had never seen him cry like that before, and I grew a little pity for him, but I was still very angry.

I got up off the floor and started destroying his belongings again. He grabbed me and told me to stop. I decided at that moment that our relationship was over. I started gathering my things to leave, but Blake stood in my way and blocked the door. He begged and pleaded and said he would never do anything like that again. I continued crying and told him that I could never forgive him for this. He refused to let me leave the room, so I sat on the bed.

I was in a state of shock. I couldn't believe it; our almost five-year relationship was down the drain just like that. I had dealt with a plethora of his bullshit, from his abuse to his chronic unemployment to his mooching. I had given up everything for this man, and this is how he repaid me? I turned around and looked at him. He was still tearful and begged again for another chance.

I felt myself begin to slip back into sadness. I began to question how I could live without this man. My life revolved entirely around him. My social circle was dead. Blake had never genuinely approved of me going to queer functions, and I had stopped attending balls. He encouraged me to cut off all contact with gay family and friends. I had abandoned my relatives. I honestly gave him my all. How could I let him go? I couldn't. I simply could not just walk away. I had invested almost five years of my life with this man.

He had promised to marry me and give me a white picket fence. He had promised me the world, and I believed him. I felt embarrassed. How could I be so stupid and naïve? If I left him, I would have to tell everyone he had cheated on me. I would have egg on my face. I knew that, as the woman, I would be blamed for Blake cheating on me. Maybe I wasn't tending to his needs. Perhaps I had lost my sex appeal. I weighed the pros and the cons and finally decided to stay with Blake. He begged me for another chance, and I gave it to him.

CHAPTER 45

THE ABSENCE OF HOPE

Shortly after I found out about the cheating, I fell into a deep depression. I couldn't even find the energy or motivation to get out of bed. I turned to Blake for support, but he gave me none. I loved him but hated his actions, which showed in my behavior. I grew distant and apathetic as he grew callous and cold. I tried to talk about the cheating and how it affected me, but he did not want to talk about it.

Still trying to process the shock of Blake cheating on me, I decided it would be best to take a break from nursing and instead get a less stressful job. So, I applied for a waitress job at Applebee's. I was on my way home from the interview and was dressed professionally. I called Blake to tell him how it went. I was still feeling pretty depressed and let him know it. He asked me what I was depressed about, and I told him I was still trying to get over him cheating on me. He snapped and began yelling at me. Finally, he told me he was sick of hearing about the cheating and said I would have to learn to move on.

It had been less than a week since he cheated on me at that point. I could not move on that easily or quickly. I hung up the phone and began crying. I started driving my car aimlessly without a destination and contemplated driving into the Passaic River. I was at the lowest point in my life and truly wanted to die. The pain was unbearable. Yet, despite my suicidal state, I still wanted to live.

I knew I needed to reach out for help and called the national suicide hotline. I told the operator that I was suicidal and was planning to drive into the river or go home and swallow a bottle of Percocet that I had left over from my top surgery. The operator convinced me to drive home.

I arrived home and went inside, still on the phone with the operator. The operator asked me if I wanted a crisis counselor to come to my house or if I wanted to be evaluated at the hospital. Worried about my family discovering what was going on, I said that I wanted to be assessed at the hospital. Shortly after, a police car pulled up, and an officer came to my front door and told me that he would escort me to the hospital.

I got in the police car and noticed he was driving to St. Joseph's Hospital in Paterson. "Can we go to another hospital?" I asked.

"No, we have to go to the closest one," he responded delicately.

"Okay," I replied. I had completed most of my clinical rotations from nursing school at St. Joseph's Hospital. I was worried I would run into someone I knew, but it seemed I had no choice.

We arrived at the hospital, and the police officer escorted me into the emergency room. He spoke to the front desk staff, told them what was happening, said goodbye, and wished me luck. The emergency room was completely packed, and no rooms were available, so I was placed in a seat in the hallway.

A nurse came up to me to take my blood pressure. "Are you on any medications?" she asked me. I remained silent and continued to cry. "Did you hear me? I need to know if you're on any medications." I continued my silence. She sighed and walked away. I was not about to announce to everyone in the hallway that I was on hormones; whatever happened to confidentiality?

About an hour later, I was escorted to a private room and was asked to change into a hospital gown. Once I had the privacy of the room, I disclosed to the staff that I was trans and told them the medications that I was on.

Shortly after, a psychiatrist came and asked me if I was suicidal and had a plan to kill myself. I told him that I did not feel safe being alone, and I worried that I might kill myself. He asked me if I wanted to be admitted to the psychiatric unit of the hospital, and I said yes. Then he told me he would start the process to have me admitted and left the room.

Soon after, another staff member told me that my Auntie Lini was in the waiting room and wanted to speak to me. I'm sure the neighbors informed her that I was taken to the hospital by the police. I knew that if I talked to her, she would try to convince me to go home, and I knew that I would undoubtedly try to kill myself if I went home.

Additionally, a part of me wanted to be admitted to get back at Blake for cheating and being so cruel to me. I thought it would make Blake feel guilty if I got admitted to the psychiatric unit, as he was the catalyst for my crisis. Also, I thought being admitted to a psychiatric unit would maybe get him to show me some compassion, as up to that point, he had shown me virtually none.

I told the staff member I did not want to talk to anyone. I fell asleep. After about four hours, I was awakened by another staff member taking my vital signs. I asked her what was taking so long. She told me they had to move some patients around to ensure I had my own room. She said they wanted to give me my own room because I was transgender and had not had SRS. She asked me if I minded having my own room.

I said, "Of course not!" About two hours later, I was finally wheeled to the psychiatric unit.

It must have been 1:00 a.m. when I finally made it onto the psychiatric unit. I was exhausted. I had cried myself into a state of total weakness. I had a splitting headache and wanted to go to bed.

The nurse who admitted me was very nice. He seemed like a young new nurse. I could tell he was very intimidated by me. The staff had discovered that I was a nurse because, for some reason, I had my LPN nursing license on me. They took my nursing license with the rest of my belongings.

I assured him that I wasn't there to judge him. I just wanted to go to bed. He asked me if I still was having suicidal thoughts, and I said, "Of course." He assured me that I was in a controlled environment and would be watched closely, so I shouldn't worry about being able to harm myself as I was in the safety of the psychiatric unit. I agreed with him and told him it would be pretty difficult to carry out a suicide plan there. But then, I told him it was still possible that I could kill myself there by hanging myself with a bedsheet. He showed me to my room, and I fell asleep.

The following day, I was awakened by a nursing student. "Can I take your blood pressure, please?" he asked. I recognized the uniform and immediately realized he was from the same community college I had just graduated from. Horrified at the discovery, I yelled at him to leave my room. He scattered in fear.

A woman in my room was sitting in a chair. "That wasn't very nice," she said.

"Who are you?" I asked.

"I'm here to watch you so you don't hurt yourself," she responded. I was confused at first, but then realized I had been given a one-to-one because I was deemed high risk for harming myself. I guess the nurse who admitted me took me saying that I could hang myself in my room very seriously and placed me on suicide watch.

Having a one-to-one didn't bother me initially, as I thought I would enjoy the company. However, I quickly realized being followed around endlessly by someone is not the most pleasant experience. I debated going to breakfast but was paranoid that I would run into more people from my college, including my nursing instructor, so I told my one-to-one that I was skipping breakfast and going back to bed.

I was awakened this time by my name being yelled over a PA system. I was being called for medications. I went to the medication window accompanied by my one-to-one. "What's this?" I asked the nurse.

"It's for your mood," she replied.

"I'm not taking that shit," I told her and walked away. I was confused as to how I was prescribed medications when I had not even been formally evaluated yet.

I returned to my room with my one-to-one and bawled my eyes out. I started to regret my decision to be admitted to the psychiatric unit. Even though I had a clear understanding of psychiatric care, I couldn't help but think of all the movies I had watched portraying psychiatric wards to be a place of horror, where you are tied down and medicated to within an inch of your life. I could not let that happen to me. I had to get out of there.

I met with the psychiatrist later. He asked me a lot of questions, including why I wasn't taking my medications. Somehow, based on what I told him, he landed on the diagnosis of bipolar disorder, as if I didn't have enough things wrong with me. Although, he did not tell me what he diagnosed me with, and I didn't ask because I presumed I was only depressed. I wouldn't discover my official diagnosis until I was discharged to aftercare. "If you want to get out of here, you're going to have to take your medication," the psychiatrist said. I agreed to do whatever it took to get the hell out of that place.

"This is extremely attractive very feminine looking woman whose only clue to the fact that she might once have been [a man] [is] that she is thin, tall and [broad] otherwise…facial features extremely feminine… voices [does] not give her birth identity away, she is crying. She is distraught."

-Hospital record excerpt

CHAPTER 46

LOVE IN THE WARD

I worried about many things while I was hospitalized, but my biggest fear was the Board of Nursing discovering my admission to the psychiatric unit. I thought for sure that my nursing license would be taken from me and I would never be able to practice nursing again. I was convinced that for the rest of my life, I would be labeled as crazy.

That's the thing about mental illness that truly sucks: the shame and the stigma. A wise person once said that the issue is that we expect people with mental illness to behave and function as if they don't have mental illness, and that's the cold, hard truth. So, I decided to confide in one of the nurses in the psychiatric ward about my concerns.

The nurse was so pretty and tall, with long blonde hair. She looked like a Barbie doll, so I called her Nurse Barbie. I told her all about my fears about having my nursing license revoked. "It's okay," she told me. "Nurses are allowed to be depressed and get help."

"Am I crazy?" I asked her.

"No," she responded. "You're just depressed."

I never forgot those kind words and the comfort they brought me.

My family visited regularly, especially my Auntie Lini. They asked if I wanted to leave, and I told them no, I wasn't ready yet. Auntie Lini brought me clothes from home and a book that I could use to study for the nursing boards, as I would have to take them soon for my RN license.

Blake even visited me a few times and looked horrified at seeing me in this state: depressed and doped up on medications. He told me he felt tremendous guilt and that he wanted nothing but to marry me and start over again. I could not believe it. *Marry me?* I thought. It seemed my plan to make Blake feel guilty had actually worked. He had told me before that he planned on marrying me but had never proposed. Maybe this time, he was serious. Perhaps we could finally start a life of our own together, him, me, some kids, and the white picket fence.

After about two days, I began to warm up to the psychiatric ward, even the one-to-ones who followed me around for the first three days. Honestly, it was a nice change being on the other side of the fence, being a patient instead of a nurse.

Most of the day was pretty dull, with nothing to do. But sometimes, there would be activities and group therapy, which I attended regularly. The best part of being a patient in the psychiatric ward was being a part of a community. We would all eat together, the patients and some hospital staff in the dining room, which was nice, and the hospital food was decent. But I spent most of the day watching TV, drifting in and out of consciousness, too sleepy from the medications I was being given.

I enjoyed talking to the other patients who were there. They were a crew of characters, and they all treated me nicely. Although, I did get into a verbal altercation with an elderly woman over the TV remote one night. (However, the altercation was one-sided, as I would not argue with an elderly woman.) She told me I was acting like a "queen" because I had my own room, a one-to-one (a "bodyguard"), and had the remote control. "I am a woman just like you!" she yelled at me. I was shocked that she was so angry with me for changing the channel, but I understood she was struggling with her issues, so I let it go and gave her the remote.

Aside from the elderly woman, the other patients seemed to like me, and I liked them too. There was one patient in particular I gravitated toward. His name was Julius. I had seen him in the emergency room before I was transferred to the psychiatric unit, but I didn't know that we would both end up in the psychiatric unit. Julius was an older Italian guy who reminded me of Cheech from Cheech and Chong. He was adorable, kind, and protective of me. I felt myself quickly falling for him. Compared to Blake, Julius was a breath of fresh air.

Of course, Julius had no idea that I was trans; in fact, no one in the unit knew. But I didn't care if Julius knew my tea or not. I was severely depressed, and being around Julius made me feel better. We would sneak and hold hands when no one was looking.

But once, we got caught touching each other in the dayroom and were scolded by a nurse. I had my head on Julius's lap, and he was stroking my hair when the nurse barged in and yelled, "No touching allowed!" I thought we were safe to touch in the dayroom, as no staff was around, but I had forgotten that cameras were everywhere. I'm sure the nurse saw us on the surveillance video at the nurse's station.

After the nurse yelled at us, Julius became upset and yelled back at her. But I laughed and removed myself from Julius's lap. I felt a little embarrassed being scolded in front of everyone, but I must admit, I felt giddy and happy, like a teenager.

Julius and I spent about four days together, falling in love on the psychiatric unit (which we fondly called "the ward") until the day came when he was discharged from the hospital. He told me he was being released earlier than I was because he didn't have insurance (I had Medicaid at the time).

I was devastated to discover he was leaving, as we were admitted on the same day. But he gave me his number before he left to keep in touch. After he left, the romantic fog cleared, and I realized that I was all alone in a psychiatric ward. I had to get out of there come hell or high water.

I spoke with the psychiatrist again, and I told him I felt ready to leave, but he told me he did not think I was prepared to go yet. Actually, he recommended I stay for another week. He said that being transgender, I was at a high risk for suicide, and I hadn't been there long enough to allow the medication time to work yet. I understood the psychiatrist's reasoning, but I was no longer suicidal at that point. But what I said didn't matter; I was not permitted to leave. The psychiatrist told me that if I wanted to leave against medical advice, I would still have to wait seventy-two hours before being released, and there was a possibility that my insurance would not cover the stay. So, I was stuck in the ward.

I called Blake later that day in tears, begging him to do something to get me out of that place. He told me not to worry and that he would handle it. The same day, Blake called the hospital, threatening to pursue legal action if I was not released. Of course, Blake was bluffing, but his bluff worked, and the next day, I was discharged from the hospital.

As soon as I was released, I called Julius to meet up. We met at a bar, and it felt amazing to be free to talk and touch without being reprimanded by anyone. We even kissed. It was magical. I had found love in the psychiatric ward, but there were two problems. One, I was still in a relationship with Blake, and two, Julius still didn't know that I was trans.

As far as Blake was concerned, I couldn't care less about cheating on him. In fact, it felt damn good after what he had done to me. So, I continued to sneak and see Julius behind Blake's back. Julius and I went on the best dates. I remember one date when we went to the state garden. It was summer, so the flowers were in full bloom. I had never seen such a majestic sight. Julius convinced me to taste a honeysuckle; it tasted amazing.

Julius was a complete gentleman, but I could tell he was becoming frustrated with us not being intimate. We had been dating for a month, and we still had not had sex. Since he didn't know my tea, I didn't do anything but kiss him hello and goodbye. I knew not telling Julius my tea and kissing him was morally wrong, but I couldn't help it; my attraction to him was intense. Still, my guilt consumed me. So, I decided I would tell Julius my truth.

It was a late summer night when I decided I was going to go ahead and tell him my tea. I had decided to spend the night at Julius's. We were eating pizza and watching a movie on his couch. "There's something I must tell you," I told him.

He paused the film. "What's up?" he asked calmly.

"There's something about me that you don't know, something I'm afraid will make you not like me."

He sat up and had a serious look on his face. "What is it?"

I began crying. I couldn't do it. I just couldn't tell him and risk him rejecting me. After about twenty minutes of crying, him consoling me, and random moments of silence, I blurted out, "I'm transgender."

"What's that?"

"It means I was born a boy."

His eyes widened as he took a moment of silence. "Yeah, I had a feeling your boobs were fake," he joked. "Did you have the other surgery too?"

"No," I replied, "I still have my birth parts."

He laughed. "I thought you would say you didn't want to see me anymore!"

"So, you don't care?" I asked.

"Well, I've never done this before, but you're the most beautiful woman I've ever seen. It doesn't bother me." I kissed him and gave him a big hug. "So that's why you didn't want to do anything?" he asked jokingly.

"Yes," I replied. The mood lightened, and we continued to eat and watch the movie. Later that night, we finally made love.

CHAPTER 47

MANIA! MANIA! MANIA!

Summer had come and gone, and fall was here. My love affair with Julius faded and came to an end. He would eventually move to another state, and I lost all contact with him. I was still in a relationship with Blake but continued to cheat on him and seek the company of other men.

But my revenge cheating had turned into something else. Something was happening to me. I kept taking my medication as prescribed, but I had become manic. I didn't know it at the time, but sexual promiscuity and risk-taking behavior are classic signs of mania.

My new community provider placed me on a new regimen shortly after my discharge from the hospital, which included eliminating the medication for bipolar disorder that I was on. I had been placed on a mood stabilizer for bipolar disorder when I was hospitalized, but I was never fully told what the medication was for; all I knew was that it was for seizures but could also help my mood. So, after I was discharged, I kept taking the mood stabilizer, as the medication seemed to have been helping with my depression.

However, my community provider didn't believe I was genuinely bipolar and thought I did not need the mood stabilizer, so it was discontinued. Although, the community provider did continue the two antidepressants that I was on. Unfortunately, this new regimen of only taking antidepressants seemed to not be working. Being taken off the mood stabilizer, I now had racing thoughts, mood swings, irritability, grandiosity, and insomnia (more classic symptoms of mania).

Concerned with my uncharacteristic behavior, I made a follow-up appointment to meet with my community provider and told her everything that had been happening. I had been a psychiatric nurse for quite some time, and I suspected that I was having signs of mania, but I was not entirely sure. After I explained all my symptoms and behaviors, the community provider told me that I actually had bipolar disorder, not just major depression.

Hearing the news that I was bipolar struck fear in me, as it made me immediately think about my mother, who also had been diagnosed with the condition. I thought back to my mother's partying and realized the possibility that she was dealing with mania. I developed mercy and empathy for my mother, as I now had experienced firsthand what it felt like to be entirely out of control during a manic episode.

My mother had decided not to take medications to manage her bipolar disorder condition, and I had seen how it made it difficult for her to function. I knew I did not want to deal with similar struggles. So, when the community provider suggested I go back on a mood stabilizer, I readily agreed. Thankfully, it seemed to work. The mania subsided, and my mood stabilized.

I had unknowingly experienced mania in the past, but it was never to that extreme; I was reckless and dangerous. As I look back on this episode of mania, I feel a sense of genuine fear. It is scary to know how wild I could be during a manic episode and how one manic episode could ruin my life completely. To this day, I continue to take my medications, as I know that I could lose everything I worked so hard for.

Before my medications were adjusted again, I was spending my money carelessly and staying up all hours of the night, cheating on Blake and having sex with a different man each night. Then, during one of my mania-driven nights, I met this one guy named Noah, who seemed very different than the other guys I had hooked up with.

Noah had responded to my casual encounters ad on Craigslist. I had received countless responses to the ad, but something about this guy fascinated me. He was White, tall and lean, very handsome, and had gray hair despite being in his mid-twenties. I was intrigued and messaged him back. We communicated via email and text for some time until we finally FaceTimed. To my surprise, he was nice, gentle, and genuinely interested in getting to know me. I knew then that this man would not be just another hookup.

Shortly after we started communicating, Noah told me that he was recovering from a chlamydia infection, and we could not have sex for about one week until he completed his course of antibiotics. You would think Noah having an STI would deter me from pursuing an intimate relationship with him, but the fact that we couldn't have sex made me desire him more.

With sex off the table, we spent all of our time really getting to know each other. I spent a lot of time with him at his house in Elizabeth, New Jersey. I got to know his family, which consisted of his eccentric mother and aunt, who both seemed to like me. We also played video games and went out on dinner dates almost every day for a whole week.

Noah was the exact opposite of Blake. Noah was gentle and kind and radiated a sense of happiness. Noah's joy was contagious, and I was on a high when I was around him. He had quickly become my safe space; before I knew it, I fell in love.

After a week passed, Noah and I finally had the green light to be physically intimate. Being intimate with Noah was amazing. After we had sex, we gathered that our relationship was going to be much more than a casual encounter. We had been dating for less than two weeks when we both realized that we loved each other and decided to become monogamous. But there was one issue: What to do about Blake?

CHAPTER 48

CRESCENDO

I called Blake the next day and told him that it was over. I told him that I had moved on and I was in a new relationship. He didn't take the news too well and demanded that I see him.

We met in a parking lot. He threatened that if I left him, he would make my life a living hell. He threatened my family and even threatened Noah, but I didn't care. I had had enough of him and his abuse. It was over, and that was that. But I would soon find out that it would not be that easy. In fact, it was worse than I could ever imagine.

Blake had truly gone off the deep end. He began calling me nonstop, making threats and pleading for me to take him back. It was New Year's Eve, and I had spent the night welcoming in 2017 with Noah at his house. Blake kept calling my phone, so I turned it off. I woke up the next day to forty missed calls from Blake and text messages saying he was at my house. I called him, and he told me he knew where I was and that if I didn't meet him at my house, he would drive to Noah's house.

I called his bluff and told him to come over if he knew where I was. Then, he said, "You're in Elizabeth with that guy." My heart stopped. He had been stalking me. Out of fear for Noah's safety, I left and drove to Paterson to meet Blake.

I met him outside my house. I tried to tell him again that it was over and that I had moved on, but he asked me if we could go inside to talk. He seemed calm, so I agreed. Once in my room, he began interrogating me. "How many guys were there?" he asked.

"A lot," I responded.

"What is this, revenge?" he barked at me.

"Yeah," I said. "You need to leave me alone."

"It's those damn pills! They're making you crazy!"

I had no idea what he was talking about. If anything, the pills were helping to keep me sane. I was on an appropriate regimen at that point and was relatively stable, psychiatrically speaking, at least. "It's not the pills. It's you!" I told him.

Then he forcefully tried to kiss me, but I pushed him away. He then pushed me on the bed and unbuttoned my pants. He pinned me down and began ripping my pants and panties off. I tried to get him off me, but he was too heavy. "What are you going to do, rape me?" I asked coolly. Then he stopped. He got up, slammed the door, and left.

***

About a week passed, and I had yet to hear from Blake. I presumed he had finally moved on, but I was very wrong. Noah had come over to spend the night at my house, and then Blake called. I rejected the call. Fed up with the constant harassment, I contacted my phone company and changed my number.

We woke up early the following day. I had started working as an RN and was scheduled to work a 7:00 a.m. – 3:00 p.m. shift. Noah walked me to my car. It was a weekday, and there was a lot of traffic, so we tried to hurry up. Then, a car pulled up and parked beside us in the middle of the street. I instantly recognized that it was Blake's blue Chevy.

He came out of the car wearing safety goggles and a long trench coat, and his hair was slicked down; he looked like the Columbine murderers. "I'm going to kill him," he said as he walked to the back of his car to open his trunk. He pulled out a large gun and pointed it right at Noah.

"Noah, run," I said with composure. Blake pointed the gun at Noah, though I was in the line of fire too and tracked him as he ran. "What are you doing?" I asked him. Then cars began honking, and Blake quickly realized he had an audience of witnesses. He put the gun back into his trunk, jumped in his car, and sped off.

Damn it, I thought. *I'm going to have to call 911.* The realization that I would need to have Blake arrested filled me with sadness and pity. He had indeed lost his mind and had clearly become a danger to Noah and me.

I called 911 and described his car to the operator. Noah had run to his car, but he returned once he saw Blake drive off, and I updated him on the situation.

Shortly after, Blake was arrested. He was easy to find as his car had a California license plate. I had been instructed by the 911 operator to remain where I was, so I did.

Soon after, the police came and interviewed Noah and me for details about what had happened. First, I went over the details of the breakup and the stalking. Then, they asked me if I knew how Blake managed to possess a gun. I informed them that he was a former border patrol agent in California, and I suspected he had acquired the weaponry there. Then, the police officers asked if I intended to press charges, and I said yes.

The police instructed Noah and me to meet them at the downtown police station to complete the paperwork. The incident had happened perpendicular to my house, and my family came out to check on me. One of my uncles said he saw the whole thing and couldn't believe that Blake would do such a thing. My Auntie Lini volunteered to call my job and tell them I wouldn't be coming to work. I was shocked and could barely think, so I was grateful for my family's help and support. Noah also took the day off from work.

Surprisingly, I had remained calm during the whole incident. I had never experienced an "out of body" experience until that day. It was as if there was a disconnect between me and reality. There was a sensation that I was looking down upon myself, observing the whole incident. Because I was in a state of trauma-induced dissociation, I didn't feel anything. It was as if I was in a dream.

I began replaying the last five years in my head. Who was this man? How could I have spent almost five years with him and not seen this coming? Of course, there were many red flags. Blake had always had a temper, and I had seen him lose it more than enough times, but I never thought he had the potential to try to kill someone.

I felt the way I had seeing Mr. W being arrested when I was a child—relief, but a sense of pity and guilt. Worse, I still felt love for Blake. Five years of commitment don't just dissipate in a few weeks. I felt guilty as I knew Blake's arrest would ruin any chance he had to return to law enforcement. In fact, the arrest and the charges to follow would shadow him for the rest of his life. I began to question if I should even pursue pressing charges, as I did not want to be responsible for putting Blake, someone I had loved so dearly, behind bars. Still, I knew it would only worsen matters for everyone involved if I didn't. Blake had to learn that his actions were wrong, dangerous, and unacceptable. So, I got into my car and headed to the downtown police station with Noah.

***

I had come out of my dissociative state and was panicking by the time we arrived at the station. I wondered what would happen to Blake. What if they released him, and he did something like this again? I also asked myself why he didn't pull the trigger. Did he simply not have the nerve, or did the severity of the consequences finally cross his mind?

I began questioning why he decided to wait until we left the house to carry out his plan. Then, all kinds of horrific images and thoughts entered my mind. I began thinking about the possibility of him actually killing me, Noah, and even my family. Without a doubt, I needed to see this through and have Blake arrested and incarcerated for everyone's protection.

All of the police officers were very sympathetic and supportive of both Noah and me. Multiple police officers informed me that

Blake had told them he was a police officer. They said it mockingly and humorously. I'm sure they were all thinking, *How could a police officer be so foolish?*

I told them that Blake was a border patrol agent in California until he returned to New Jersey sometime around the early 2010s when we started dating. They thanked me for the information and said they would contact the California Border Patrol for further information.

Noah and I sat in a secluded room, writing our statements in silence. Noah held my hand and told me everything was going to be alright. I felt safe with Noah being there. He stayed with me the entire day and provided vital emotional support. My love for him intensified through the ordeal. We completed our statements, and the police officers returned.

One of the officers stated with a chuckle, "So, were you aware that Blake was fired from border patrol?"

"No," I responded, "he never told me that. He always said he quit and returned to New Jersey because he missed his family."

No wonder he couldn't get another job as a police officer. I couldn't believe that for almost five years, Blake had been lying to me. I began wondering what else he had lied about. The police officers also told us that Blake was distraught and refused to cooperate with them.

They gave us some details on the arrest. They said they had found him in a parking lot about ten minutes up the road from my house. He was inside the car with the doors locked, crying. The car had been surrounded by police officers, all with their guns drawn. Blake was instructed to open the door or the window, but he refused. They said he remained in the car for about twenty minutes, resisting arrest. Finally, he had been forcefully removed from the vehicle. The police discovered that he had a fully loaded handgun with a ten-round magazine plus one round in the chamber. They also found an AR-15 rifle with two loaded thirty-round magazines.

The police officers left us again for a while. Then, they returned to give us an update on Blake's charges. They informed us that he had been charged with a multitude of offenses, including harassment under domestic violence, unlawful possession of a weapon, terrorism, and resisting arrest. For the first time that day, I felt a sense of relief. Given that Blake was charged with all of those offenses, I knew that he would remain incarcerated for at least six months.

The police officers then asked me if I wanted to file a restraining order, and of course, I said yes. Once we finished our statements, the police officers escorted us to a waiting room for individuals filing restraining orders. I had to sit in front of a judge and give a statement validating my need for a temporary restraining order against Blake. I would then have to attend another court session to get the official restraining order. I was also told that my testimony would be recorded and used later for Blake's official trial. Because my testimony would be recorded, I did not have to attend Blake's trial. Instead, they would just play my recorded testimony.

As we were walking to the waiting room, one of the officers had a call come in on his walkie-talkie. "Uh-oh," he said. He paused and continued, "Would you be okay seeing Blake? He's going to pass us in the hallway. They're taking him to his cell."

I began shaking. "No," I responded.

"Alright, I'll just have you turn around as they escort him in."

I turned around as instructed. I began hearing Blake's voice. He argued with the officers, questioning why he couldn't speak to me. Then, he was asked to remain quiet, and he did. Obviously, I couldn't see him, but I could hear the jangling of the handcuffs and chains. My heart broke. I did not want this; I did not want to have Blake arrested. I began to cry, and Noah consoled me.

"Alright, he's gone," the police officer said. We continued walking to the waiting room.

We sat in the waiting room in silence. We were surrounded by other people also waiting to see the judge. About an hour later, I was called in to see the judge. I was a bundle of nerves. The room was cold and sterile, and the judge sat at his podium. No one was in the room except the judge, a court stenographer, and myself.

The judge was very kind to me and encouraged me to give my statement as much time as needed. He reminded me that my account would be recorded to play later at Blake's trial. He wanted a complete history of the relationship between Blake and me. I was sworn in and began giving my statement. I detailed the history of our relationship without pause. I described all the details clearly and concisely.

I told the judge of the time that Blake pushed me. I told him of times that he destroyed my property in rage, invoking fear and terror in me. I detailed how he had pinned me down and ripped open my pants and panties to potentially rape me. I spared no details of anything. I told the judge how Blake had stalked me and that he threatened to harm my family, Noah, and myself on multiple occasions. I even managed to recall the incidents in chronological order. I freed my mind, and the words poured like a river.

When I finished, about twenty minutes later, the judge told me he believed every word I said. He told me he was impressed by my bravery. He continued and said that he was also impressed by my ability to recall everything calmly, confidently, and precisely. He didn't know that I was fueled by fear and concern over the safety of my loved ones.

The temporary restraining order was granted. I felt some sense of safety from the temporary restraining order, but not much. It's nothing but a piece of paper, especially for a perpetrator. What brought me the most comfort was knowing that Blake was behind bars. I finally felt a sense of peace.

CHAPTER 49

DECRESCENDO

The day came that I would have to show up to court to be granted an official restraining order against Blake, as the temporary restraining order is just that—temporary. Luckily, I had managed to get a lawyer pro bono, who was a lovely lady who did domestic violence cases.

Noah was unable to accompany me to court as he had to work. I was all by myself, and I was terrified. I wore a gray suit from H&M with a black pump. My face was beat with a red lip. I looked snatched. Looking especially good was important that day. I often relied on my looks to present a façade of confidence, and that day the façade was vital.

My lawyer reviewed the case details with me in the waiting room and prepared me for what was to come. She told me she would do most of the speaking but encouraged me to chime in whenever necessary.

Finally, we walked into the courtroom. My heels clacked fiercely with each step. Blake was sitting on the right, and I was to sit on the left. His mother was sitting in the front row, looking care-worn. "Here she comes; just stay calm and don't look at her," I heard her whisper to him. I saw the back of his head as I walked into the room. Then, the judge entered. We were sworn in and took our seats. Then, the lawyers began talking.

Blake's lawyer did not have much to say. What was there to defend? Blake was caught red-handed with his deadly weapons.

He obviously was a danger to me. The lawyer could not deny it or accuse me of lying. Seeing that his lawyer wasn't doing much to defend him, Blake became upset. He began interrupting his lawyer and speaking directly to the judge. The judge asked him several times to remain quiet, and he did.

Finally, my lawyer began to describe the events and their effects on me. Blake interrupted my lawyer. By that point, the judge had obviously become fed up with Blake. My lawyer stated that she would allow me to make a statement to the court, but the judge deemed that unnecessary because he had already made his decision. He granted me the final restraining order against Blake.

I was overcome with emotions upon hearing the judge's decision. It was as if time stood still. The voices in the courtroom became muffled, but I could clearly hear Blake's mother crying. I didn't know if I wanted to cry, smile, or frown. I was grateful that the judge granted me the restraining order, but at the same time, my heart broke.

They escorted Blake out of the courtroom. "Well, that was quick!" my lawyer said to me. I thanked her for all her help, as she was a blessing. I walked out of the courtroom and made it to my car, where I wept uncontrollably.

For so long, Blake had been my safe place. He had fulfilled many roles in my life: lover, friend, mentor, and protector. I wished to God that our relationship had not ended this way. I wished that Blake had just moved on peacefully, but that was not the case. The reality was that Blake had committed multiple crimes, which he had to be held accountable for.

Blake's big court date was months after the gun incident. I did not attend. I did not want to put myself through that level of trauma, but I was informed by the courts that Blake was found guilty on most of the charges and sentenced accordingly.

I blamed myself for what had happened. The guilt followed me for years. I felt that I had pushed Blake to the point of mental breakdown. It took me years of therapy to accept that what had happened was not my fault and that I was not responsible for the actions of anyone, including Blake.

***

About a year passed. I had moved out of my grandparents' house into a small one-bedroom apartment with Noah. We were so much in love. About two months after we moved in, we got a dog. He was a cute brown Pomeranian whom we named Frankie. I was the happiest I had been in a long time. We decorated the apartment with all kinds of quirky knickknacks.

It was my first time living independently, and I was glad I had someone like Noah to share that experience with. I also began working full time at a psychiatric hospital. It was an exciting new job, and I loved it. Everything seemed to be going well until I got a call one day from my Auntie Lini.

She told me that a court summons had come in the mail for me. My heart began racing. I knew it was something related to Blake. I asked her what the letter said. She opened it and told me that Blake had challenged my restraining order and claimed that I had falsified information. The letter detailed a mandatory court appearance in about a month. I couldn't believe it. A year had passed, but Blake refused to move on. He was still trying to control my life.

I drove to my grandparents' house the next day to pick up the letter and called the number listed to get more information. I was informed that if I did not show up on the court date, Blake would win the case by default, and the restraining order would be null and void. Once I learned that information, I knew I was obligated to appear.

I began wondering why Blake wanted to challenge the restraining order. The only logical reason I could think of is that he wanted to contact me, but why would he need to? I knew that this was about control and power. Blake had always remained in control of our relationship. I knew that this was just an attempt to regain control over me, and I wouldn't allow it.

I contacted the same pro bono lawyer, and she agreed to represent me again. Blake had claimed that I made false statements in my testimony, and I had no idea what he was referring to. He showed up with a gun, for God's sake! What was there to lie about? I started feeling paranoid that Blake would somehow weaponize my being trans to make some point about me being dishonest.

I had not disclosed at any point that I was trans as I didn't think I needed to reveal my transness to the court. What difference would it have made anyway? Blake was still a danger to me, trans or not, and I needed that restraining order against him. I became paranoid and decided to disclose my tea to my lawyer. She reassured me that I did not have to disclose that I was trans, and it made no difference in what had happened because Blake still did what he did.

***

A month had passed since I got the letter, and it was time for me to appear in court again. Noah offered to accompany me, but I told him that I was fine on my own. By that point, I was sick of Blake and his nonsense. I would show up because it was mandatory, but I would not give in to his manipulation. Of course, I looked stunning.

I went into the courtroom, and it was the same. Blake was on the right, in handcuffs, and I was to sit on the left. I only saw the back of his head and refused to look at or talk to him. The judge came in, and we began. This time, Blake was alone, without a lawyer. He said I had lied in my statement, and that he had not threatened me. He tried to use all types of legalese but came off as incompetent.

My lawyer then began speaking. "Your Honor," she said, "my client is the victim here. Mr. Blake showed up at her residence with deadly weaponry, threatening my client and her current partner. I believe this is just an attempt to gain access to my client."

The judge interrupted my lawyer. He turned to Blake and said, "Why are you looking at Ms. K.? Are you aware that she has a restraining order against you?"

Blake responded, "I have eyes, Your Honor. Am I not allowed to look at her?"

"No," the judge replied.

My lawyer continued and was interrupted again by the judge. He questioned Blake, "Why are you still looking at her? Did I not tell you not to look at her?"

"I didn't realize looking at someone was a crime," Blake responded with arrogance.

The judge replied, "If you look at her again, I'm adding more time to your sentence." I did not think that was possible, but apparently Blake did as he stopped looking at me.

Shortly after, the judge declared that the restraining order would remain. Also, he said that if Blake tried to challenge it again or contact me, it would be considered a violation of the restraining order, and more time would be added to his current sentence. Blake complied, and I never heard from him again.

CHAPTER 50

CONCLUSION

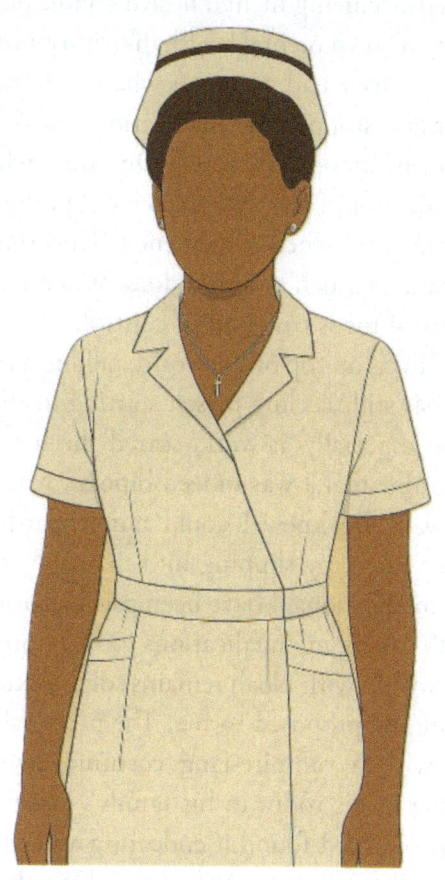

After obtaining my Associate of Science in Nursing (ASN) degree and becoming an RN, I returned to school to complete a Bachelor of Science in Nursing (BSN) degree. I then completed a Master of Science in Nursing (MSN) degree to become a psychiatric nurse practitioner. Finally, in 2023, I obtained a Doctor of Nursing Practice (DNP) degree. Yes, I am a doctor. Who would have thought little old LPN me would go on to do that? I began my nursing career working with underserved and disadvantaged communities and still serve this population. Currently, as a nurse practitioner, I provide psychiatric care predominantly to individuals with substance use disorder, treating their co-occurring mental health conditions.

Regarding my own mental health, like most individuals with bipolar disorder, I have had moments where I questioned if I was indeed bipolar and stopped my medication. But I would always have a rebound in mood symptoms. One time when I stopped taking my medication, I felt myself slowly slipping into a manic episode. I was at work when it happened. Truthfully, depression does not scare me as much as mania does. When I am in a manic state, every part of me is truly out of control.

Suddenly, I was on top of the world, talking a mile a minute, and I couldn't sit still. Feeling myself starting to slip back into a manic episode, especially at work, scared the hell out of me. I knew at that point that I was indeed bipolar, which was a hard pill to swallow. I also knew I could not jeopardize my safety, relationship, or career by slipping into mania again. So, I went right back on medications. I have been psychiatrically stable and compliant with taking my medications for over one year now.

My relationship with Noah remains solid. Actually, after two weeks of dating, he proposed to me. The proposal was comical, as he did it with a vampire-fang costume jewelry ring. He proposed to me in his room in his family's basement. While it was a simple proposal, I found it endearing and agreed to marry him. Then, on the following Valentine's Day that year, Noah decided to propose again, but this time, he gave me a real diamond ring. I was ecstatic and said yes again. After six years of engagement, Noah and I finally married in July of 2023.

We did a courthouse wedding with a small reception. During our vows, I told Noah that he had changed my life the way that light changed a dark room, and I meant every word as he had truly been the sunshine of my life. He fills my days with joy and love and is unquestionably my eternal soulmate. I am blessed to have someone like Noah with whom I can spend the rest of my life.

Both of my parents attended the wedding. I have forgiven my father for being absent for most of my life, as well as for the choking incident. We have been building our relationship together, and it has been wonderful.

My relationship with my mother is also improving. She still struggles with the demon of addiction, and each day, she fights for her recovery. She is still learning to navigate my trans identity but accepts and loves me as her child.

I have not spoken to my brother in almost ten years. He has moved on with his life and now lives in Georgia. I attempted to contact him once, and he said he did not want contact with anyone from our family. Surprisingly, he said he had no ill feelings toward me, but he preferred to avoid any chance of being contacted by our mother.

My sisters on my mother's side both decided to forgive me for abandoning them when I was eighteen. My relationship with my youngest sister is estranged, but I am close to the older sister. I am also becoming close to my sisters on my father's side.

Fortunately, I was able to repair the relationship with most of my family members after my relationship with Blake ended. It was most important to me to fix the relationship with my dear Auntie Lini, who unfortunately passed in 2022 from an unknown cause at the age of fifty. I was devastated by this loss, and I still mourn her to this day. I was honored to give the eulogy at her funeral. Happily, before her sudden and unexpected passing, we (her, me, and some of my female cousins) went on a girl's trip to Virginia, which was a blast. I cherish that memory and all my memories of my Auntie Lini dearly, and I look forward to the day that we meet again.

Mending the relationship with my chosen queer family was just as important to me as mending the relationship with my biological family. However, it would not be as easy (I guess blood is thicker than water). I have lost contact with most of my queer siblings except Abbey, my chosen sister. My relationship with Abbey is unshakable, and she remains my best friend and was maid of honor at my wedding. I attempted to mend the relationship with my chosen mother, Mother Aaliyah, but this was ultimately unsuccessful. We contacted each other sporadically throughout the years, but our mother-daughter relationship could not be salvaged. We simply grew apart, but we remain in contact on social media.

Regarding ballroom, I have slowly been making my way back into the scene. I have attended some balls, walking femqueen realness, and even won. However, I do not see myself continuing to walk realness, as I believe the category is outdated and not in touch with the current trans revolutionary movement that says that trans women are women, regardless of whether we are passable or not. I now aspire to transition to walking femqueen face. Who knows, maybe someday I'll be deemed legendary femqueen face.

Noah and I would eventually move out of our apartment, purchase a large home, and adopt two other Pomeranians named Foxy and Lucky. We are currently in the process of starting a family through in vitro fertilization (IVF), which entails getting an egg donor as well as a gestational carrier (surrogate). We are taking our time with this process, as it is very costly, but we look forward to having children of our own one day.

Because I would be using my sperm to conceive a child, I had to come off hormones. I was sterile at first, but luckily, my body eventually resumed making viable sperm. After being off hormones for two years, I was able to have enough viable sperm to freeze and was able to resume my HRT. Being off hormones was scary at first, but I did not see any significant changes or masculinization, aside from some facial hair growth, which I addressed successfully with laser hair removal. However, I lost some of the curves I gained from being on HRT, but I am hopeful they will return. I also plan on eventually getting a fat transfer (BBL) after removing the loose silicone from my buttocks.

For the most part, my life is quiet, routine, and drama-free. Things are going great, and I couldn't be happier. When I look back on my life, writing this book, I realize how far I have come and how much bravery and nerve it took to get to this place of happiness and stability. The future looks bright, and I cannot wait to see what life and God have in store for me.

I'm Not Angry Anymore

Anger is a cancer

That attacks its host

This I know the most

Like rhythm to a dancer

Is madness to sadness

Anger is secondary, so they say

It takes you away

And drowns you in an ocean of emotions

Hues of reds, yellows, and blues

Anger is a sickness that will kill you

And kill others too

From mothers to lovers

Friends to strangers

Anger is a danger

I once would get serious

I once would get furious

I once would get defeated

And allow myself to get heated

But with age

I have learned to let go of rage

For there is no need to debate

No need to get irate

I could be bitter

I could be annoyed

But what would I do that for?

I'm not angry anymore

EPILOGUE

While my gender transition remains a significant part of my life, I have many more experiences that define who and what I am. Transgender people are much more than our gender transition. Yes, I am a trans woman, but I am many other things: a nurse, a wife, a friend, and an aspiring mother. However, most importantly, I am a spiritual being having a human experience.

At this point in my life, I have realized that life is a journey, and everyone, regardless of gender identity, will go through their own transition to become better and fully realized versions of themselves. Transition is the great equalizer and a universal human experience that everyone must endure. Transition is a lifelong process that starts from birth and continues until we take our last breath and make the ultimate and final transition to the afterlife.

Through all my trauma, trials, and tribulations, I have found my true and honest self, and that is simply amazing. For so long, I hated being me. Coming to a place of self-love is no easy task, for the world often exclusively tells us what is wrong with us rather than celebrating our differences and unique beauty.

I used to think that happiness was a lie, for so much of my life was spent in misery, but now I am hopeful for the future. Finding hope after being stuck in a hopeless place is nothing short of a miracle. Coming to this place of happiness was challenging and required much hard work, including self-reflection and self-acceptance.

I have learned to accept myself fully and view my flaws as beauty marks rather than moles. Learning to love yourself is a continuous process, and yes, there will be times when you fall.

What is important is to remember to get up, continue to fight, and always show yourself mercy and forgiveness.

In many ways, I am still getting to know myself. I am not to the point of total enlightenment, but I have garnered true wisdom. The girl I kept hidden inside me has finally been fully realized and released to the world. She is beautiful, happy, and emboldened to live.

Reflecting on my life, I must remember all the ugly truths and face the reality of my failures and regrets. Still, I am also pushed to celebrate my accomplishments. My life has been filled with many days of darkness, but I am moving forward to happier days filled with love, laughter, and light.

Remembering where I started while writing this book was truly difficult. For so long, I have kept my past hidden from the world. Writing this book has helped break the shackles of shame that have held me down practically all my life. I hope that more than anything, this book helps someone stand in their truth and show their sparkling true selves, as having the bravery to be yourself is, perhaps, the true meaning of freedom.

ACKNOWLEDGEMENTS

There are many people who I must thank for making this book possible. I would like to thank my husband for his support during this project and for guiding me in telling my truth to the world. I would like to thank my chosen sister, Abbey, for her constructive feedback, which helped make this book a work of art. I thank and acknowledge Hannah Elnan for her hard work and assistance editing this book. Most importantly, I would like to thank God for giving me the strength to revisit my traumatic past and instilling in me the desire to help others navigate this crazy world and life. I would like to thank you, the reader, for taking the time to read my life story; I hope it was a good one! Lastly, I want to thank myself for revealing myself in a way I never have before and allowing myself to be vulnerable and brave.

Made in United States
North Haven, CT
08 March 2026

89593297R00183